Lecture Notes in Computer Science 6303

Commenced Publication in 1973
Founding and Former Series Editors:
Gerhard Goos, Juris Hartmanis, and Jan van Leeuwen

Editorial Board

David Hutchison
  Lancaster University, UK
Takeo Kanade
  Carnegie Mellon University, Pittsburgh, PA, USA
Josef Kittler
  University of Surrey, Guildford, UK
Jon M. Kleinberg
  Cornell University, Ithaca, NY, USA
Alfred Kobsa
  University of California, Irvine, CA, USA
Friedemann Mattern
  ETH Zurich, Switzerland
John C. Mitchell
  Stanford University, CA, USA
Moni Naor
  Weizmann Institute of Science, Rehovot, Israel
Oscar Nierstrasz
  University of Bern, Switzerland
C. Pandu Rangan
  Indian Institute of Technology, Madras, India
Bernhard Steffen
  TU Dortmund University, Germany
Madhu Sudan
  Microsoft Research, Cambridge, MA, USA
Demetri Terzopoulos
  University of California, Los Angeles, CA, USA
Doug Tygar
  University of California, Berkeley, CA, USA
Gerhard Weikum
  Max Planck Institute for Informatics, Saarbruecken, Germany

Leonardo Bottaci   Gordon Fraser (Eds.)

Testing – Practice and Research Techniques

5th International Academic and Industrial Conference
TAIC PART 2010
Windsor, UK, September 3-5, 2010
Proceedings

Volume Editors

Leonardo Bottaci
University of Hull, Department of Computer Science
Hull, HU6 7RX, UK
E-mail: l.bottaci@hull.ac.uk

Gordon Fraser
Saarland University, Department of Computer Science
66123 Saarbrücken, Germany
E-mail: fraser@cs.uni-saarland.de

Library of Congress Control Number: 2010933352

CR Subject Classification (1998): D.2, F.3, D.3, D.2.4, C.2, K.6

LNCS Sublibrary: SL 2 – Programming and Software Engineering

ISSN	0302-9743
ISBN-10	3-642-15584-7 Springer Berlin Heidelberg New York
ISBN-13	978-3-642-15584-0 Springer Berlin Heidelberg New York

This work is subject to copyright. All rights are reserved, whether the whole or part of the material is concerned, specifically the rights of translation, reprinting, re-use of illustrations, recitation, broadcasting, reproduction on microfilms or in any other way, and storage in data banks. Duplication of this publication or parts thereof is permitted only under the provisions of the German Copyright Law of September 9, 1965, in its current version, and permission for use must always be obtained from Springer. Violations are liable to prosecution under the German Copyright Law.

springer.com

© Springer-Verlag Berlin Heidelberg 2010
Printed in Germany

Typesetting: Camera-ready by author, data conversion by Scientific Publishing Services, Chennai, India
Printed on acid-free paper   06/3180

Preface

A Message from the TAIC PART 2010 General Chair

TAIC PART is a unique event that strives to combine aspects of a conference, a workshop and a retreat. Its purpose is to bring together industrialists and academics in an environment that promotes fundamental collaboration on problems in software testing. Among the wide range of topics in computer science and software engineering, software testing is an ideal candidate for academic and industrial collaboration because advances in research can have such wide-ranging and far-reaching implications for industry. Conversely, the advances in computing and communications technology and the growth of the associated software engineering activity are producing new research challenges at an increasing rate.

The problems that arise in software testing are related to the problems that arise in many other areas of computing. As such, testing research combines a wide range of elements encompassing the theoretical work of program analysis and formal methods and the associated representations such as finite-state machines and dependence graphs. The inherent complexity of software testing has led to the involvement of heuristic methods. Software testing is also a human activity and has thus seen the involvement of psychology, sociology and even philosophy. This astonishing breadth and depth have made the problems of software testing appealing to academics for several decades.

Industrial activities are, of course, the fundamental source of the software testing problems to which research is directed. Software now controls safety-critical systems from chemical plants and national nuclear defence systems, through sophisticated fly-by-wire commercial aircraft, to the airbag and brake controllers in our motor cars. These problems have a strong technical aspect but they also have economic and social aspects. This explains the variety of disciplines that have contributed to software testing research. Industrialists are not only the source of research problems but they are also significant contributors to the solutions of these problems, particular in the development of tools and methods. Many of the industrial tools used in software testing today are based on research ideas and research prototypes.

The consequences of software failure can be severe, and so it is with these pressing concerns in mind that TAIC PART seeks to bring academics and industrialists together in a retreat setting, allowing for interaction, extended discussion and joint work that is not possible in the rushed schedule of a conventional conference format. The organizers have aimed to ensure that there is a productive mix of academic and industrial involvement in this rather special event. We are delighted that we have been able to secure industrial sponsorship for the event, ensuring the committed participation of the industrial community. We would like to thank our TAIC PART sponsors: CREST and LDRA.

June 2010   Anthony Simons

A Message from the TAIC PART 2010 Programme Chairs

This volume contains the proceedings of Testing: Academic and Industrial Conference–Practice and Research Techniques (TAIC PART 2010), held during September 3–5 in Cumberland Lodge, Windsor, UK, the fifth conference in a series of highly successful events.

A special thank you is due to the Programme Committee, which worked hard to ensure that the event lived up to the standards of academic rigor, ensuring that the event engaged fully with the academic community. Putting together the programme was both enjoyable and challenging. The event received 40 paper submissions and we would like to thank everyone who submitted a paper. After a rigorous reviewing process in which each paper was reviewed by at least two reviews followed by Programme Committee discussions, 15 full papers and 7 abstracts were accepted. Three of the papers were from industry. The papers originate from 13 countries in North and South America, Europe and Asia.

A special thank you is due to the Programme Committee for the outstanding quality of their reviews, which were produced promptly to a short deadline. We believe that for the authors (irrespective of whether their papers were accepted) this is the most sincere and valuable reward for their hard work and expertise. TAIC PART seeks to encourage and facilitate high-quality reviewing, since it plays such a vital role in the development of this subject. In addition to the submitted papers, TAIC PART had three outstanding invited speakers, Wolfgang Grieskamp of Microsoft, USA, Sir Tony Hoare of Microsoft Research, UK and Bertrand Meyer of the Swiss Federal Institute of Technology, Switzerland, who we thank for their contributions and for attending the conference.

We are very grateful to the international community for their participation. A complex event like TAIC PART cannot be organized without the help of a committed team of organizers. We would therefore like to extend a very warm thanks to all the staff at the Cumberland Lodge. The event would not be nearly so appealing without their support, kindness and professionalism. We would also like to thank the staff at the Springer who have been very helpful in supporting us to collect and organize the material required to produce the proceedings. We are also very grateful to R.N. Horspool and A.J. Wellings, the editors of *Software: Practice and Experience* for agreeing to a special section of extended selected papers from TAIC PART. Finally, thanks also to Easychair, which makes the life of Programme Chairs so much easier.

June 2010
Gordon Fraser
Leonardo Bottaci

Keynote Speakers

Bertrand Meyer is Professor of Software Engineering at ETH Zurich (the Swiss Federal Institute of Technology), which he joined in 2001 and was chairman of the computer science department from 2004 to 2006. He remains Chief Architect of Eiffel Software, the company he founded in California in 1985. He is the author of a number of books translated into many languages, including "Object-Oriented Software Construction" (Jolt Award 1997), "Reusable Software", "Introduction to the Theory of Programming Languages", "Eiffel: The Language" and several others, as well as many articles and over 60 edited conference proceedings. He has led the design and implementation of numerous tools and libraries used in production applications, including the open-source EiffelStudio environment, and serves as consultant to industry and government agencies. He is the principal designer of the Eiffel language and method, and the editor of the Eiffel language standard, accepted by the International Standards Organization in 2006. His research interests range over object-oriented analysis, design and programming, concurrency (SCOOP model), object persistence, development environments, software project management, software verification, automatic testing, formal methods, programming language semantics, and educational issues. He is the recipient of the Dahl-Nygaard object technology award and, in 2007, of the ACM Software System Award.

Sir Charles Antony Richard Hoare (Tony Hoare or C.A.R. Hoare, born January 11, 1934) is a British computer scientist, probably best known for the development in 1960 of Quicksort (or Hoaresort), one of the world's most widely used sorting algorithms, Hoare logic, the formal language Communicating Sequential Processes (CSP) used to specify the interactions between concurrent processes, structuring computer operating systems using the monitor concept, and the axiomatic specification of programming languages. He is now an Emeritus Professor at the Oxford University Computing Laboratory, and is also a senior researcher at Microsoft Research in Cambridge, England. He received the 1980 ACM Turing Award for "his fundamental contributions to the definition and design of programming languages".

Wolfgang Grieskamp is a principal architect and researcher in the Protocol Engineering Team at Microsoft, Server Tools and Business, which aims to create tools and engineering methods that enable software engineers to build, test, and maintain interoperable products from Microsoft Technical Documentation. To achieve this goals they apply modeling, model-based testing, and other advanced technologies. Before joining Microsoft he worked for six years at Microsoft Research, developing MBT technology and the Spec Explorer family of MBT tools. Spec Explorer has moved together with him from Microsoft Research to Windows, where it is successfully productized and maintained.

Conference Organization

General Chair

Anthony Simons   University of Sheffield, UK

Programme Chairs

Leonardo Bottaci   University of Hull, UK
Gordon Fraser   Saarland University, Germany

Programme Committee

Rui Abreu   University of Porto, Portugal
Paul Baker   Motorola, UK
Sigrid Eldh   Ericsson, Sweden
Michael Ernst   University of Washington, USA
Mark Harman   King's College, UK
Rob Hierons   Brunel University, UK
Daniel Hoffman   University of Victoria, Canada
John Hughes   QuviQ, Sweden
Timea Illes-Seifert   University of Heidelberg, Germany
Gregory Kapfhammer   Allegheny College, USA
Wes Masri   American University of Beirut, Lebanon
Phil McMinn   University of Sheffield, UK
Atif Memon   University of Maryland, USA
Manuel Nunez   Universidad Complutense de Madrid, Spain
Jeff Offutt   George Mason University, USA
Alexander Pretschner   Fraunhofer IESE, Germany
Filippo Ricca   Università degli Studi di Genova, Italy
Marc Roper   University of Strathclyde, UK
Paul Strooper   The University of Queensland, Australia
Nikolai Tillmann   Microsoft Research, USA
Hasan Ural   University of Ottawa, Canada
Neil Walkinshaw   University of Sheffield, USA
Elaine Weyuker   AT&T Research Labs, USA

External Reviewers

Alejandro Russo   Chalmers University of Technology, Sweden
Cesar Andres   Universidad Complutense de Madrid, Spain
Dan Haitao   Brunel University, UK
Joern Guy Suess   University of Queensland, Australia
Margaret Wojcicki   University of Queensland, Australia
Mercedes Merayo   Universidad Complutense de Madrid, Spain

Table of Contents

Keynote Addresses

Automatic Testing and Fixing for Eiffel (Extended Abstract) 1
  Bertrand Meyer

Testing and Proving, Hand-in-Hand 5
  Sir Tony Hoare

Microsoft's Protocol Documentation Program: A Success Story for
Model-Based Testing 7
  Wolfgang Grieskamp

Full Papers

Masking Boundary Value Coverage: Effectiveness and Efficiency 8
  *P. Vijay Suman, Tukaram Muske, Prasad Bokil, Ulka Shrotri, and
  R. Venkatesh*

Model-Checking Erlang - A Comparison between EtomCRL2 and
McErlang 23
  Qiang Guo, John Derrick, Clara Benac Earle, and Lars-Åke Fredlund

Bad Pairs in Software Testing 39
  *Daniel Hoffman, Chien-Hsing Chang, Gary Bazdell,
  Brett Stevens, and Kevin Yoo*

Localizing Defects in Multithreaded Programs by Mining Dynamic Call
Graphs 56
  *Frank Eichinger, Victor Pankratius, Philipp W.L. Große, and
  Klemens Böhm*

Filtering Test Models to Support Incremental Testing 72
  Antti Jääskeläinen

Does Testing Help to Reduce the Number of Potentially Faulty
Statements in Debugging? 88
  Mihai Nica, Simona Nica, and Franz Wotawa

Linguistic Security Testing for Text Communication Protocols 104
  Ben W.Y. Kam and Thomas R. Dean

Tool Papers

An Open-Source Tool for Automated Generation of Black-Box xUnit
Test Code and Its Industrial Evaluation 118
    *Christian Wiederseiner, Shahnewaz Amin Jolly, Vahid Garousi, and
Matt M. Eskandar*

TeCReVis: A Tool for Test Coverage and Test Redundancy
Visualization 129
    Negar Koochakzadeh and Vahid Garousi

A Fault Injection Tool for Testing Web Services Composition 137
    *Fayçal Bessayah, Ana Cavalli, Willian Maja, Eliane Martins, and
Andre Willik Valenti*

Synthesis of On-Line Planning Tester for Non-deterministic EFSM
Models 147
    Marko Kääramees, Jüri Vain, and Kullo Raiend

A Generic Approach to Run Mutation Analysis 155
    Siamak Haschemi and Stephan Weißleder

Challenge Paper

The Practical Assessment of Test Sets with Inductive Inference
Techniques 165
    Neil Walkinshaw

Experience Reports

Mining API Popularity 173
    Yana Momchilova Mileva, Valentin Dallmeier, and Andreas Zeller

Automatic Discovery of Unspecified Behaviors in Automotive Control
Software 181
    Muzammil Shahbaz and Robert Eschbach

Fast Abstracts

An Empirical Evaluation to Study Benefits of Visual versus Textual
Test Coverage Information 189
    Vahid Garousi and Negar Koochakzadeh

A Multi-criteria Decision Making Framework for Real Time
Model-Based Testing 194
    *Mohammad Saeed Abou Trab, Bachar Alrouh, Steve Counsell,
Rob M. Hierons, and George Ghinea*

Improved Testing through Refactoring: Experience from the ProTest
Project 198
    Huiqing Li and Simon Thompson

Towards Run-Time Monitoring of Web Services Conformance to
Business-Level Agreements 203
    Konstantinos Bratanis, Dimitris Dranidis, and Anthony J.H. Simons

A New Approach for Software Testability 207
    Lydie du Bousquet

DOM Transactions for Testing JavaScript 211
    Phillip Heidegger, Annette Bieniusa, and Peter Thiemann

The GZoltar Project: A Graphical Debugger Interface 215
    André Riboira and Rui Abreu

Author Index 219

Automatic Testing and Fixing for Eiffel
(Extended Abstract)

Bertrand Meyer

Chair of Software Engineering, ETH Zurich
Eiffel Software, Santa Barbara
http://se.ethz.ch/~meyer, http://www.eiffel.com

Abstract. Key aspects of software development, in particular testing and debugging, still commonly rely on manual techniques. If the programs contain enough built-in correctness information, in the form of contracts, it is possible to automate some of the most tedious and error-prone aspects of testing, and even to perform *corrections* automatically.

At both ETH and Eiffel Software we have developed such techniques and integrated them into Eiffel programming environments, in the form of tools for automated program testing and automated program fixing: the AutoTest and AutoFix frameworks.

Some of the work is still research in progress, but many results have already been integrated in the production version of the EiffelStudio environment.

Keywords: software testing, automatic program testing, automatic program fixing, Design by Contract, Eiffel, AutoTest, AutoFix.

1 Automated Program Testing

Progress in software engineering has occurred for a large part through the same technique that has made computer technology successful in so many other areas of human endeavor: automation.

The typical candidate for automation is a task that when performed manually is both labor-intensive and error-prone.

Software testing abounds with suitable examples:

1. If you have a test case, especially one that failed — the interesting case from the software tester's Mephistophelic perspective —, it should remain part of the project's test base. More specifically, it should join the *regression test suite* (so called because projects must be careful to avoid the case, known as a "regression", of a corrected fault that reappears in a later version). Inclusion of failed and corrected tests into the regression test suite is a prime candidate for automation.

2. In a large project, tests are likely to be numerous. The mere task of *running* all these tests, for example before a new release, is tedious and subject to human mistakes. It can largely be automated. Of all the tasks listed here, this one has the best support in today's environments, thanks to tools of the "XUnit" class.

3. Preparing the large number of test cases required for credibility of the test process — *test generation* — is perhaps the most time-consuming and tricky task of all.
4. A competing candidate for that distinction is the preparation of *test oracles*: the mechanisms that analyze the results of test runs. Tests are only useful if it is possible, in each case, to decide whether a test run has passed or failed. With the amount of testing necessary for a realistic project, devising oracles is a major challenge when performed manually.
5. Sometimes an execution fails without having been explicitly prepared as a test case; the typical case is a failure occurring while a developer is trying out the program interactively. In the absence of tools such as those described below, this important event of project history will be forgotten: the mistake will be corrected and development will continue. It is desirable, however, to remember the fault as part of the project's history and, more specifically, as part of regression testing. *Test extraction* is the task of automatically producing test cases from failed executions.

Task 2 is, as noted, a solved problem in modern development environments. The other tasks remain manual for most programmers. Over the past years, the Eiffel environment has been extended with techniques, now integrated in the EiffelStudio environment [1] (open-source and commercial versions) addressing the corresponding needs. Collectively, they are known as the AutoTest framework. AutoTest fundamentally relies on the presence of Eiffel's contracts (preconditions, postconditions, class invariants and other assertions) in programs. The framework supports the following applications, detailed in a recent article [2]:

- Test case generation. Provided with a set of classes, AutoTest generates instances automatically, and calls all the routines of the class with targets and arguments generated according to various strategies (detailed in the many publications on AutoTest, see the bibliography in [1] and in the author's online publication list). The most important characteristic of this process is that it is entirely automatic ("push-button"); no programmer intervention is required to produce test cases. Programmers may, of course, add manual test cases if they wish. The purposes are complementary [3]: automatically generated test cases are good for breadth; they trigger many cases that people might forget. Human testers are good for depth: they exercise software in ways that resemble some of the actual executions by users.
- Automatic oracles. AutoTest evaluates contracts during execution, and flags violations of postconditions and class invariants, which always denote faults. This is the primary mechanism for finding faults.
- Test extraction. If the developer has turned on the corresponding option, AutoTest will, after any failed execution, create a test case that reproduces that execution.
- Regression testing. AutoTest maintains a repository of tests — generated or extracted through the previous techniques, as well as any manually prepared test cases — and on request will run these collected tests.

While research and development continue to refine these techniques, they have already proved their worth by detecting hundreds of faults, some quite subtle, and some in code that had been released and was thought to have been debugged.

Automated testing cannot completely replace manual techniques. Empirical studies show [3] that they are complementary; automatic tools such as AutoTest, human testers, and users in the field tend to report different kinds of bugs. This observation does not remove the duty to make automatic techniques as extensive as possible, so that humans can focus their efforts on the tasks for which they are irreplaceable.

2 Automated Program Fixing

It is good to automate tests; what about the next step in debugging, correcting the faults? The idea of applying automation here may at first sound like science-fiction, but three reasons make it eminently reasonable.

The first is the mere power of computers: model checking, among other developments, has demonstrated that previously unthinkable approaches, based on exhaustive exploration, can be realistic.

The second reason is the realization, from empirical analysis of large project repositories, that even when the cause of an error is subtle the fix is in many cases simple: adding an instruction before a call, switching two instructions. Combined with the previous observation, this property suggests techniques that will try out many such transformations until one is found that fixes the problem.

These ideas would not yield a satisfactory approach to automatic correction without some guarantee that the fixes will not be haphazard but will preserve the essential semantics of the program; in particular, that they do not endanger the successful executions. Hence the third observation: contracts enable us to distinguish promising fixes from arbitrary ones.

The result of this analysis is our AutoFix framework [4], part of a joint project with Andreas Zeller's group at Saarbrücken, which builds on AutoTest to propose fixes (corrections) after a program failure. The fixes are tried on a body of successful tests maintained by AutoTest, and are validated against the program's contracts. While the project is still in its early phases, first results are encouraging; in a significant proportion of cases, the automatically suggested fixes are those a programmer would have applied after thoughtful analysis. We are also assessing the approach on older bugs, by comparing the suggested fixes against those that programmers actually applied, as recorded in the project repository of EiffelStudio; here too the first results, although partial, suggest that the approach is realistic.

The intended use of AutoFix is as an advisory tool, which will suggest corrections rather than apply them blindly. The final decision must rest with the programmer. Having an automatic mechanism is useful not only to save debugging time, but also to make sure that if the programmer does approve a suggested fix it will be applied correctly — rather than introducing a new fault, a regrettably common case.

3 Assessment

Software development efforts, especially the delicate tasks of testing and debugging, still involve many repetitive, error-prone parts. Automation is the key to improving this state of affairs, with obvious benefits for software engineering goals of quality and productivity. While many issues remain open, the AutoTest and AutoFix frameworks outlined above show that programmers can expect considerable help from automated tools, if they use a programming language such as Eiffel where contracts are an integral component of all stages of the development process.

References

1. EiffelStudio environment, `http://www.eiffel.com`
2. Meyer, B., Ciupa, I., Leitner, A., Fiva, A., Wei, Y., Stapf, E.: Programs that Test Themselves. IEEE Computer 42(9), 46–55 (2009)
3. Polikarpova, N., Ciupa, I., Meyer, B.: A Comparative Study of Programmer-Written and Automatically Inferred Contracts. In: ISSTA 2009: International Symposium on Software Testing and Analysis, Chicago (July 2009)
4. Wei, Y., Pei, Y., Furia, C., Silva, L., Buchholz, S., Meyer, B., Zeller, A.: Automated Fixing of Programs with Contracts. To appear in ISSTA 2010: Proceedings of the International Symposium on Software Testing and Analysis, Trento (Italy), July 12-16. ACM Press, New York (2010)

Testing and Proving, Hand-in-Hand

Sir Tony Hoare

Microsoft Research
Cambridge, UK

The motivating ideal of my lifetime's scientific research has been that of program correctness, achieved with the aid of mathematical proof. As suggested by Turing, Floyd, and others, the proofs would be based on the decoration of a program with assertions, that would be proved true if ever they were evaluated at the point where they were written in the code. During my long academic career, I regarded program testing as the main rival technology, and feared that improvement in the practice of testing would delay development and application of the superior technology of proof.

When I retired, I was offered the opportunity to join Microsoft Research at Cambridge. I was not expecting to see any application in current Microsoft program development practice of the topics or results of my lifetime's research. So when I first visited the Microsoft program development centre in Redmond, I was delighted to find a number of senior developers actually making regular use of assertion macros in the code which they wrote and delivered to their customers.

But I was shocked to find that they were being used not for proof, but only as test oracles to help in overnight program testing,. The assertions were designed to detect programming errors as close as possible to the point at which they were made. At that moment the scales fell from my eyes. Testing and proving are not rivals: they are just two ends of a scale of techniques available to the software engineer to collect evidence for the validity and serviceability of delivered code. Both technologies are worthy of development by research, and should be used in combination. Furthermore, they both use the same underlying framework of logic and mathematics which have been developed by research. It is not the business of a researcher to recommend one over the other. The engineer is the person to decide in what proportions to combine them, depending on the characteristics of the current project.

So I encouraged developers to use assertions during testing, and hoped that this would prepare the ground for other uses of assertions as program documentation, and eventually proof: maybe we could persuade programmers to write important interface assertions as contracts, even before the code was written.

And so it has come to pass. In the last ten years, interface assertions have been included in all of Microsoft's supported programming languages. Furthermore, automated tools to generate test cases now seek the cases most likely to violate the assertions, and they use proof technology to do so. Nearly all Microsoft software is now subjected to program analyses, which attempt to construct assertions, and use them to detect likely coding errors, even before the programs are tested. All the tools combine testing with the technology of proof. Verifying compilers have recently become available for two programming languages, concurrent C and a variant of C# . Furthermore, every attempt is made to ensure that these tools can be used in combination, at the discretion of the software engineer.

I will describe some of the current Microsoft programming, which have been assembled in a collection called RiSE, and which are now being offered for use outside Microsoft by researchers into programming theory, correctness, and testing.

Microsoft's Protocol Documentation Program: A Success Story for Model-Based Testing

Wolfgang Grieskamp

Windows Interoperability Engineering Team
Microsoft Corporation, USA

Microsoft is producing interoperability documentation for Windows client-server and server-server protocols. The Winterop team in the Windows organization is responsible for verifying the documentation to ensure its quality. Various test-driven methods are being applied including, when appropriate, a model-based approach. This talk describes core aspects of the quality assurance process and tools that were put in place, and specifically focuses on model-based testing (MBT), using Microsoft's Spec Explorer technology. Though MBT has been applied successfully to features and products before, this is the first attempt to use it in such a large scale and in the context of a business-critical area within Microsoft, and to the best of the author's knowledge throughout the whole industry. Empirical results confirm that MBT not only works and that it scales, provided it is accompanied by good tool support and clear methodological guidance, but also that it delivers significant productivity gains when compared to traditional testing in a similar domain and with the same people resources. The method to measure this is based on the effort per end-to-end tested requirement (including not only test design, but also test harnessing and test execution), over a probe of 9,844 requirements in test suites using MBT and 8,728 requirements in non-MBT test suites, with an average effort of 1.39 person days for MBT-tested requirement, and 2.37 person days for traditionally-tested requirement, documenting a productivity gain of 42%. A detailed account of this work is scheduled to appear in the journal for Software Testing and Verification (STVR) under the title Model-based Quality Assurance of Protocol Documentation: Tools and Methodology.

Masking Boundary Value Coverage: Effectiveness and Efficiency

P. Vijay Suman, Tukaram Muske, Prasad Bokil, Ulka Shrotri, and R. Venkatesh

TRDDC
54B, Hadapsar
Industrial Estate,
Pune 411 013, India

Abstract. Boundary value testing in the white-box setting tests relational expressions with boundary values. These relational expressions are often a part of larger conditional expressions or decisions. It is therefore important, for effective testing that the outcome of a relational expression independently influences the outcome of the expression or decision in which it is embedded. Extending MC/DC to boundary value testing was proposed in the literature as a technique to achieve this independence. Based on this idea, in this paper we formally define a new coverage criterion - masking boundary value coverage (MBVC). MBVC is an adaptation of masking of conditions to boundary value testing. Mutation based analysis is used to show that test data satisfying MBVC is more effective in detecting relational mutants than test data satisfying BVC.

In this paper, we give a formal argument justifying why test data for MBVC is more effective compared to that for BVC in detecting relational mutants. We performed an experiment to evaluate effectiveness and efficiency of MBVC test data relative to that for BVC, in detecting relational mutants. Firstly, mutation adequacy of the test set for MBVC was higher than that for BVC in 56% of cases, and never lower. Secondly, the test data for MBVC killed 80.7% of the total number of mutants generated, whereas the test data for BVC killed only 70.3% of them. A further refined analysis revealed that some mutants are such that they cannot be killed. We selected a small set of mutants randomly to get an estimate of percentage of such mutants. Then the extrapolated mutation adequacies were 92.75% and 80.8% respectively. We summarize the effect of masking on efficiency. Details of the experiment, tools developed for automation and analysis of the results are also provided in this paper.

1 Introduction

Bugs in software can be very expensive and can result in loss of life in the case of safety-critical software, product recalls in the case of embedded software and loss to business in other cases. Ensuring that a software application is bug-free is very difficult. Formal specification and verification of the entire software of such systems could be one way of demonstrating that an application is bug-free. However formal specification of the complete software is often unavailable, and in many cases not derivable. Moreover, when the program is complex, formally showing its correctness is often intractable.

Software testing serves as a practical and economic alternative to detect bugs in software. Testing methods have been extensively studied in the literature [13]. Testing typically assesses the end-to-end quality of a software by exercising the software on a representative set of test set to check if it meets the specified requirements. However, it is impossible to check program performance on all possible input data. An ideal test set should be large enough to effectively exercise most of the program executions, yet small enough so that the tester can comfortably run the program on it and compare the actual outputs with the expected outputs.

Generating effective test data efficiently is a challenging task. Test generation is usually done with respect to some coverage criterion. The coverage could be either functional coverage such as boundary value analysis (BVA) or structural coverage of the code. There are various types of structural coverage criteria [9] such as statement, condition, decision, condition/decision, modified condition/decision coverage (MC/DC), multiple condition coverage (MCC). Ensuring that a test set satisfies a coverage criterion is an indirect measure of its effectiveness [10].

Boundary value analysis is a functional testing technique in which tests include boundary values of relational expressions. A test set covers the boundary values for a relational expression `e relop c`, where `c` is a constant if `e` evaluates to `c`, `c+1` and `c-1` for some test in the set. A test set is said to achieve boundary value coverage (BVC) for a program if it covers every boundary value of every relational expression. BVC is useful for uncovering bugs in relational conditions where either an incorrect operator is used or there is an off-by-one error.

Relational expressions in a program often occur as part of a larger conditional expression or decision. In such cases a test case that covers a boundary value of the expression should ensure that the expression has an independent effect on the outcome of the larger conditional expression or decision. Masking of conditions, as introduced in the context of masking MC/DC [9], can be applied to achieve this independent effect. A condition `c` in a decision `d` is said to be masked if the values of the other conditions in `d` are such that changing the value of `c` will have no impact on the result of `d`. The idea of extending MC/DC to relational testing was proposed in [4]. In this paper we formalize this idea by defining a new coverage criterion called masking boundary value coverage (MBVC) that extends boundary value coverage with masking. In MBVC each test set that covers a relational expression for boundary values also ensures that the values of other conditions in the decision are such that the relational expression of interest is the one that influences the outcome of the decision. For example, consider the function `func` given in Figure 1. The relational condition of interest is (`inp1 > 10`) in line number 4. The difference between the two test sets for BVC and MBVC will be in the value of `inp2`. The test set for MBVC will ensure that the value of `inp2` is `non-zero` so that the relational expression has an independent effect, whereas the test set for BVC could have any value for `inp2` including `zero`.

The paper presents a more rigorous comparison of the effectiveness of test sets generated for BVC and MBVC using mutation analysis [2,4,7,11]. We do this using a mutation operator that introduces off-by-one errors and relational operator errors in the code. We compare the two sets by their effectiveness in detecting erroneous versions, and how efficiently they can be generated. A formal argument is presented to show that

```
1. int inp1, inp2, op;
2. void func()
3. {
4.     if( ( inp1 > 10 ) && inp2 )
5.         op = 1;
6.     else
7.         op = 0;
8. }
```

Fig. 1. Running Example

where MBVC test data for a boundary value cannot be generated, the corresponding mutants cannot be killed by the BVC test data. Furthermore, when MBVC test data for a boundary value can be generated it ensures that the intermediate states in the corresponding mutants are different from that of the original, which is not necessarily true with BVC test data. It is still theoretically possible that test data for BVC would kill a mutant, but test data for MBVC would fail to kill the same mutant. However, this is not a side-effect of using masking, but rather an incidental possibility. For our experiments we chose a random set of 74 functions (which we refer to as *representative set*) from an embedded automotive application. Since we used a restricted mutation operator we could do an exhaustive mutation analysis as opposed to selecting a set of mutants randomly. This removes the repeatability requirement from our method of analysis.

This paper...

- formally defines boundary value coverage,
- introduces masking boundary value coverage,
- describes a white-box method to generate at unit level, test data satisfying MBVC,
- analyses the effectiveness and efficiency of masking in detecting relational mutants,
- describes the experimental setup and the tools used to perform the experiment, and
- presents the findings of the experiment along with a detailed analysis.

Related Work: Boundaries are common locations for errors that result in software faults and hence they need to be exercised by the test set. There have been studies comparing BVA with equivalence partitioning [15], and it is widely believed that BVA is very effective and necessary. Traditionally BVA is applied to the input specification to detect bugs in specification of input ranges. Automatic white-box generation of test data satisfying boundary value coverage (with or without masking) has never been attempted before. Masking of conditions has been used as a mechanism to achieve MC/DC coverage [1,3], however, masking by itself is useful in generating more effective test data. Extending MC/DC to relational testing with boundary values was proposed in [4]. However, neither formal nor experimental analysis of effectiveness of masking in detecting was done as part of the paper. There are numerous works which use mutation analysis to experimentally compare the effectiveness and efficiency of various testing techniques. See [2,11,7] for instance. The closest work to ours among these is that of [7]. However, our approach differs from these works in two ways. Firstly, we have not come across a mutation based comparison of coverage criteria like ours where the test data satisfying both the criteria are exhaustively generated using a white-box technique. This is different from more prevalent techniques of black-box generation where test data is generated randomly until a satisfactory level of required coverage is achieved. Secondly, we use a specific mutation operator which simulates only relational bugs. This is because we did not have access to appropriate mutation analysis tools at the point of conducting these experiments, in order to consider a more comprehensive set of mutation operators [16]. This reduces the total number of possible mutants, and enables us to give a formal argument why test set satisfying MBVC is more effective in detecting relational mutants. On the flip-side, this might not give an accurate comparison with respect to detecting mutants in general. However, we believe that MBVC test data would still turn out to be relatively more effective than BVC test data, if the experiments were repeated with a comprehensive set of mutation operators.

The primary contributions of our current work are the following. (1) We describe a white-box technique to generate test sets for both boundary value coverage and masking boundary value coverage. (2) We give a case wise analysis of scenarios wherein test data for MBVC kills more mutants than that for BVC. We also show a purely theoretical and incidental scenario where the vice-versa holds. (3) Our detailed experimental analysis demonstrated that MBVC test set is more effective in detecting relational mutants.

2 Masking Boundary Value Coverage

In this section we formally define boundary value coverage and masking boundary value coverage. We use the example function func in Figure 1 to illustrate the basic ideas. The input variables for func are inp1 and inp2, whereas op is the output variable.

2.1 Boundary Value Coverage

A relational condition in the programming language C is an expression using a relational operator ($==, !=, <, >, <=, >=$) to compare two entities. To test whether a relational condition is coded correctly, the recommended approach is to generate test data which exercise its boundary situations. The hypothesis is that boundary test cases find (1) *off-by-one* errors and (2) *incorrect operator* errors. An off-by-one error is an instance where one of the operands is either one less or one more than the intended. Any instance where the intended relational operator was replaced by another operator, is referred to as an incorrect operator error. A *relational bug* is the presence of either an off-by-one error or an incorrect operator error. Relational testing is testing intended to find relational bugs.

Consider the condition (inp1 > 10) in line 4 of the function given in example code shown in Figure 1. The condition has an off-by-one error if the constant in the comparison should have been 9 or 11. To detect this bug, test set should be generated such that inp1 takes the values 10 and 11, respectively. Similarly, for the instances of incorrect operator errors to be found, test set should be generated such that inp1 takes the values 9 and 10. In other words, it is necessary to generate test set with inp1 taking values 9, 10 and 11 to detect all relational bugs.

Let r be a relational condition of the form $e_1 \sim e_2$ at program point p in a function $f(i_1 \ldots, i_n)$ where,

- $\sim$ is a relational operator and
- e_1 and e_2 are arbitrary integral expressions
- $i_1, \ldots, i_n$ are inputs to f

Definition 1 (BVC). *A test set TS satisfies BVC for r iff there exist three test vectors $t_1, t_2, t_3 \in TS$ such that e_1 evaluates to $e_2 - 1$, e_2 and $e_2 + 1$ at p for t_1, t_2 and t_3 respectively. Each t_i is a tuple of values $(v_1 \ldots v_n)$ for the input variables $i_1 \ldots i_n$.*

A test set that satisfies BVC for each relational condition in a function is said to provide *boundary value coverage* for that function. This definition can be similarly extended for a program.

It is noteworthy that the boundary value test set would not be sufficient to detect instances where both kinds of errors can occur simultaneously. For instance, the conditions (inp1 > 10) and (inp1 == 11), have uniform truth value for the three test set entries described above.

2.2 Masking Boundary Value Coverage

When a relational expression occurs as part of a larger conditional expression, BVC may not be sufficient to detect relational bugs. To address this problem we introduce masking boundary value coverage, which adopts the idea of masking from masking MC/DC to BVC. Let d be a decision with several conditions in it and let r be one condition in it. If the test set generated is such that the value of r does not have an independent effect over the outcome of d, then the effect of r is not seen on the output either. To ensure this independent effect, other conditions in d should be masked while generating test set for r.

Let $r = e_1 \sim e_2$ be an atomic relational condition in a decision d at program point p in a function $f(i_1 \ldots i_n)$. Let $d^{r'}$ represent the decision generated by replacing the condition r by r', and let d_t represent the truth value of d at program point p with the test vector t.

Definition 2 (MBVC). *A test set TS satisfies MBVC for r iff there exist three test vectors $t_1, t_2, t_3 \in TS$,*

1. *e_1 evaluates to $e_2 - 1$, e_2 and $e_2 + 1$ respectively at p, for t_1, t_2 and t_3 respectively. Each t_i is a tuple of values $(v_1 \ldots v_n)$ for the input variables $i_1 \ldots i_n$ and*
2. *for each t_i, $d^r_{t_i} = \neg d^{\neg r}_{t_i}$.*

A test set that satisfies MBVC for each relational condition in a function is said to provide *masking boundary value coverage* for that function. This definition can be similarly extended for a program.

For example, consider the decision in line 4 in the afore-mentioned code. To ensure BVC for the condition (inp1 > 10), the test set should be such that this condition is exercised with inp1 taking the values 9, 10 and 11. At the same time, to see the effect of a coding error on the output, it is necessary that `inp2` takes a non-zero value in this test set.

Claim: Test data generated for MBVC is more effective at detecting relational mutants than that generated for BVC.

3 Mutation Analysis

Observability based techniques such as mutation analysis are most suitable to compare different coverage criteria. Mutation analysis has been used in the past to determine test suite adequacy [12,11] and also to compare test coverage criteria [2,7].

Mutation [12] is a way of purposely modifying code of a function so as to change its external behaviour. The modified function is called a mutant. Mutation operators define the way in which a particular programming construct gets modified. For instance, a mutation operator can be defined which replaces the operator in a randomly selected relational condition with a different one. Depending on which program unit is selected and how it is mutated different mutants of the same function can be created. For instance, if there are n relational operators in a function, there would be $5n$ possible mutants of this function with the above mutation operator. Note that we work under the assumption that a mutant contains exactly one fault [12,6].

A test set is said to *kill* a mutant iff there exists a test data entry in the test set such that

- Both the original program and the mutant terminate on the test data, and
- The output of the mutant is different from the output of the original program when run with this test data.

Note that a test data entry kills a mutant only if both the following conditions hold [12].

1. It causes different program states for the mutant and the original program (*Weak Mutation* [8]).
2. This difference in state propagates to the output of the program.

The number of mutants killed by a test set is a measure of effectiveness of the test set. Mutation adequacy ratio represents this effectiveness. Formally -

Definition 3 (Mutation Adequacy Ratio). *Let TS represent a test set, and let td represent a test set input. A mutant f' of the program f is said to be killed by a test set TS iff $\exists td \in TS$ such that the output of f and f' are not equal when run with the input td. The mutation adequacy ratio of a test set TS, $\mathcal{AM}_{\mathcal{F}}(TS)$, is the fraction of mutants killed by it in a given set of mutants $\mathcal{F}$.*

The code shown in Figure 2 gives one possible mutant of our running example. The constant used in the relational condition is perturbed by one.

BVC and MBVC are both coverage criteria intended to find relational bugs and hence for our experiments we use a mutation operator that only changes operators and operands in relational expressions. Using such a restricted mutation operator as opposed to using a comprehensive set of mutation operators helps in greatly reducing the number of possible mutants to only those that are of direct interest to the coverage criteria under consideration.

```
1. int inp1, inp2, op;
2. void func()
3. {
4.     if( ( inp1 > 9 ) && inp2 )
5.         op = 1;
6.     else
7.         op = 0;
8. }
```

Fig. 2. An Example Mutant

Formally given a relational condition $e_1 \sim e_2$ the mutation operator is defined as

$$\mu(e_1 \sim e_2) = \begin{cases} e_1 \sim' e_2 \text{ where } \sim' \neq \sim \text{, or} \\ e_1 \sim e_2' \text{ where } e_2' \text{ is either } e_2 - 1 \text{ or} \\ e_2 + 1 \end{cases}$$

4 Generation of Test Sets and Mutants

This section describes the tools used for automatic test set generation and mutant generation.

4.1 Test Set Generation

We have extended our tool AutoGen [3], to accept additional criteria BVC and MBVC and automatically generate test set for that criterion thus reducing the time and effort required to achieve coverage. AutoGen also attempts to generate a non-redundant test set by continuously performing an analysis of coverage that has already been achieved by the test set generated at each step and generating additional test data only for uncovered coverage units.

AutoGen transforms the source program to include statements that generate non-deterministic values for input variables and adds assert statements, the violation of which will result in a condition getting covered. To generate test set that violates these asserts the transformed program is analyzed using C Bounded Model Checker (CBMC) [5]. Given a C program and an assert statement, CBMC checks if the assert is valid and generates a trace that violates the assert if it is not valid.

CBMC is a SAT-based bounded model checker for programs written in Ansi-C and C++. Note that since property checking is undecidable in general, for some cases CBMC may not terminate or may run out of resources. For our experiments we considered only code for which CBMC terminates successfully for both BVC and MBVC.

The functions for which CBMC did not terminate were mostly ones with loops. Generating test data for these functions is necessary to keep our analysis fair. However, doing this would require techniques which are out of scope of this paper.

```
1.  int inp1, inp2, op;
2.  int nondet_int();
3.  void func()
4.  {
5.      inp1 = nondet_int();
6.      inp2 = nondet_int();
7.      assert (!((inp1)==(10+1)));
8.      if( ( inp1 > 10 ) && inp2 )
9.          op = 1;
10.     else
11.         op = 0;
12. }
```

Fig. 3. Annotated Code for $e_1 \sim e_2$

Code transformation: Source code transformation is explained using the example function func of Figure 1. A transformed code is shown in Figure 3. The code has been modified for generating values for input variables and for inserting assert statements. Please refer to [3] for detailed description of the transformation. The tool first identifies the set of input variables needed in the function and then the code is modified such that input variables take non-deterministic values at the start of execution of the function. Any function whose name has the prefix "nondet_" is treated as a special function by CBMC. Let type be the data type of the return value of such a function. CBMC assumes that the return value of this particular function can be any valid value in the range defined by type. Hence lines 5 and 6 of the instrumented code in Figure 3 essentially communicate to CBMC that it has to check executions of func, wherein inp1 and inp2 can both be assigned any two independent values from the data type int.

The input code is also annotated with assert statements which are of the form assert(expr), where expr is any expression allowed by the Ansi-C syntax. To model check this assertion, CBMC tries to check whether there exists an assignment to the input variables, which causes the execution to satisfy (expr==0) when the corresponding line is reached. If so, the assertion is said to be violated, and CBMC reports the same along with a counter-example trace. The required test set is nothing but the values assigned to the input variables in the trace.

Asserts for BVC: Line 7 in Figure 3 shows the assert annotation. When the annotated C code in Figure 3 is given as input to CBMC, it produces a counter-example trace with 11 as the value for inp1 and 0 as the value for inp2.

Asserts for MBVC: The test set for BVC is generated without considering the fact that inp2 is part of the same decision (see line 4 in Figure 1). As explained in Section 2.2, one can use masking of conditions to overcome this limitation. To generate test set for MBVC, we need to ensure that inp2 takes a non-zero value in the entire test set. In order to achieve this, we instrument the code further such that the assert statement is guarded by an appropriate if statement. The condition corresponding to this if statement is such that when the test set is generated, the effect of other conditions is masked.

In case of our running example, line 7 in Figure 3, should be replaced by the following two lines.

```
if(inp2)
    assert (!((inp1)==(10+1)));
```

When the annotated C code with above mentioned modification is given as input to CBMC, it produces a counter-example trace with `11` as the value for `inp1` and `1` as the value for `inp2`.

4.2 Mutant Generation

To generate mutants we have developed a tool that implements the mutation operator μ. The tool takes C source code as input and the mutant is generated by applying the mutation operator μ to each relational condition in the function. The tool also generates the `main` function which executes the mutated function on a given test set, and records the values of the output variables after each invocation.

In general, the number of possible mutants of a function can be quite large. However, we take the *do fewer* approach suggested in [12], by restricting to a particular mutation operator. The number of possible mutants of a function with n relational operators is only $7n$ using our mutation operator. Hence we generate the mutants of each function exhaustively for our analysis. It is noteworthy that the mutation operator emulates the kind of erroneous functions intended to be detected by the test sets generated for both BVC and MBVC.

4.3 Test Sets

The original code (Figure 1) of the actual function and the mutant code (Figure 2) is executed with the generated test set. Table 1 (on the left) shows the test set generated for BVC and it also shows the output of actual function and the mutant code. In this case it is an accident that our test data generator generated 0 for `inp2`.

Table 1. Test Data for BVC and MBVC

inp1	inp2	Function Output	Mutant Output
9	0	0	0
10	0	0	0
11	0	0	0

inp1	inp2	Function Output	Mutant Output
9	1	0	0
10	1	0	1
11	1	1	1

Table 1 (on the right) shows the test set generated for MBVC and it also shows the output of actual function and the mutant code. It is easy to see that the mutant of Figure 2 gets killed by test set for MBVC but not by test set for BVC.

5 Formal Analysis of the Effect of Masking

This section presents a formal analysis of how masking of conditions helps in achieving additional effectiveness in detecting relational mutants. We consider an arbitrary mutant and do a case-wise analysis on the basis of generatability of each type of test data.

Let f be the function of interest, and let f' be one of its mutants. Let r be the relational condition $e_1 \sim e_2$ in decision d, which was changed by μ and let r' represent the variant of r and d' the modified decision. Let b represent a boundary value which differentiates r from r', and let τ_b and t_b respectively represent any MBVC and BVC test data for coverage of b.

Case 1. Neither τ_b nor t_b exist. The mutant cannot be detected by either of the test sets.

Case 2. τ_b exists, but not t_b. This contradicts the definition of MBVC, as any test data entry that satisfies MBVC, by definition satisfies BVC.

Case 3. t_b exists, but not τ_b. If t_b kills the mutant then since f and f' differ only in r, $r = \neg r'$ and $d = \neg d'$ must be true. Then t_b also satisfies MBVC for r which contradicts our assumption. Hence t_b cannot kill the mutant.

Case 4. Both τ_b and t_b exist.

(a) t_b kills f' and τ_b does not. We give an example of such a function and a mutant in Figure 4 to argue that this is a valid possibility. The commented code on line 6 represents one possible application of μ to (inp1 > 10). For this example $b = 10$. Table 2 shows two possible test data entries for this boundary value, one satisfying MBVC and the other satisfying BVC. This shows one possible instance where the mutant is killed by t_b but not by τ_b. Note that the same example can be used to show how τ_b kills a mutant that t_b does not.
(b) All the other sub cases do not contradict our claim and hence we do not analyze them.

All the cases are in favour of MBVC, except Case 4(a). Note that Case 4(a) is an instance where the test data for MBVC could not ensure the second condition for mutant to be detected (see Section 3). However, since inp2 is a condition independent of the mutated condition, it is highly improbable that inp2 has different values in the two test data entries, especially when test data is generated automatically using a fixed algorithm. Furthermore, if the value of inp2 was same in the two test data entries, it cannot happen that BVC test data detects the mutant but MBVC test data does not. This argument is supported by our experimental data which contains no occurrences of scenarios similar to Case 4(a).

```
1. int inp1, inp2, op;
2. void func()
3. {
4. int local;
5.     if( inp1 > 10 )
6.     //if( inp1 > 9 )
7.         local = 1;
8.     else
9.         local = 0;
10.    if( local || inp2 )
11.        op = 1;
12.    else
13.        op = 0;
14. }
```

Fig. 4. Counter-Example

Table 2. Test Data

Coverage	inp1	inp2	Function Output	Mutant Output
MBVC	10	1	1	1
BVC	10	0	0	1

6 Experiment

To validate our theory an experiment based on mutation analysis was conducted. In this section we describe our experimental setup, and then present the empirical data supporting our claim. Section 6.2 gives the figures obtained in our experiments.

6.1 The Setup

To make our experiment more realistic we chose some modules of an embedded application. The application is a C program intended to control the battery in a car. The application has around 22 modules of which we randomly chose 12 for our analysis. Among the functions in these modules the number of functions which had logical combinations of relational conditions, and were amenable to our analysis was 74. The total number of lines of code for these 74 functions is 3646.

Let $\mathcal{F}$ represent the set of 74 functions we analyzed. The following steps were executed on each function f in $\mathcal{F}$.

1. Identify the set of output variables of f.
2. Generate test sets for f satisfying BVC and MBVC.
3. Generate a random subset of all possible mutants of f.

4. Compile and execute each of the mutants on both the test sets, and record independently the number of mutants killed by each of them. In our setup, since the test sets are executed on the same set of mutants, we can consider the number of mutants killed as a direct measure of their mutation adequacy ratios.

6.2 Empirical Data

Table 3 summarizes the empirical data collected from our mutation analysis. A description of the contents of various rows in the table is as follows:

- The first row gives the total number of functions in our representative set. Note that only functions involving decisions with logical combination of relational conditions were considered.
- The second row gives the number of functions for which MBVC killed more mutants than BVC.
- The third row gives the number of functions for which BVC killed more mutants.
- The fourth row gives the number of functions for which both BVC and MBVC killed the same number of mutants.
- The fifth row gives the total number of mutants generated using our mutation operator.
- The sixth row gives the number of mutants killed by test data satisfying MBVC.
- The seventh row gives the number of mutants killed by test data satisfying BVC.

The rest of the rows are explained below.

We did a further (manual) investigation of why 893 of these mutants were not killed by any of the generated test data. We had the time to analyze 153 of them, and it was revealed that 103 of these were not killed because the test data that can kill these mutants cannot be generated. For instance, the actual relational condition in a function was of the form `b==1`, whereas that in the mutant was `b>=1`. The boundary value that can kill this mutant is `2`. But the variable b was a bit field of size `1`. Extrapolating these numbers the total number of mutants that can be killed comes down to 4026. And hence the mutation adequacies of test data satisfying MBVC and BVC are 92.75% and 80.8% respectively. The rows 8,9 and 10 in Table 3 quote these numbers.

Table 3. Empirical Data from Mutation Analysis

No.	Category	Number	Percentage
1	Representative Set	74	-NA-
2	$\mathcal{AM}(TS_M) > \mathcal{AM}(TS)$	42	56
3	$\mathcal{AM}(TS_M) < \mathcal{AM}(TS)$	0	0
4	$\mathcal{AM}(TS_M) = \mathcal{AM}(TS)$	32	44
5	Total Mutants	4627	-NA-
6	Mutants killed by MBVC test data	3734	80.7
7	Mutants killed by BVC test data	3253	70.3
8	Number of Detectable Mutants (Extrapolated)	4026	-NA-
9	Mutants killed by MBVC test data	3734	92.75
10	Mutants killed by BVC test data	3253	80.8

```
1. int inp1, inp2, op;
2. void func()
3. {
4. int local;
5.     if( inp1 > 10 && inp2)
6.     //if( inp1 > 11 && inp2)
7.         local = 1;
8.     else
9.         local = 0;
10.    if( local || inp3 )
11.        op = 1;
12.    else
13.        op - 0;
14. }
```

Fig. 5. Hindrance in Propagation

Propagation. The reason for the other mutants not getting killed by test set satisfying MBVC was that the change in state induced by the test data did not propagate to the output. This was because of masking by a condition in an independent decision. For instance consider the code given in Figure 5. The commented line 6 is a mutated version of the code in line 6. The boundary value for `inp1` that can detect this mutant is `11`. However, if the test values that were generated for `inp1`, `inp2` and `inp3` were `11`, `1` and `1`, the output of the mutated function does not differ from that of the original. Note that the change in state is observed at line 5. But this fails to propagate to the output due to the input variable `inp3` taking the value `1`. It is noteworthy that the condition `inp3` is part of an entirely different decision.

Efficiency. Using masking for relational testing comes with the following added costs. For the functions wherein the conditions use logical operators,

- the **size** of the test set for MBVC was 28.65% more than that for BVC. This happens mostly when there are more than one relational expression in a decision. In such cases the probability of a test vector generated for covering one component of a decision covering some other component also goes down in presence of masking. Hence more test vectors are required to provide MBVC coverage.
- the **time** taken to generate the test set for MBVC was 9.38% more than that taken to generate for BVC. The average time taken for generating test data for MBVC was 95.19 seconds per function, as opposed to 86.26 seconds per function for BVC. This was expected because the constraint that is generated by the model checker will be stronger when masking is used. Computing a satisfiable assignment for this constraint is expected to be relatively expensive.

However, these costs should be acceptable as the probability of detecting a bug goes up considerably and although the time taken for MBVC is more, the entire generation is automatic.

In the industrial code we tried to target, there were functions which could not be analyzed using our approach. For example, there were instances where the model checker ran out of resources. We completely excluded data corresponding to any such function.

7 Conclusions and Discussions

Mutation analysis validated the claim that MBVC is more effective than simple BVC in detecting mutants. We restricted our attention to the test set generated for BVC of relational conditions occurring in the code. Masking is likely to be beneficial in other contexts too such as the data flow coverage criteria p-use [14].

Our experiments, modulo the limitations (see Section 7.1), suggest that using masking when generating boundary value test data is more effective and at the same time insignificantly inefficient. Following are some of our observations.

- Test data for MBVC is strictly more effective in 56% of the cases.
- The average mutation adequacies of MBVC test data and BVC test data are 80.7 and 70.3 respectively. A further investigation revealed that there were mutants that could not be killed, because test data for killing these cannot be generated. Discounting these, with some extrapolation, the mutation adequacies turned out to be 92.75 and 80.8 respectively.
- The average size of the test data generated increased by 28.65% and the average time taken to generate the test data increased by 9.38%. Given the increase in chances of detecting a bug, these added prices are acceptable. Moreover, the test data generation was automated in the form of a tool and hence required insignificant manual effort.
- The defects that could not be detected by MBVC test data were diagnosed to be those in which the change in state induced by the test data was hindered from propagating to the output by an independent condition occurring in a decision other than the one of interest.

We would like to point out that when none of the conditions in the code is such that it is a logical combination of atomic conditions, masking has neither positive nor adverse effects.

7.1 Limitations of Our Approach

- One prominent limitation of our approach is that we consider only those functions for which the model checker terminated. A more fair analysis would require significant efforts towards loop abstraction and is out of scope of this paper.
- Another factor which could have improved the credibility of our analysis is keeping the size of the test sets being compared same. This could be achieved by padding more test data to the BVC test set to make it as big as the test set for MBVC.

7.2 Future Directions

- Other coverage criteria such as p-use can be extended with masking of conditions. We intend to do more rigorous experimental study of how effective masking would be in those cases.
- Using specific mutation operators to assess the effectiveness of a test suite in finding the bugs it is intended to find, is an interesting idea by itself. When the category of bugs to be detected is clearly defined, this approach is a useful alternative to using a comprehensive set of mutation operators. A systematic study of how effective our alternative approach is in the spirit of [16] needs to be done.
- We would like to point out that the test data generation is at unit level and does not take procedure preconditions into account.

References

1. Do-178b: Software considerations in airborne systems and equipment certification (1982)
2. Andrews, J.H., Briand, L.C., Labiche, Y., Namin, A.S.: Using mutation analysis for assessing and comparing testing coverage criteria. IEEE Trans. Softw. Eng. 32(8), 608–624 (2006)
3. Bokil, P., Darke, P., Shrotri, U., Venkatesh, R.: Automatic test data generation for c programs. Secure System Integration and Reliability Improvement, 359–368 (2009)
4. Chilenski, J.J.: An investigation of three forms of the modified condition decision coverage (mcdc) criterion. Technical Report DOT/FAA/AR-01/18, Office of Aviation Research (2001)
5. Clarke, E., Kroening, D., Lerda, F.: A tool for checking ANSI-C programs. In: Jensen, K., Podelski, A. (eds.) TACAS 2004. LNCS, vol. 2988, pp. 168–176. Springer, Heidelberg (2004)
6. De Millo, R.A., Lipton, R.J., Sayward, F.G.: Hints on test data selection: Help for the practicing programmer. Computer 11(4), 34–41 (1978)
7. Gupta, A., Jalote, P.: An approach for experimentally evaluating effectiveness and efficiency of coverage criteria for software testing. Int. J. Softw. Tools Technol. Transf. 10(2), 145–160 (2008)
8. Howden, W.E.: Weak mutation testing and completeness of test sets. IEEE Trans. Softw. Eng. 8(4), 371–379 (1982)
9. Hayhurst Kelly, J., Veerhusen Dan, S., Chilenski John, J., Rierson Leanna, K.: A practical tutorial on modified condition/decision coverage. Technical Report NAS 1.15:210876 (2001)
10. Myers, G.J.: The Art of Software Testing. Wiley, New York (1979)
11. Namin, A.S., Andrews, J.H.: The influence of size and coverage on test suite effectiveness. In: ISSTA 2009: Proceedings of the eighteenth international symposium on Software testing and analysis, pp. 57–68. ACM, New York (2009)
12. Jefferson Offutt, A., Untch, R.H.: Mutation 2000: uniting the orthogonal, pp. 34–44 (2001)
13. Perry, W.: Effective methods for software testing. Wiley-QED Publishing, Somerset (1995)
14. Rapps, S., Weyuker, E.J.: Selecting software test data using data flow information. IEEE Trans. Softw. Eng. 11(4), 367–375 (1985)
15. Reid, S.C.: An empirical analysis of equivalence partitioning, boundary value analysis and random testing. In: METRICS 1997: Proceedings of the 4th International Symposium on Software Metrics, p. 64. IEEE Computer Society Press, Washington (1997)
16. Namin, A.S., Andrews, J.H., Murdoch, D.J.: Sufficient mutation operators for measuring test effectiveness. In: ICSE 2008: Proceedings of the 30th international conference on Software engineering, pp. 351–360. ACM, New York (2008)

Model-Checking Erlang – A Comparison between EtomCRL2 and McErlang

Qiang Guo[1], John Derrick[1], Clara Benac Earle[2], and Lars-Åke Fredlund[2]

[1] Department of Computer Science,
The University of Sheffield,
Regent Court, 211 Portobello, S1 4DP, UK
{Q.Guo,J.Derrick}@dcs.shef.ac.uk
[2] Facultad de Informática,
Universidad Politécnica de Madrid
Boadilla del Monte 28660, Madrid, Spain
{cbenac,fred}@babel.ls.fi.upm.es

Abstract. Model-checking programs is important in the development of a reliable software system. Two approaches might be applied to model-check a system at a source code level. One is to directly apply model-checking algorithm to the programming language; the other to abstract the program source codes into a formal specification, upon which some standard model-checkers can be used to verify system's properties. Both methods have recently been investigated for model-checking the functional programming language Erlang. Correspondingly, two Erlang model-checkers McErlang and Etomcrl2 are developed. This paper evaluates the two model-checkers by applying them to verify a a distributed and concurrent example - telecoms implemented in Erlang/OTP. A number of system's key properties are model-checked with both tool-sets. Advantages and disadvantages upon the uses of Etomcrl2 and McErlang are compared and summarized. Through such a case study, we intend to evaluate the two model-checkers on their effectiveness when verifying distributed and concurrent systems, and propose suggestions for their future work.

Keywords: Erlang, Model Checking, Program Source Code, Etomcrl2, McErlang.

1 Introduction

Model checking has been widely used in system design and verification. It has become a standard technique at both the design level as well as for finite-state hardware components, and much recent research has been concerned with extending its applicability to programming languages. This is increasingly necessary since as the complexity of systems grow, implementations of concurrent and distributed systems sometimes contain fatal errors such as deadlocks, despite the existence of careful designs. One example is demonstrated in the analysis of

NASA's Remote Agent Spacecraft Control System [15]. Thus to derive a reliable system, it is essential not only to verify the system design, but also to model check its implementations. This paper reviews and compares the existing techniques that have been applied to model-check applications written in the functional programming language Erlang [7] at a source code level.

There are essentially two approaches to model checking Erlang applications at a source code level. The first is to directly implement verification algorithms to the Erlang programming language; the other to abstract the Erlang programs into a formal specification, upon which a standard model checker can be applied to verify the system's properties. Both methods have advantages and disadvantages. The first approach requires less effort in computing the state space. However, developing verification algorithms is usually hard and time consuming. The second approach verifies the system's properties with the support of some existing tool-sets (model checkers). These tool-sets are usually standard and optimised, and thus efficient to use. However, in order to make use of a model checker, one has to model every aspects of Erlang and the Open Telecom Platform (OTP) components in a formal specification language that is supported by the model checker.

Fredlund *et al.* [8] investigate the first approach and develop a tool-set McErlang to model-check distributed systems written in Erlang. The tool-set McErlang makes use of a standard on-the-fly depth-first model checking algorithm [16] where the properties under evaluation can be represented by Büchi automata. The Erlang tool LTL2Buchi [17] is used to translate a Linear Temporal Logic (LTL) formulas into a Büchi monitor.

Arts *et al.* [2] initiate the strand of the second approach where Erlang and the OTP components are modeled in the process algebra μCRL [10] and verified via the standard model checker CADP [6]. A set of rules is defined to abstract the behaviour of Erlang syntax, OTP *gen_server*, *supervisor* and *gen_fsm* into μCRL. A small tool-set Etomcrl [2] is developed to automate the process of translation. Guo *et al.* extend the work by defining rules to model OTP *gen_fsm* [11] and the Erlang *timeout* events [12] in μCRL. Guo *et al.* [13] further study the ways to transform the existing rules to a set of new rules that is able to model Erlang and the corresponding OTP components in mCRL2 [9]. mCRL2 is a new version of μCRL that is extended with higher-order data-types, standard data-types, multi-actions and local communication. Compared to μCRL, mCRL2 is more applicable in practice. The tool-set Etomcrl is upgraded to Etomcrl2 where mCRL2 is used as the formal specification language for system modeling.

This work evaluates and compares the Erlang model-checker Etomcrl2 and McErlang. A telecoms case study is designed with a server-client infrastructure and implemented making use of Erlang OTP design patterns. A number of system's key properties is verified via Etomcrl2/CADP and McErlang respectively. Experimental results suggest that both model-checkers are effective in verifying the majority of system properties; both are able to distinguish the faulty implementations from the design. A number of limitations on the uses of the tool-sets are summarised. Etomcrl2 has to make use of a third-party toolset such as CADP to model-check an Erlang application. In order to make Etomcrl2 a mature toolset, modeling of all OTP components in mCRL2 are necessary; McErlang is unable to model-check *timeout* related properties due to it implements neither a discrete nor a real-time semantics. To improve the usability of the toolset, timing scheme needs to be developed. Through such a case study, we intend to provide suggestions for their future work.

The rest of paper is organised as follows: Section 2 introduces Erlang and OTP with a telecoms example; Section 3 reviews the existing Erlang model-checkers Etomcrl2 and McErlang; Section 4 applies Etomcrl2 and McErlang to model-check our telecoms example; Section 5 compares the model checker Etomcrl2 and McErlang; the work is summarised in Section 6.

2 Telecoms: An Illustration of Erlang Application

2.1 An Introduction to Erlang and OTP

Erlang [7] is a concurrent functional language with specific support for the development of distributed,fault-tolerant systems with soft real-time requirements. It was designed from the start to support a concurrency-oriented programming paradigm and large distributed implementations that this supports. The Open Telecom Platform (OTP) is a set of Erlang libraries for building large fault-tolerant distributed applications. With the OTP, Erlang applications can be rapidly developed and deployed across a large variety of hardware platforms, and this has caused it to become increasingly popular, not only within large telecoms companies such as Ericsson, but also with a variety of SMEs in different areas such as Yahoo! Delicious, and the Facebook chat system [7].

To further illustrate how a distributed and concurrent system is constructed using Erlang and OTP, in the following subsections, we demonstrate a telecoms example that is designed and implemented making use of Erlang OTP design patterns.

2.2 The Case Study

The telecoms system is designed using a client-server structure. It configures a number of functional servers (FS) to process clients' requests. Each FS is defined with a capacity that specifies the maximum number of mobile phones to be connected.

A client can communicate with any FSs and perform some functional operations such as *calling* and *top-up*. Each client has an account maintained by the system. In order to make a phone call, a client needs to preset enough money in its account. Before performing any functional operations, a client needs to connect

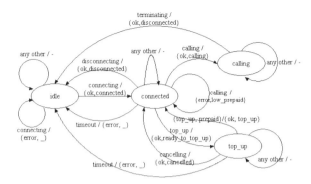

Fig. 1. The mobile phone behaviour modeled as an FSM

to an FS. A client can only be connected to one FS, and if a client has connected to an FS and tries to connect to another FS, the request will be denied.

The behaviour of a client (mobile phone) is modeled as a finite state machine (FSM), and the initial design is shown in Figure 1. There are four states: *idle*, *connected*, *calling* and *top_up*, where initially, the system is set to the *idle* state. The FSM defines the behaviour of a number of operations: *connecting*, *disconnecting*, *calling*, *terminating*, *top_up* and *canceling*. Before performing any operations, a client FSM needs to connect to an FS through sending the *connecting* request.

A client FSM has a timing restriction applicable when in the state *connected* or *top_up*. Specifically, when the FSM is directed to the state *connected* or *top_up*, a timer will be instantiated which enables the timing process. If, within the predefined time period, no action is performed by the client, a *timeout* event will be generated to trigger the corresponding process.

2.3 Erlang Implementations

The telecoms example is implemented, making use of the OTP design patterns as is common practice. The FS is implemented using the Erlang/OTP *gen_server* module. A generic server is implemented by providing a *callback module* where (*callback*) functions are defined to specify the concrete actions such as server state handling and response to messages.

The client behaviour is realized using the OTP *gen_fsm* module. In accordance with the design, four state functions are defined: *idle*, *connected*, *calling* and *top_up*.

The state function *idle* initiates a *connecting* request to an FS. If the FS replies the FSM with {*ok,connected*}, the request is accepted and the connection is set up. The FSM moves to the state *connected*; otherwise, the request is denied and the FSM remains unchanged.

```
idle(AT,{MB,RS,CSs})→                            :    action:show({MB,already_connected}),
  PT1 = gen_server:                              :    {next_state,connected,
    call(hd(CSs),{request,AT,MB}),               :           {MB,RS,CSs},20000};
  case PT1 of                                    :   {error,busy}→
    {error,invalid_mobile}→                      :    action:show({RS,sever_busy}),
      action:show({MB,invalid}),                 :    idle(AT,{MB,RS,
      {next_state,idle,{MB,RS,CSs}};             :        lists:append(tl(CSs),[hd(CSs)])});
    {ok,connected,CalledFS}→                     :   _Other→
      action:show({MB,connected,CalledFS}),:    action:show({AT,invalid}),}
      {next_state,connected,                     :    {next_state,idle,{MB,RS,CSs}}
             {MB,CalledFS,CSs}, 20000};          :  end.
    {error,already_connected}→                   :
```

Once the client is connected to an FS, an event will trigger the state function *connected*, which evaluates the request and then makes decisions for the consequent actions. For example, if a *calling* request is made, the function will call the FS to evaluate the client's state. If the client has enough money in its account, {*ok,calling*} will be returned to approve the calling process, and upon receiving the reply, the FSM moves to the state *calling*.

```
connected(timeout,{MB,RS,CSs})→                  :    action:show({MB,calling_enabled}),
  gen_server:call(RS,{request,timeout,MB}),:    {next_state,calling,
  action:show({MB,timeout}),                     :           {MB,RS,CSs}};
  {next_state,idle,{MB,nil,CSs}};                :   {error,low_prepaid}→
connected(AT,{MB,RS,CSs})→                       :    action:show({MB,low_prepaid}),
  case AT==terminating of                        :    {next_state,connected,
    true →                                       :           {MB,RS,CSs},20000};
      action:show({AT,invalid}),                 :   {ok,ready_to_top_up}→
      {next_state,connected,                     :    action:show({MB,ready_to_top_up}),
             {MB,RS,CSs},20000};                 :    {next_state,top_up,
    false →                                      :           {MB,RS,CSs},20000};
      Flag=gen_server:call(RS,{request,AT,MB}): _Other →
      case Flag of                               :    action:show({MB,invalid}),
        {ok,disconnected}→                       :    {next_state,connected,
          action:show({MB,disconnected}),        :           {MB,RS,CSs},20000}
          {next_state,idle, {MB,RS,CSs}};        :  end
        {ok,calling_enabled}→                    : end.
```

When in the state *calling*, only the *terminating* action can stop the calling process. This prevents the calling process from being disrupted by any unintended actions.

```
calling(AT,{MB,RS,CSs})→                         :           {MB,nil,CSs}};
  case AT of                                     :   _Other →
    terminating →                                :    action:show({AT,invalid}),
      gen_server:call(RS,{request,AT,MB}),:    {next_state,calling,
      action:show({MB,call_terminating}), :           {MB,RS,CSs}}
      {next_state,idle,                          :  end.
```

When being connected to an FS, the client can ask to top up its account by sending the *top_up* request to the FS. If {*ok,ready_to_top_up*} is replied, the top up process is enabled, and the FSM moves to the state *top_up*. An action will trigger the state function *top_up* to either start the transaction by {*top_up*, *Prepaid*} operation (*Prepaid* is the amount of money the client is about to transfer), or cancel the process by sending the *canceling* request.

top_up(timeout,{MB,RS,CSs})→	:	{ok,cancelled} →
gen_server:call(RS,{request,timeout,MB}),:		action:show({MB,top_up_cancelled}),
action:show(MB,timeout),	:	{next_state,connected,
{next_state,idle,{MB,nil,CSs}};	:	{MB,RS,CSs},20000};
top_up(AT,{MB,RS,CSs})→	:	_Other →
case gen_server:call(SVR,{request,AT,MB}) of:		action:show({AT,invalid}),
{ok,top_up} →	:	{next_state,top_up,
action:show({MB,top_up_ready}),	:	{MB,RS,CSs},20000}
{next_state,connected,	: end.	
{MB,RS,CSs},20000};	:	

When an FSM moves to the state *connected* and *top_up*, a timer is initiated. The timer is set to 20,000ms. If within the time period, no action is performed, a *timeout* event will be generated and sent to the FS. The FSM is reset to the state *idle*.

3 Erlang Model-Checking Tool-Sets

This section reviews the existing Erlang model checker Etomcrl2 and McErlang.

3.1 Etomcrl2

Etomcrl2 [13] is a tool-set that automatically translates the source codes of an Erlang application into an mCRL2 [9] specification, upon which the standard model checker CADP [6] is used to generate a (finite) state space to check the system properties against the designs. The process algebra μCRL (micro Common Representation Language) [10] is an extension of the process algebra ACP [3]. It was developed with equational *abstract data types* being integrated into the process specification, which enables the specification of both data and process behaviour. The language [1]mCRL2 is a new version of μCRL that is extended with higher-order data-types, standard data-types, multi-actions and local communication. Compared to μCRL, mCRL2 is more applicable in practice.

The tool-set Etomcrl2 is comprised of three functional modules: the *Preprocess* module, the *mCRL2 translation* module and the *mCRL2 initialization* module. These functional modules work together to automatically translate the source codes of an Erlang application into an mCRL2 specification, upon which the standard model checker CADP is used to check system's properties.

3.2 McErlang

McErlang [8] is a tool-set that is developed to model-check Erlang programs, particularly concurrent applications. The main idea behind McErlang is to re-use as

---
[1] Instead of μCRL2, the newly release language is named as mCRL2.

much of a normal Erlang programming language implementation as possible, but adding a model checking capability. To do so, the tool-set replaces the part of the Erlang runtime system that implements concurrency and message passing without modifying the runtime system for the evaluation of sequential executions.

The tool-set takes an Erlang function as its input. This function specifies the entry of the Erlang application under verification, a call-back module (written in Erlang) that defines the behavioural safety property[2] to be checked (called the *monitor*), and the algorithm used to check the property. When a property is checked with McErlang, the tool-set either returns a positive reply, confirming that property holds, or a negative one with a counterexample (a trace leading to the problem state).

McErlang also supports model checking programs against full Linear Temporal Logic (LTL) formulas. The LTL2Buchi tool [17] is used to translate an LTL formulas into a Büchi monitor, which are then checked using a standard on-the-fly depth-first model checking algorithm [16].

4 Illustrative Example – The Tools in Use

There are two groups of experiments. In the first group, a number of properties are checked against the implementationd and, in the second, two types of faulty implementations are constructed to examine the capability of the model-checkers on fault detection.

To instantiate the simulation process, we configure the system with three FSs (svr_1, svr_2 and svr_3) and five clients (m_1, m_2, m_3, m_4 and m_5). The capacity of every FS is set to 1 and the minimal cost for making a call is set to £2. Here, we define that, when the system is modeled with an mCRL2 specification (using Etomcrl2), the passing of one time unit is specified as 10,000ms, represented by one *tick* action.

4.1 Property Verification

We first devise two experiments to verify the properties on making a call. In the first experiment, the client m_1 attempts to make a phone call with its account being preset with £1; while, in the second, m_1 tries to make a call with its account being preset with £3. In both experiments, all other clients are idle. Through these two experiments, we intend to check (1) whether the communication between FS(s) and the client(s) is running correctly; (2) whether the logics of making a call extracted from the behaviour of the FS(s) and the client(s) comply with their designs; and (3) the logics of *timeout* event have been correctly implemented.

These properties are first verified using Etomcrl2 and CADP. The Labeled Transition Systems (LTSs) derived from the experiments are shown in Figure 2 and Figure 3 respectively. It can be seen that, in both experiments,both LTSs present the logics that comply with the designs.

---

[2] A safety property expresses that nothing bad ever happens, which can be expressed as "always(not P)" in linear temporal logic (where "P" is the bad event).

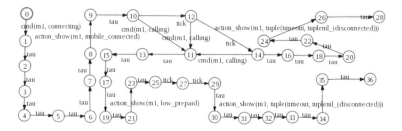

Fig. 2. LTS: m_1 tries to make a call with low prepaid and the request is denied

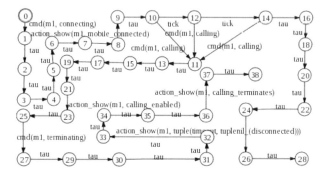

Fig. 3. LTS: m_1 tries to make a call with enough prepaid and the request is enabled

The system properties can be formalized with a set of LTL formulas. For example, in the above experiments, the property "without being connected to an FS, m_1 cannot make a phone call." is formalized as:

[not(action_show(m_1, mobile_connected))*. action_show(m_1, calling_enabled))] false

Similarly, to check "when m_1 is connected to an FS, without delaying enough time (two *tick* actions being consecutively performed), a *timeout* event cannot be generated.", the property is formalized as:

[true*. action_show(m_1, mobile_connected)*]
<not('tick.tick')*. action_show(m_1, tuple(timeout,tuplenil(disconnected)))> false

By applying the formulas to CADP, verification of the system properties can be automated.

The above properties are then verified using McErlang. Since McErlang is not capable of checking the *timeout* event, we will only examine the properties of communication between FS(s) and the client(s) and the logics of making a call. Before the experiments start, a number of transition labels has been inserted to the system's source codes using McErlang *mce_erl:probe* function. McErlang provides the ability to visualize LTSs using the graphviz set of drawing tools. In the following experiments, however, we will only report the verification results.

First, we will check the connection relation between client m_1 and the FSs. The property is defined as "without being connected to an FS, the functional operation *calling* performed by m_1 is invalid" and constructed in McErlang as shown:

property1_1() →
  mce:start(#mce_opts
    {program = {action,startSimulation,[[{[m_1,m_2,m_3,m_4,m_5],[1,2,3,4,5]},
                                         [svr_1,svr_2,svr_3],2,3]]},
     monitor = {mce_ltl_parse:ltl_string2module_and_load(
       "always(((not P) and Q) ⇒ eventually R)",messenger_mon),
       {void,[{'P',basicPredicates:show_message({m_1,mobile_connected})},
              {'Q',basicPredicates:receive_cmd({calling,m_1})},
              {'R',basicPredicates:show_message({m_1,action_invalid})}]}},
     algorithm = {mce_alg_buechi,void}}).

We then evaluate "after m_1 is connected to an FS and tries to make a phone call, the request will be denied with a reply *low_prepaid*". The property is defined in a verification run as:

property1_2() →
  mce:start(#mce_opts
    {program = {action,startSimulation,[[{[m_1,m_2,m_3,m_4,m_5],[1,2,3,4,5]},
                                         [svr_1,svr_2,svr_3],2,3]]},
     monitor = {mce_ltl_parse:ltl_string2module_and_load(
       "always(P and Q) ⇒ eventually R)",messenger_mon),
       {void,[{'P',basicPredicates:show_message({m_1,mobile_connected})},
              {'Q',basicPredicates:receive_cmd({calling,m_1})},
              {'R',basicPredicates:show_message({m_1,low_prepaid})}]}},
     algorithm = {mce_alg_buechi,void}}).

After running the checks of these two properties in McErlang, the tool-set returns "Execution terminated normally.", with total 1377 and 18201 states being explored respectively. The experimental results imply that both properties are held in the implementation.

Next, we construct an experiment to examine the system's behaviour where more than one clients are active. Two clients m_1 and m_2 request to connect to a FS simultaneously. Since the capacity of the FS is set to 1, according to the design, when an FS, for example svr_1, accepts the request of a client, say m_1, it should reply the other m_2 with *server_busy*; the client m_2 should afterwards request a connection to another FS, say svr_2.

The property is first checked using Etomcrl2 and CADP. The LTS derived from the experiment is illustrated in Figure 4. The graph is symmetric and shows that if m_1 is firstly connected to an FS and m_2 requests to connect to the same FS, m_2 will receive a reply *server_busy*. After trying a different FS, m_2 is connected to the FS; or, if m_2 is firstly connected to an FS and m_1 requests to connect to the same FS, m_1 will receive a reply *server_busy*. After trying a different FS, m_1 is connected to the FS. The logics extracted from the LTS comply with the system design.

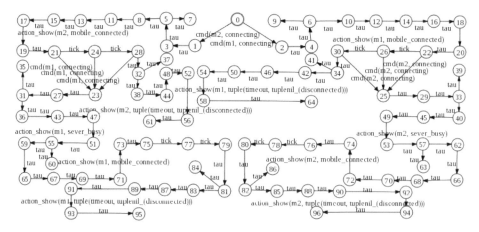

Fig. 4. LTS: m_1 and m_2 request to connect to an FS simultaneously with the capacity of svr_1 is set to 1

A number of properties can then be automatically verified via CADP. For example, to check "when m_1 is connected to an FS and m_2 requests to connect to the same FS, m_1 will receive reply *server_busy*.". The property is formalized as:

<true*. action_show(m_1, mobile_connected) *. cmd(m_2, connecting) *. action_show(m_2, server_busy)> true

Another property we want to check is formalized as:

<true*. cmd(m_2, connecting) *. action_show(m_2, server_busy) *. cmd(m_2, connecting) *. action_show(m_2, mobile_connected)> true

stating that "when m_2 requests to connect to an FS and receives the reply of *server_busy*, it will request to connect to another FS and its request will be accepted."

The property is then verified using McErlang. The above two properties are configured as:

```
property2_1() →
  mce:start(#mce_opts
    {program = {action,startSimulation,[[{[m_1,m_2,m_3,m_4,m_5],[1,2,3,4,5]},
                                        [svr_1,svr_2,svr_3],1,3]]},
     monitor = {mce_ltl_parse:ltl_string2module_and_load(
                  "always((O and P) and Q) ⇒ eventually R)",messenger_mon),
                  {void,[{'O',basicPredicates:receive_cmd({connecting,m_1})},
                         {'P',basicPredicates:show_message({m_1,mobile_connected})},
                         {'Q',basicPredicates:receive_cmd({connecting,m_2})},
                         {'R',basicPredicates:show_message({m_2,server_busy})}]}},
     algorithm = {mce_alg_buechi,void}}).
```

property2_2() →
  mce:start(#mce_opts
    {program = {action,startSimulation,[[{[m_1,m_2,m_3,m_4,m_5],[1,2,3,4,5]},
                                          [svr_1,svr_2,svr_3],1,3]]},
     monitor = {mce_ltl_parse:ltl_string2module_and_load(
                  "always(R and Q) ⇒ eventually P)",messenger_mon),
                  {void,[{'P',basicPredicates:show_message({m_2,mobile_connected})},
                         {'Q',basicPredicates:receive_cmd({connected,m_2})},
                         {'R',basicPredicates:show_message({m_2,server_busy})}]}},
     algorithm = {mce_alg_buechi,void}}).

After the two properties being checked in McErlang, the tool-set returns "Execution terminated normally." with 11412 states being explored. The properties are concluded to be held in the implementation.

4.2 Fault Detection

This subsection evaluates the capabilities of Etomcrl2 and McErlang on fault detection. Two types of faulty implementations are devised, one of which is designed with a coding fault while the other a configuration error.

A. Detecting a Coding Error. The telecoms system takes use of a number of FSs. These FSs should be configured in a list [svr_1, ..., svr_(k-1), svr_k]. A faulty implementation is devised where the FS list is coded in the format of [svr_1, ..., svr_(k-1)|svr_k]. Such a coding pattern is syntactically legal and will not cause any errors or exceptions in the state of compiling. However, the injected fault could give rise to a serious problem since, when trying to connect to an FS, instead of **svr_k**, a client may send the request to the list [**svr_k**]. [**svr_k**] is not recognised as an FS entity, which could make the telecoms system crashed.

The faulty implementation is then model-checked using Etomcrl2 and McErlang respectively. The fault is immediately captured when the implementation is compiled by McErlang to derive the core files for model-checking. Thanks to the fact that McErlang implements the Erlang semantics directly on the model checker, the location of the fault in the code and the interleaving of the actions that caused the error are layed out clearly, which provides clues to fix it.

The fault is also detected by Etomcrl2 and CADP. After the implementation source codes are translated into an mCRL2 specification, CADP is used to verify the system's properties. It is discovered that there exists *deadlock* in the generated state space. By examining the execution traces, it is concluded that the *deadlock* is induced by the fact that clients send requests to the FS [**svr_k**]. Compared to McErlang, when using Etomcrl2 to debug Erlang programs, it is more difficult to locate the error in the original code.

B. Detecting a Configuration Error. A configuration error is devised in this section. Here, we define the telecoms is constructed with two FSs (svr_1 and svr_2) and four clients (m_1, m_2, m_3 and m_4) where four clients simultaneously request a connection to an FS. Both svr_1 and svr_2 are meant to be designed with a capacity of 2, and we assume that one (say svr_2) by mistakenly implemented with a capacity of 1. This could cause serious problems as one client will iteratively make a request to connect to the system without knowing whether he/she will ever get through.

One way to detect such a problem is to check whether the four clients are successfully connected to the FSs. Since the system is designed with the capacity of 4, all four clients should have connected to an FS. Thus, for each client m_i, $i \in \{1,2,3,4\}$, The properties can be defined as "when client m_i sends *connecting* request to the system, its request will be fairly accepted by an FS (svr_1 or svr_2)". The properties are constructed in Etomcrl2 and McErlang as shown:

[true*. "cmd(m_i, connecting)" *]
(<true* "action_show(m_i, connected)"> or
<true* "action_show(m_i, connected)">) true

property3() →
  mce:start(#mce_opts
    {program = {action,startSimulation,[[{[m_1,m_2,m_3,m_4,m_5],[1,2,3,4,5]},
                                         [svr_1,svr_2,svr_3],1,3]]},
     monitor = {mce_ltl_parse:ltl_string2module_and_load(
                 "always(R and Q) ⇒ eventually P)",messenger_mon),
                 {void,[{'P',basicPredicates:receive_cmd({connecting,m_i})},
                        {'Q',basicPredicates:show_message({m_i,mobile_connected})}]}},
     algorithm = {mce_alg_buechi,void}}).

Using these properties, Etomcrl2/CADP and McErlang can correctly distinguish the correct and faulty implementations based upon the design we wish to check against.

5 Comparisons between Etomcrl2 and McErlang

This section makes a comparison between Etomcrl2 and McErlang.

5.1 Effectiveness in System Verification

The experimental results suggest that both Etomcrl2/CADP and McErlang are effective in verifying the system properties. In terms of fault detection, both model-checkers are able to isolate the faults from the faulty implementations and provide clues to fix them. However, McErlang is unable to verify properties related to *timeout* event, since it implements neither a discrete nor a real-time semantics for Erlang program. This could decrease its applicability to some examples for classes of systems where exact timing is crucial for correctness. Etomcrl2 introduces a discrete clock into the mCRL2 specification, which makes it possible to simulate the timing process.

Etomcrl2 takes use of a static/fixed state space for system verification, that is, before the process of verification starts, the tool-set generates a complete state space and uses the state space throughout any stages of system verification; while, McErlang applies on-the-fly to dynamically generate a small/partial state space for a property under evaluation, that is, when a property is about to be checked, the tool-set generates a partial state space that is sufficient to check the property's correctness.

Both Etomcrl2 and McErlang can be applied to check for the presence of *deadlock* in the scenarios, where the size of system components incrementally grows. It can be seen that, when McErlang is used for *deadlock* checking and the telecoms system is free from *deadlock*, McErlang generates a complete state space. All experiments are run in a desktop of DELL OPTIPLEX 760 (Memory: 2.0Gib, Processor: Intel(R) Core(TM)2 Duo CPU E8400 @ 3.00GHz). The numbers of states and the times used to generate such state spaces are illustrated in Table 1 where "<" stands for *less than*.

Table 1. State spaces and the times used for their generations

Clients	States (E2Crl)	Times (E2Crl)	States (McErl)	Times (McErl)
1	20	21 sec	38	< 5 sec
2	77	23 sec	214	< 5 sec
3	286	32 sec	5163	< 5 sec
4	1217	172 sec	543358	46 sec
5	6176	2747 sec	1801308	2385 sec

Table 1 shows (1) Etomcrl2 generates fewer states than McErlang does. McErlang defines function calls as state changes. Transitions depicted in McErlang are interpreted as function calls. By contrast, Etomcrl2 highly abstracts Erlang and OTP behaviour in mCRL2, where modeling rules are used to concisely encapsulate the executions of Erlang and OTP functions with a set of actions. Compared to McErlang, Etomcrl2 can use fewer states to model some system functionalities; (2) McErlang delivers answers faster than Etomcrl2. This is due to the fact that McErlang applies on-the-fly techniques for system verification, and (3) when the complexity of the system under investigation arrives at a certain degree, both model-checkers come to a bottle-neck and become less efficient in the generation of state spaces. These problem is currently being addressed in McErlang by defining partial order reductions that decrease the number of states.

5.2 Usability

Etomcrl2 is a tool-set that has to take use of a third-part model-checker such as CADP to perform model-checking. CADP is a standard model-checker, and it allows Linear Temporal Logic (LTL) formulas to be directly used for modeling system behaviour. This makes the process upon the verification of an Erlang application (using Etomcrl2 and CADP) a standard model-checking process. By defining the system's properties in a set of LTL formula, one can easily model-check the Erlang application, without further learning about Erlang.

The limitation upon the use of Etomcrl2 is that every aspect of Erlang and OTP components has to be modeled in mCRL2. So far, Etomcrl2 has included the abstract schema for Erlang syntax, OTP modules *gen_server*, *supervisor*, *gen_fsm*, and *timeout* event. To make Etomcrl2 a more comprehensive tool-set, abstract rules for other OTP components such as *event* need to be developed.

By contrast, it is a much easier task to add support for new OTP components in McErlang as such components can be written directly in Erlang.

Moreover, when using Etomcrl2 it is usually more difficult to identify the reason for an error, and location in the source code where it was introduced, than when using McErlang. This is because for Etomcrl2 errors are discovered in the mCRL2 specification *generated* from the Erlang program rather than in the original Erlang program itself.

In comparison, McErlang is an independent model-checker that directly applies model-checking algorithms in system verification. McErlang uses on-the-fly techniques for checking a system property. This has the potential for making McErlang a faster model-checker for some verification problems. When examining a system property, McErlang produces a tree of executions and allows the executions to be performed step by step. This provides a means to track and analyse the execution traces from the property under evaluation.

There exists some potencial limitations on the use of McErlang. McErlang reimplements a number of model checking algorithms whereas Etomcrl2 reuses an already available mature implementation in mCRL2 and CADP of a set of model checking algorithms. This brings the advantage that the developers of Etomcrl2 can focus only on the problem of translating Erlang to the specification language of the model checker. In general one would expect that as a result of using a mature model checker, Etomcrl2 would be faster than McErlang[3]. Early experiments reported here do not show such a slow-down of McErlang compared to Etomcrl2, but if improvements are made to mCRL2 or CADP, the Etomcrl2 tool would benefit too without having to write new code. Besides, McErlang is particularly developed for model-checking Erlang applications, where system properties must be described partly in Erlang. This is in fact an advantage since facilitates the use of McErlang for Erlang programmers.

6 Summary

Model-checking programs is important in the development of a reliable software system. This paper evaluates and compares the Erlang model-checker Etomcrl2 and McErlang by applying them to verify a telecoms case study. The telecoms is designed with a server-client infrastructure and is implemented making use of the OTP components *gen_server*, *supervisor* and *gen_fsm* and the *timeout* event. A number of system's key properties are outlined and verified by using Etomcrl2 and McErlang. Experimental results show both model-checkers are effective in verifying the majority of these properties. In terms of fault detection, both model-checkers are able to distinguish the devised faulty implementations from the design. Early benchmark results indicate that McErlang delivers answers quicker than Etomcrl2.

We have compared the two model-checkers with their usabilities. A number of limitations on the uses of the tool-sets are summarised. Through such a case

---

[3] Especially since mCRL2 is largely implemented using C++ compared to McErlang which is implemented using Erlang.

study, we propose suggestions for both toolsets in their future work. Etomcrl2 has to make use of a third-party toolset such as CADP to model-check an Erlang application. This requires every aspect of Erlang and OTP components to be modeled in mCRL2. To make Etomcrl2 a mature model-checker, it is necessary to develop abstract rules for the other OTP components such as *event*.

McErlang is not capable of verifying some properties related to timing, since it implements neither a discrete nor a real-time semantics for Erlang program. As such, it is an item for future work to extend McErlang with an implementation of a timed semantics. On the other hand, there are classes of systems and properties which require real-time model checking algorithms too, for which the discrete clock implementation in Etomcrl2 is not sufficient.

It has been noticed that, when the complexity of the system under investigation arrives at a certain degree, both model-checkers come to a bottle-neck and become less efficient in the generation of state spaces. To overcome such a problem, for both tool-sets, more work need to be carried out. In particular, there is some work in progress in using some partial order reductions in McErlang.

Acknowledgements

This work was funded by the FP7 project *ProTest*, number 215868: www.protest-project.eu.

References

1. Armstrong, J., Virding, R., Wikström, C., Williams, M.: Concurrent Programming in Erlang, 2nd edn. Prentice-Hall, Englewood Cliffs (1996)
2. Arts, T., Benac-Earle, C., Penas, J.J.S.: Translating Erlang to μCRL. In: Kishinevsky, M., Darondeau, P. (eds.) 4th International Conference on Application of Concurrency to System Design, pp. 135–144. IEEE Computer Society, Los Alamitos (June 2004)
3. Baeten, J.C.M., Weijland, W.P.: Process Algebra. Cambridge University Press, Cambridge (1990)
4. Benac-Earle, C., Fredlund, L.-Å.: Verification of Language Based Fault-Tolerance. In: Moreno Díaz, R., Pichler, F., Quesada Arencibia, A. (eds.) EUROCAST 2005. LNCS, vol. 3643, pp. 140–149. Springer, Heidelberg (2005)
5. Benac-Earle, C., Fredlund, L.-Å., Derrick, J.: Verifying Fault-Tolerant Erlang Programs. In: Sagonas, K., Armstrong, J. (eds.) Proceedings of ACM SigPlan Erlang 2005 Workshop, pp. 26–34. ACM Press, New York (September 2005)
6. CADP, http://www.inrialpes.fr/vasy/cadp/
7. Cesarini, F., Thompson, S.: Erlang Programming. O'Reilly Media, Sebastopol (2009)
8. Fredlund, L., Svensson, H.: McErlang: a Model Checker for a Distributed Functional Programming Language. In: Hinze, R., Ramsey, N. (eds.) 12th ACM SIGPLAN International conference on functional programming (ICFP 2007), pp. 978-1-59593-815-2 (2007)
9. Groote, J.F., Mathijssena, A., van Weerdenburga, M., Usenkoa, Y.: From μCRL to mCRL2. Electronic Notes in Theoretical Computer Science 162, 191–196 (2006)

10. Groote, J.F., Ponse, A.: The syntax and sematics of µCRL. In: Ponse, A., Verhoef, C., van Vlijmen, S. (eds.) Algebra of Communicating Processes 1994, Workshop in Computing, pp. 26–62 (1995)
11. Guo, Q.: Verifying Erlang/OTP Components in µCRL. In: Derrick, J., Vain, J. (eds.) FORTE 2007. LNCS, vol. 4574, pp. 227–246. Springer, Heidelberg (2007)
12. Guo, Q., Derrick, J.: Verification of Timed Erlang/OTP Components Using the Process Algebra µCRL. In: Thompson, S., Fredlund, L.-Å. (eds.) 6th ACM SIGPLAN Erlang Workshop, pp. 55–64. ACM Press, New York (2007)
13. Guo, Q., Derrick, J.: Formally Based Tool Support for Model Checking Erlang Applications. International Journal on Software Tools for Technology Transfer (2010) (under review)
14. Guo, Q., Derrick, J., Hoch, C.: Verifying Erlang Telecommunication Systems with the Process Algebra µCRL. In: Suzuki, K., Higashino, T., Yasumoto, K., El-Fakih, K. (eds.) FORTE 2008. LNCS, vol. 5048, pp. 201–217. Springer, Heidelberg (2008)
15. Havelund, K., Lowry, M., Penix, J.: Formal Analysis of a Space-Craft Controller Using SPIN. IEEE Transactions on Software Engineering 27(8), 749–765 (2001)
16. Holzmann, H.: Design and Validation of Computer Protocols. Prentice-Hall, Englewood Cliffs (1991)
17. Svensson, H.: Implementing an LTL-to-Büchi translator in Erlang: a protest experience report. In: 8th ACM SIGPLAN Erlang Workshop, pp. 63–70. ACM Press, New York (September 2009)

Bad Pairs in Software Testing

Daniel Hoffman[1], Chien-Hsing Chang[1], Gary Bazdell[2],
Brett Stevens[2], and Kevin Yoo[3]

[1] University of Victoria, Dept. of Computer Science, Victoria BC V8W 3P6, Canada
{dhoffman,chichang}@cs.uvic.ca
[2] Carleton University, Dept. of Math. and Statistics, Ottawa ON K1Y 1Z4, Canada
{gbazdell,brett}@math.carleton.ca
[3] Wurldtech Security Technologies Inc., Vancouver BC K1Y 1Z4, Canada
kyoo@wurldtech.com

Abstract. With pairwise testing, the test model is a list of N parameters. Each test case is an N-tuple; the test space is the cross product of the N parameters. A pairwise test is a set of N-tuples where every pairwise combination of the parameter values is contained in at least one of the N-tuples. Well-known algorithms generate pairwise test sets far smaller than the test space. Pairwise testing has good tool support and is widely known in industry and academia. Empirical results have shown the effectiveness of the approach. While pairwise testing is used to generate test inputs, we propose a novel analysis of the test outputs. We focus on bad pairs: those which always result in a failed test case. We experimentally evaluate the frequency of occurrence of bad pairs using mutation testing with 1 and 2 faults per mutant. The results provide useful insights into two important relationships: (1) between faults and bad pairs and (2) between input selection and bad pairs. We then apply the approach to an industrial example in network vulnerability testing. We also present *error-locating arrays*, a recent theoretical result providing a powerful tool for bad pairs analysis.

Keywords: software testing, pairwise testing, covering and error-locating arrays.

1 Introduction

The occurrence of software failures due to multiple conditions has been considered in a variety of contexts. In the world of telephony, feature interaction problems have long been studied [11]. Failure-triggering fault interactions have been identified in software in a variety of domains [12]. A recent study categorized field errors according to the smallest combination of conditions sufficient to reveal the errors [16]

Pairwise testing is a technique for exposing failures caused by a combination of two conditions. We illustrate the approach with a hypothetical test suite for VoIP software. Suppose that field error reports have shown the software to be

Table 1. Pairwise testing for a VoIP product

	CallerOS	ServerOS	CalleeOS
1	*Mac*	*Lin*	*Mac*
2	Mac	Lin	Win
3	Mac	Sun	Mac
4	*Mac*	*Sun*	*Win*
5	Mac	Win	Mac
6	*Mac*	*Win*	*Win*
7	Win	Lin	Mac
8	*Win*	*Lin*	*Win*
9	*Win*	*Sun*	*Mac*
10	Win	Sun	Win
11	*Win*	*Win*	*Mac*
12	Win	Win	Win

sensitive to combinations of the operating system versions used by the calling phone, the VoIP server, and the called phone.

There are three parameters: CallerOS, ServerOS, and CalleeOS. Table 1 shows the test space. The rows shown in italics, taken together, are a pairwise test [20] because every pairwise combination of parameter values is present in at least one of the rows. To demonstrate this, we must consider the combinations of each of the three pairs of parameters. Consider the cross product of CallerOS and CalleeOS: {⟨Mac, Mac⟩, ⟨Mac, Win⟩, ⟨Win, Mac⟩, ⟨Win, Win⟩}. The first pair is found in row 1 of Table 1. The other three pairs are found in rows 4, 8, and 9 of Table 1. To complete the demonstration, the same exercise must be carried out for CallerOS × ServerOS and for ServerOS × CalleeOS.

While pairwise testing focuses on the test inputs, bad pairs analysis focuses on the relationship between the test inputs and outputs. Suppose that a number of test cases are run and that whenever CallerOs is Lin and ServerOS is Win, the result is always 'fail'. Then [(CallerOs,Lin),(ServerOs,Win)] is a bad pair. Would that information be interesting to a debugger? If there were a lot of failed test cases, would a test case containing a bad pair be more useful than one without? The remainder of the paper pursues these and other related questions.

In Section 2, we present and illustrate the key terms. Section 3 presents a set of experiments using mutation testing to explore the occurrences of bad pairs in mutants with one and two faults. Section 4 describes similar experiments on a somewhat larger target program. Section 5 applies bad pairs analysis to an industrial example in network vulnerability testing. Section 6 briefly describes error locating arrays and their relationship to bad pairs analysis. Section 7 contains the related work.

2 Definitions

A *test input table* is a set of n-tuples, often shown in tabular form. Each row in a test input table represents a test case and each column corresponds to one of the

Table 2. Bad pair analysis examples

Test Input Table			Results Vector
a	b	c	Pass or Fail
1	1	1	F
1	2	2	F
2	1	2	P
2	2	1	P
2	2	2	F

(a) Test input table and results vector

a	b	c
1	•	•

(b) A bad singleton

a	b	c
1	2	•
1	1	•
1	•	2
1	•	1
•	1	1
•	2	2

(c) Bad pairs

a	b	c
1	2	•
1	1	•
1	•	2
1	•	1

(d) Dependent bad pairs

a	b	c
•	2	2
•	1	1

(e) Independent bad pairs

Line	Failure Ratio	a	b	c	Type
1	1.0	1	2	•	dependent
2	1.0	1	1	•	dependent
3	1.0	1	•	2	dependent
4	1.0	1	•	1	dependent
5	1.0	•	2	2	independent
6	1.0	•	1	1	independent
7	0.5	2	2	•	
8	0.5	2	•	2	
9	0.0	2	1	•	
10	0.0	2	•	1	
11	0.0	•	2	1	
12	0.0	•	1	2	

(f) Failure ratios for all pairs

n parameters. A *results vector* is a one-dimensional array where each element is either 'P' (pass) or 'F' (fail). Bad pairs analysis is conducted on a test input table with k rows and a results vector with k elements. Consider a hypothetical program with three integer inputs: a, b, and c. Table 2(a) shows a test input table containing five test cases and a results vector showing the results of executing each test case.

The remaining terms are defined with respect to a test input table T with n columns and k rows, and a results vector R with k elements. A *singleton* is a value for a specific parameter. In this paper, we represent a singleton in two ways: as an n-tuple where all the elements except one contain '•', or as an explicit column/value pair. In the test input table in Table 2(a), for example, both $(•, 2, •)$ and $(b, 2)$ denote value 2 for parameter b. A *bad singleton* is a singleton which always results in a failure, i.e., whenever test case $T[i]$ contains the singleton, then $R[i]$ is 'F'. Table 2(b) shows a bad singleton: in every row in which parameter a has value 1, the result is 'F'. Table 2(a) contains no other bad singletons.

A *pair* is a pair of parameter values. As with singletons, we represent a pair in two ways: as an n-tuple where all the elements except two contain '•', or as a pair of column/value pairs. For example, in the test input table in Table 2(a), $(1, •, 2)$ denotes the pair with value 1 for parameter a and value 2 for parameter c. The same pair can be specified by $[(a, 1), (c, 2)]$. A *bad pair* is a pair which always results in a failure. For example, Table 2(c) shows all of the bad pairs from Table 2(a). The pair $(1, •, 2)$ is a bad pair because the only row containing it has an 'F' in the results vector. However, $(2, •, 2)$ is *not* a bad pair because it is in two rows, one of which has a 'P'. Finally, a *good pair* is a pair which always results in a pass.

We divide bad pairs into two types:

1. A *dependent bad pair* is a bad pair which contains one or two bad singletons. Table 2(d) shows the four dependent bad pairs from Table 2(a).
2. An *independent bad pair* is a bad pair which contains no bad singletons. Table 2(e) shows the two independent bad pairs from Table 2(a).

Intuitively, an independent bad pair is a bad pair because of the interaction between the two parameter values, while a dependent bad pair is a bad pair because of the presence of the bad singleton(s) it contains. Our analysis focuses on independent bad pairs.

Table 2(f) summarizes the test results by presenting the failure ratios for each pair in Table 2(a). A bad pair has a failure ratio of 1 while a good pair has a failure ratio of 0.

3 Bad Pairs in the Triangle Program

The long term goal of this research is to determine the most important relationships between independent bad pairs and faults. In this paper, we address several preliminary questions:

- How common are independent bad pairs?
- What is the influence of input selection on the occurrence of bad pairs?
- What is the effect of using a threshold to identify pairs that fail, say, 90% of the time?

3.1 The Code-under-Test

Our first experiments use a Java implementation of the well-known triangle program [8], shown in Figure 1. The function `triangle` takes three integer inputs, interpreted as the lengths of the sides of a triangle, and determines whether the inputs correspond to an equilateral, isosceles, scalene, or illegal triangle.

Starting from the "gold version" in Figure 1, the muJava mutation tool [14] was used to create 213 mutants, each seeded with a single fault. In one of the mutants, for example, the == operator in line 6 of the gold version is changed to the > operator.

```
1  public static String triangle(int side1, int side2, int side3) {
2      int triang;
3      if (side1 <= 0 || side2 <= 0 || side3 <= 0)
4          return "illegal";
5      triang = 0;
6      if (side1 == side2)
7          triang = triang + 1;
8      if (side1 == side3)
9          triang = triang + 2;
10     if (side2 == side3)
11         triang = triang + 3;
12     if (triang == 0)
13         if (side1 + side2 <= side3 ||
14             side2 + side3 <= side1 ||
15             side1 + side3 <= side2) {
16             return "illegal";
17         } else
18             return "scalene";
19     if (triang > 3)
20         return "equilateral";
21     else if (triang == 1 && side1 + side2 > side3)
22         return "isosceles";
23     else if (triang == 2 && side1 + side3 > side2)
24         return "isosceles";
25     else if (triang == 3 && side2 + side3 > side1)
26         return "isosceles";
27     return "illegal";
28 }
```

Fig. 1. Triangle source code: the "gold" code

```
for each mutant M
    open log file L_M
    for each test case t
        run M with input t
        run the gold code with input t
        if M and the gold code produce the same output
            write t followed by 'P' to L_M
        else
            write t followed by 'F' to L_M
    close log file L_M
```

Fig. 2. Execution pseudocode

The test inputs consist of all (a, b, c) triples where a, b, and c are between 0 and 5. In other words, the test inputs consist of the 216 triples in $[0..5] \times [0..5] \times [0..5]$. As shown in Figure 2, each mutant is tested on each of the inputs, with the gold code serving as test oracle. At the end of a test run, there are 213 log files, one per mutant. Each log file contains 216 lines, each containing an (a, b, c) triple followed by 'P' or 'F'.

3.2 Test Results: Single Mutation Per Mutant

When we analyzed the log files, we found that there were no bad pairs—dependent or independent—for any of the mutants. We found this result surprising and studied several of the log files.

Consider the mutation M in which the == operator in line 6 of Figure 1 is changed to the > operator. This fault causes, for example, a scalene triangle with $a > b$, e.g., $(5, 2, 4)$, to be incorrectly classified as isosceles. Indeed, M's log file contained the line:

5 2 4 F

Thus, we expected $(5, 2, \bullet)$ to be a bad pair. We discovered that other inputs containing $(5, 2, \bullet)$, e.g., $(5, 2, 0)$, passed. The reason is that M correctly classifies $(5, 2, 0)$ as illegal; for this test case, the code containing the fault is never reached.

When we looked further, we found this situation recurring in many log files: many pairs were bad when considering only legal inputs, but not when illegal inputs were considered. When test cases representing illegal triangles are filtered out, independent bad pairs were present for 103 of the 213 mutants.

Figure 3 summarizes the contents of the 213 log files, restricted to legal triangles. The X axis represents the number of independent bad pairs; the Y axis represents the number of mutants with the corresponding number of independent bad pairs. For instance, 44 of the 213 mutants have 8 independent bad pairs. Nearly half of the mutants have at least one independent bad pair.

We also tested the triangle code using pairwise testing. The test input table consisted of a two-cover of $[0..5] \times [0..5] \times [0..5]$. The results are shown in Figure 4. The total number of independent bad pairs is about the same, although they are distributed more evenly across the mutants.

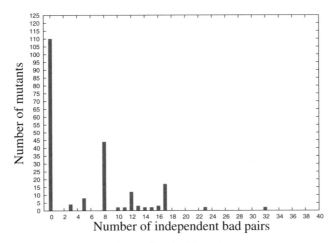

Fig. 3. Single Mutation

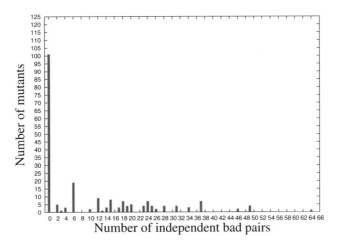

Fig. 4. Single Mutation with pairwise inputs

A bad pair has a failure ratio equal to 1. It might be useful to use a threshold to identify "nearly bad pairs," e.g., pairs with failure ratio 0.9 or larger. With tests run on the full cross product, there are still no bad pairs with threshold 0.9. With thresholds 0.8 and 0.7, 49 mutants have at least 1 independent bad pair. Using legal triangles only, there is no change in the independent bad pairs found until threshold 0.7.

3.3 Two-Fault Mutants

We expected that mutants with two faults would have more bad pairs than mutants with a single fault, due to fault interactions. The double-fault mutants were created by selecting 3 of the 213 single-fault mutants, and running MuJava on them again. The three mutants were chosen to vary the mutation operator used to create the first fault: one mutant was chosen from each of relational operator replacement (ROR), conditional operator replacement (COR), and arithmetic operator replacement (AOR). The result is three sets of 212 mutants each, one set from each one of the three selected single-fault mutants. There are 212 two-fault mutants because one of the 213 double-fault mutants is the gold program: the second mutation corrected the first one. The same test procedure was followed, with only legal triangles as inputs, producing three sets of 212 log files each.

Figure 5 summarizes the results for the ROR-based double-fault mutants. Figure 5 shows that 76 of the 212 mutants have 11 independent bad pairs, and only 7 of them do not have any independent bad pairs. We observed the same trend—a significant increase in independent bad pairs—for the COR-based and the AOR-based double-fault mutants.

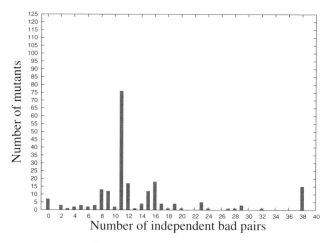

Fig. 5. Double Mutation ROR

3.4 Discussion

No independent bad pairs are observed when the test results from all 216 test cases are considered. When only legal triangles are considered, however, independent bad pairs are common; nearly half of the 213 mutants have at least one. Clearly, test case selection has a significant practical impact on bad pairs analysis. Independent bad pairs are common in mutants with one fault, although the number of them varies among the mutants. In addition, the number of independent bad pairs increases significantly when the mutants contain two faults rather than a single fault. Finally, the number of mutants with no independent bad pairs decreases drastically when the mutants contain two faults rather than a single fault.

4 Bad Pairs in TCAS

As with the triangle code, we use mutation testing to measure the occurrence of independent bad pairs. Here the target code is significantly larger: more lines of code, more parameters, and a much bigger test space.

The gold code is the TCAS program from the Siemens collection, hand converted from C to Java. There are 7 functions and 109 lines of executable code. We used MuJava to generate 250 mutants.

TCAS has 12 input parameters. While most of the parameters have type `int`, the code clearly divides each of these into a small number of ranges, where all values in a range are treated identically. We selected 3–5 values for each parameter, using equivalence partitioning. Because the cross product of the parameters sets has 6,220,800 elements, testing the full cross product against all the mutants is impractical. Instead, we generated a pairwise test set containing 34 cases.

As shown in Figure 6, 46 mutants have no independent bad pairs; most of the remaining 204 have 17.

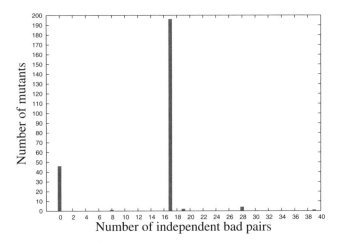

Fig. 6. TCAS: single mutation with pairwise inputs

5 Bad Pairs in Network Vulnerability Testing

Industrial control systems (ICSs) are used to control processes such as power distribution and generation, manufacturing, and oil refining. These systems consist of specialized field controllers and general-purpose workstations. The field controllers are located on the plant floor and control local operations such as opening and closing valves, and collecting data from sensors. The workstations are physically located further from the industrial process, and they are used by engineers to program and monitor the field controllers. Initially, ICSs did not use the ubiquitous TCP/IP protocol suite, but instead used proprietary network protocols. Furthermore, ICS networks were physically separated from traditional IT networks.

These two factors provided a considerable degree of protection from network attacks, as the networks were extremely difficult to access and the protocols in use were unknown to the vast majority of potential network attackers. In the past fifteen years the situation has changed dramatically [4]. ICSs now use TCP/IP and are connected to IT and business networks. Systems that were designed and implemented without much consideration for network security are now exposed and vulnerable to the myriad issues that are faced by traditional IT systems.

One solution to the problem of ICS network security is to employ network vulnerability testing [21,10,18]. Network vulnerability testing is the process of sending potentially problematic network traffic to a device-under-test (DUT). The purpose of network vulnerability testing is to find and correct device vulnerabilities before they are deployed, thereby resulting in more robust and secure devices. To support the vulnerability testing process, Wurldtech Security Technologies has developed an automated testing tool called the Achilles Satellite. The Satellite is capable of sending the network attack types previously described across a range of protocols. Test results are determined through the Satellite Monitors. A Satellite Monitor continually observes one particular aspect of the DUT. For instance, there is an ICMP Monitor that sends ICMP echo requests to the DUT, and checks that corresponding ICMP echo replies are being received. If echo replies are received as expected, the monitor state is normal. If the replies are no longer received, the state changes to warning. There are multiple monitors; together they determine the test results.

5.1 Test Setup

The Achilles Satellite was used to test an ICS field controller. The test bench consists of the controller (DUT), the Achilles Satellite, and the workstation used to interface with the vendor control server (VCS), as shown in Figure 7. Note how the Satellite is connected to the DUT and the VCS via ports 1 and 2, respectively. Ports 1 and 2 are bridged, i.e., traffic sent from the DUT destined for the VCS will be forwarded from port 1 to port 2, and vice-versa. Test traffic is only sent from port 1 to the DUT. Finally, the digital output of the DUT is monitored by the Achilles Satellite. During real use, a controller's digital output controls actuators on the plant floor. For our tests, the digital output is programmed to produce a periodic signal which can be monitored by the Satellite.

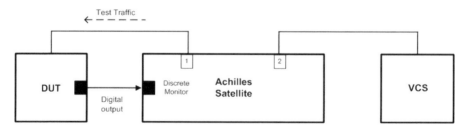

Fig. 7. Test bench diagram

A test session consists of the following four steps:

1. *Environment Configuration*: selection of Achilles Satellite monitors and specification of logistical details such as DUT IP address.
2. *Service Discovery*: execution of TCP and UDP port scans to determine open ports.
3. *Test Selection*: selection and parameterization of test cases.
4. *Test Execution*: automatic execution of selected test cases.

A wide range of tests across a number of protocols was run against the DUT. In the next subsection, we will examine in detail the results of one particular test, the IP Grammar Field Fuzzer.

5.2 Test Results

The IP Grammar/Field Fuzzer generates invalid packets using a combination of IP header values taken from a predefined list. In all, the test sends 4734 distinct packets. Upon running this test, the Satellite's ICMP Monitor observed that echo responses were not being received. Upon further investigation, it was determined that the DUT's network stack was restarting during the test. The next step was to determine which of the 4734 packets was causing this behavior. Through additional testing, it was discovered that the DUT would power cycle when sent packets numbered 4188 and 4220. The remaining 4732 packets had no effect.

Table 3. IP parameters

Version	header length	TOS	total length	id	flags	offset	TTL	protocol	source	destination
0	0	0	0	0	0	0	0	0	0x00000000	0x00000000
1	4	1	19	1	1	1	1	1	0xc0a86401	0xc0a8644d
4	5	3	20	65534	2	1479	2	2	0xc0a8644d	0xc0a86401
6	6	5	1499	65535	4	1480	3	3	0xc0a864ff	0xc0a864ff
7	14	7	1500		7	1481	31	5	0xefffffff	0xefffffff
	15		1501		3	1499	32	6	0xffffffff	0xffffffff
			3001		5	1500	33	7		
			65534		6	1501	63	16		
			65535			8190	64	17		
						8191	65	18		
							127	37		
							128	59		
							129	64		
							254	65		
							255	254		
								255		

5.3 Bad Pairs Analysis

Manual analysis was able to narrow the search for the cause of the failure to just two packets out of 4734. It remained unclear, however, what was special about those two packets.

To apply bad pairs analysis, we extracted the IP header fields from each packet. The resulting 11 parameter sets are shown in Table 3. The analysis yielded two bad pairs, both independent. The failures occur precisely when the total length is 0 and the protocol is ICMP, or when the total length is 0 and the protocol is TCP. With $\binom{11}{2} = 55$ pairs per test case, manual analysis of this kind was impractical.

6 Graph-Based Algorithms

In this section we discuss another input selection method, Error Locating Arrays (ELA), which is a pairwise test input table with additional tests cases which allow us to isolate bad pairs. ELA's require more test cases than pairwise tests but still have logarithmic growth on the number of tests cases.

6.1 Parameter Sets and Bad Pairs

To discuss ELA's, we model the parameter space of a system as a graph. In Table 4 we see the parameter space for the triagle program and the same space modeled as a graph in Figure 8.

Table 4. Triangle System

	Parameters		
	a	b	c
	0	0	0
	1	1	1
	2	2	2
Values	3	3	3
	4	4	4
	5	5	5

	Parameters		
	a	b	c
	$a,0$	$b,0$	$c,0$
	$a,1$	$b,1$	$c,1$
Values	$a,2$	$b,2$	$c,2$
	$a,3$	$b,3$	$c,3$
	$a,4$	$b,4$	$c,4$
	$a,5$	$b,5$	$c,5$

Fig. 8. Vertex set of Triangle System

Fig. 9. A bad singleton

Fig. 10. Bad Pair

Since each vertex represents a singleton, edges can be used to represent bad singletons and bad pairs. A bad singleton is a self-loop in the graph, as shown in Figure 9, while a bad pair can be seen as an edge between two vertices, as shown in Figure 10. In graph theory language [2], every system with a set of n parameters can be modeled as an n-partite graph where each part i has the same size as the number of values for parameter i.

In terms of graphs, each row in the test input table can be viewed as a selection of n vertices from an n-partite graph, one per part. For example, the test case $(0, 1, 2)$ is equivalent to the set of vertices $(a, 0)$, $(b, 1)$ and $(c, 2)$ in the simplest mathematical model. Choosing a set of vertices such that the set contains one or more edges, including self-loops, will cause a test case to fail. For example, if the test case was $(0, 1, 2)$ but $(b, 1)$ and $(c, 2)$ were a bad pair, i.e., were connected by an edge, then this test would fail.

6.2 Two-Way Locatable n-Partite Graph

In order to *locate* an independent bad pair, the pair must be in a failing test such that the only reason for the failure is from that pair. More precisely, the test case must contain no bad singletons and exactly one bad pair. For example, in Figure 2(a) Section 2, $(\bullet, 2, 2)$ is a locatable bad pair. Test $(1, 2, 2)$ is not locatable because it also contains the bad singleton $(1, \bullet, \bullet)$.

In a *two-way locatable n-partite graph*, for each pair of vertices from different parameter sets:

- The pair does not contain a loop on either vertex.
- There exists a set of $n - 2$ vertices from different parameter sets such that, when combined with the pair, the only edge in the set, if any, is from the pair itself.

From Figure 11, suppose we wanted to locate the pair $v_{a,2}$ and $v_{b,2}$. We need to be able to pick a vertex in part c such that it does not form an edge with either of the two already chosen vertices. Since $v_{c,5}$ contains a loop it is not a possible choice. It is easily seen that any other choice of vertex from part c would be an acceptable choice. Such a test case is said to *verify* the pair. In order for Figure 11 to be a locating graph, all pairs would need to be verified. In a similar way, bad sets of larger size can be modeled as Hypergraphs which are a generalization of a graph where an edge can connect any number of vertices.

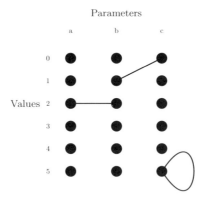

Fig. 11. Error Graph - Triangle System

6.3 Why Is a Locatable Graph Useful?

An error locating test case is a case which contains at most one independent bad pair. Error locating test cases are interesting for two reasons:

1. *Practical utility.* Suppose that test case T is an error locating test case containing independent bad pair P, and that cases containing P, and only those cases, reveal the fault. Then T locates the fault, in the sense that the statement containing the fault will be executed by T. A test case T' which contains two or more bad pairs might not have this property.
2. *Algorithm support.* An error locating array is a test table containing an error locating test case for every pair in the cross product. Under certain restrictions, efficient algorithms exist for generating error locating arrays [15].

6.4 Error Locating Arrays (ELA)

Suppose a system could fail due to the combination of t interactions. An ELA, in its most general form, is an array such that every t-tuple appears in at least one row of the array (which represents a test) and where this t-tuple can be the only reason for the failure of the test.

For example, consider a system that has four parameters: two parameters have 2 values and the rest have 3. Figure 12 shows a set of errors in the system (edges connection specific vertices), a test input table and a result vector. The bold values in the first three rows represent the edges in the graph in Figure 12. Because each non-bad pair can be found by a passing test, each bad pair can be uniquely identified: it is the only pair to be not found non-faulty in the row containing the bad pair. Verifying the remaining interactions clearly shows that the test input table is an ELA for the graph in Figure 12.

For example, the test $(0, 1, 1, 0)$ is a failing test. Since none of these are found to be bad singletons, there are six options for failing interactions. $(\bullet, \bullet, 1, 0)$ was found non-faulty in test 10, $(\bullet, 1, 1, \bullet)$ was found non-faulty in test 8, $(0, \bullet, 1, \bullet)$ was found non-faulty in test 11, $(0, \bullet, \bullet, 0)$ was found non-faulty in test 4 $(\bullet, 1, \bullet, 0)$ was found non-faulty in test 7. Thus the only remaining pair is $(0, 1, \bullet, \bullet)$ and we conclude it an independent bad pair.

Factors:	(1) Printer	(2) File format	(3) Colours	(4) File size
test 1	0	1	1	0
test 2	1	0	1	0
test 3	1	2	0	0
test 4	0	0	0	0
test 5	0	0	0	1
test 6	1	0	0	2
test 7	1	1	0	0
test 8	1	1	1	1
test 9	1	1	0	2
test 10	1	2	1	0
test 11	0	2	1	1
test 12	0	2	1	2

Outcome
fail
fail
fail
pass
pass
pass
pass
pass
pass
pass
pass
pass

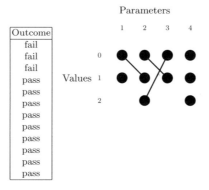

Fig. 12. Test Suite

7 Related Work

7.1 Fault Interactions

The occurrence of software failures due to multiple conditions has long been studied. Modern telephony software has been plagued by feature interaction problems, e.g., call forwarding and VoIP work well on separate calls but fail when present on the same call, perhaps only on certain releases of the VoIP software [11]. Kuhn, et al' [12] summarize empirical studies of software from a variety of domains, focusing on the failure-triggering fault interaction (FTFI) number: the number of conditions required to trigger a failure. The studies showed that the FTFI number is often relatively small. FTFI numbers are usually 1 or 2 and are rarely larger than 6. Moritz describes an empirical study of field errors [16]. Each error was replicated in a lab and analyzed to determine the minimum number of conditions required to generate the error.

In the studies just described, the concept of "condition" is quite general, with each condition typically described in one or two prose sentences. In this paper, and in all work based on covering arrays, conditions are restricted by the tabular test model, i.e., each condition is a value for a parameter. While this restriction narrows the applicability of the approach it also allows us to apply sophisticated analysis algorithms.

7.2 Covering Arrays

Grindal et al. [9] survey and classify combinatorial test strategies, including work on orthogonal and covering arrays. Many approaches [20,19,7] and tools [5,13] have been proposed for generating covering arrays. Some of the approaches only work for covering arrays in which all domain sizes are the same, problematic in testing applications where the domain sizes typically vary. Algorithms mixed-level covering arrays, in which domain sizes can vary, have been described by Moura et al. [17].

7.3 Error Locating Arrays

ELA's can be used to expose failures caused by a combination of any number of conditions. Martínez et al. [15] gave three constructions for ELA's.

First, higher strength covering arrays provide the additional overlap needed to locate errors. Constructions for covering arrays of strength 2 have been extensively covered [6]. Bazdell [1] presents an efficient single approach construction for mixed-level covering arrays of strength 2 with for any arbitrary number of parameters and values. For strength greater than 3, Colbourn and Bryce [3] present a one-test-at-a-time greedy algorithm for t-tuple coverage that grows logarithmically with the number of parameters.

"Safe values" for a system are values that are known in advance not to be part of any error. The second construction gives an adaptive algorithm that locates faults when safe values are known and each parameter must contains at least one.

Lastly, when a system has parameters that take only 2 values each, binary, Martínez et al. [15] characterize the family of locatable graphs and give an algorithm that adaptively builds tests that locate all errors.

8 Conclusions

While pairwise testing is used to generate test inputs, we have presented a novel analysis of the test outputs, focusing on bad pairs: those which always result in a failed test case. We have experimentally evaluated the frequency of occurrence of bad pairs providing useful insights into the relationships between faults and bad pairs, and between input selection and bad pairs. We also applied the approach to an industrial example in network vulnerability testing. Finally, we presented the main results in error-locating arrays, a powerful tool for bad pairs analysis.

References

1. Bazdell, G.P.: Projection—product and asymptotic constructions of mixed level covering arrays. Master's thesis, Carleton University, Ottawa, Canada (2009)
2. Bondy, J.A., Murty, U.S.R.: Graph Theory. Springer, Heidelberg (2008)
3. Bryce, R.C., Colbourn, C.J.: A density-based greedy algorithm for higher strength covering arrays. Softw. Test. Verif. Reliab. 19(1), 37–53 (2009)
4. Byres, E., Carter, J., El Ramly, A., Hoffman, D.: Worlds in collision—Ethernet and the factory floor. In: Proc. ISA Emerging Technologies Conf. (October 2002)

5. Cohen, D.M., Dalal, S.R., Fredman, M.L., Patton, G.C.: The AETG System: An Approach to Testing Based on Combinatorial Design. IEEE Trans. Soft. Eng. 23(7), 437–444 (1997)
6. Colbourn, C.J.: Combinatorial aspects of covering arrays. Matematiche (Catania) 59(1-2), 125–172 (2004)
7. Colbourn, C.J., Martirosyan, S.S., Van Trung, T., Walker II, R.A.: Roux-type construction for covering arrays of strengths three and four. Designs, Codes and Cryptography 14, 33–57 (2006)
8. Demillo, R.A., Lipton, R.J., Sayward, F.G.: Hints on test data selection: help for the practising programmer. Computer 11(4), 34–41 (1978)
9. Grindal, M., Offutt, J., Andler, S.F.: Combination testing strategies: a survey. Journal of Software Testing, Verification, and Reliability 15(3), 167–199 (2005)
10. Hoffman, D., Kube, N.: Automated testing of SCADA protocols. In: Proc. SCADA Scientific Security Symposium (2007)
11. Keck, D., Kuehn, P.: The feature and service interaction problem in telecommunications systems: a survey. IEEE Trans. Soft. Eng. 24(10), 779–796 (1998)
12. Kuhn, D.R., Wallace, D.R., Gallo Jr., A.M.: Software fault interactions and implications for software testing. IEEE Trans. Soft. Eng. 30(6), 418–421 (2004)
13. Lei, Y., Kacker, R., Kuhn, D.R., Okun, V., Lawrence, J.: IPOG: a general strategy for t-way software testing. In: Proc. of the 14th Intl. Conf. on the Engineering of Computer-Based Systems, pp. 549–556 (2007)
14. Ma, Y.S., Offutt, J., Kwon, Y.R.: MuJava: an automated class mutation system. Journal of Software Testing, Verification, and Reliability 15(2), 97–133 (2005)
15. Martínez, C., Moura, L., Panario, D., Stevens, B.: Locating errors using ELAs, covering arrays, and adaptive testing algorithms. SIAM J. Discrete Math. 23(4), 1776–1799 (2009)
16. Moritz, E.: Case study: how analysis of customer found defects can be used by system test to improve quality. In: Proceedings of the International Conference on Software Engineering, pp. 16–24 (2009)
17. Moura, L., Stardom, J., Stevens, B., Williams, A.: Covering arrays with mixed alphabet sizes. Journal of Combinatorial Designs 11(6), 413–432 (2003)
18. Peltier, T., Peltier, J., Blackley, J.: Managing a Network Vulnerability Assessment. CRC Press, Boca Raton (2003)
19. Sherwood, G.B., Martirosyan, S.S., Colbourn, C.J.: Covering arrays of higher strength from permutation vectors. Journal of Combinatorial Designs 14(3), 202–213 (2005)
20. Tai, K.C., Lie, Y.: A test generation strategy for pairwise testing. IEEE Trans. Soft. Eng. 28(1), 109–111 (2002)
21. Tal, O., Knight, S., Dean, T.: Syntax-based vulnerability testing of frame-based network protocols. In: Proc. Conf. Privacy, Security, and Trust (2004)

Localizing Defects in Multithreaded Programs by Mining Dynamic Call Graphs

Frank Eichinger[1], Victor Pankratius[1],
Philipp W.L. Große[2], and Klemens Böhm[1]

[1] Karlsruhe Institute of Technology (KIT), Germany
{eichinger,victor.pankratius,klemens.boehm}@kit.edu
[2] SAP AG, Walldorf, Germany
philipp.grosse@sap.com

Abstract. Writing multithreaded software for multicore computers confronts many developers with the difficulty of finding parallel programming errors. In the past, most parallel debugging techniques have concentrated on finding race conditions due to wrong usage of synchronization constructs. A widely unexplored issue, however, is that a wrong usage of *non-parallel* programming constructs may also cause wrong *parallel* application behavior. This paper presents a novel defect-localization technique for multithreaded shared-memory programs that is based on analyzing execution anomalies. Compared to race detectors that report just on wrong synchronization, this method can detect a wider range of defects affecting parallel execution. It works on a condensed representation of the call graphs of multithreaded applications and employs data-mining techniques to locate a method containing a defect. Our results from controlled application experiments show that we found race conditions, but also other programming errors leading to incorrect parallel program behavior. On average, our approach reduced in our benchmark the amount of code to be inspected to just 7.1% of all methods.

1 Introduction

Present-day computers with several cores on a single chip require developers to write multithreaded applications in order to exploit the full performance potential. Compared to sequential software development, programmers are now additionally confronted with nondeterminism and parallel-programming failures, such as race conditions or deadlocks [15,19].

Today, static and dynamic debugging aids for parallel shared-memory programs are widely available [10,13,20,22,23,25,26]. They focus on identifying atomicity violations, race conditions or deadlocks due to wrong or inconsistent locking. However, these tools are usually heavily specialized on a particular class of parallel programming errors. Little attention has been paid so far to other causes (e.g., originating from *non-parallel* constructs) that might be incorrectly used to produce wrong *parallel* program behavior. For example, suppose that a programmer forgets or incorrectly specifies a condition when creating threads in a thread pool. This might lead to an unbounded creation of threads, uncontrolled program behavior and wrong program outputs. Clearly, there is a need for more general defect localization techniques to fill such gaps. Advances in this area are of great importance for industrial practice.

This paper addresses this problem and proposes a novel defect localization technique for multithreaded shared-memory programs. It is designed to detect a wider range of defects that affect parallel execution rather than just race conditions. Our approach is based on analyzing anomalies in program behavior. To this end, we employ a data-mining technique building on call graphs of multithreaded applications. This extends our previous work addressing sequential programs [12]. In particular, we compare the structure of the call graphs and the call frequencies from correct and incorrect program executions to isolate the methods containing defects. We also discuss different call-graph representations for multithreaded programs and develop a solution with edge annotations that is more robust with respect to varying thread schedules and more compact in situations in which different threads execute replicated tasks. Contrary to race detectors that produce many warnings (most of which are false positives) in some arbitrary order, our technique produces a ranking of methods ordered by the likelihood of containing a defect. Our controlled experiments with typical applications show that an upper bound of several hundred program executions is enough to pinpoint the actual defects. In addition, our approach was able to localize a previously unknown (and undocumented) error in an open-source download tool.

Paper organization: Section 2 explains the principles of call-graph-based defect localization. Section 3 discusses appropriate extensions for representations of call graphs for multithreaded programs. Section 4 introduces our novel approach to mine these graphs and use the results for defect localization. Section 5 evaluates the approach, and Section 6 gives a detailed illustrative example. Section 7 contrasts our approach to related work, while Section 8 compares our technique to selected alternative approaches. Section 9 provides a conclusion.

2 Dynamic-Call-Graph-Based Defect Localization in Sequential Programs

We distinguish between *defects*, *infections* and *failures*, according to [28]: *Defects* are the positions in the source code which cause a problem, an *infection* is an incorrect program state (usually triggered by a defect), and *failures* are an observable incorrect program behavior (e.g., a user obtains wrong results).

For sequential software, Liu et al. [18] and Di Fatta et al. [9] have proposed graph-mining techniques for defect localization, working on call graphs that represent program execution traces. The techniques assume that a collection of test cases is available and that it is possible to decide if a program is executed correctly or not. Both approaches deal with *occasional bugs*, i.e., defects that lead to both correct and failing executions. In these works, this behavior depends on the input data, but it could be caused by varying thread interleavings, too. Furthermore, they focus on *non-crashing bugs*.

A detailed survey of call-graph-mining-based defect localization is presented in [11]. The basic idea of most approaches is to mine for patterns in the call graph that are characteristic for incorrect executions. Thereafter, they calculate for each method its likelihood of being defective. The call graphs may become huge, so it is necessary to work on a compact representation. In [12] we observe that the representations in [6,9,18] lose the information how many method calls an edge reprsents in the call-graph. We therefore extend the graphs with edge weights representing call frequencies in [12]. We also demonstrate that data-mining analyses based on such graphs increase the defect-localization precision and detect defects that other approaches cannot deal with.

Other recent approaches introduce call graphs with several granularity levels, instead of one at the level of methods, such as the the basic-block level in [6]. It facilitates more detailed defect localizations.

The mentioned sequential techniques cannot be applied to multithreaded software right away, as they do not define call graphs of multithreaded programs. Thus, two extensions are necessary: (1) Find an appropriate graph representation for multithreaded programs, and (2) adapt the mining scheme. We address both issues in the following sections.

3 Dynamic Call Graphs for Multithreaded Programs

We now present the call-graph representation we employ for our technique and contrast it with other possible choices. We also sketch how to generate the call graphs for a multithreaded application.

3.1 Representation of Call Graphs in Our Approach

Unreduced call graphs. Call graphs are based on program executions and therefore need to be derived at runtime. Our approach uses call graphs at the granularity level of methods, i.e., nodes refer to methods and edges to method calls. Furthermore, in the multithreaded case, every method can be executed several times in more than one thread. Therefore, in unreduced call graphs, we initially label the nodes with the thread ID as a prefix and with the method name. Figure 1(a) contains an example call graph. This example represents the method calls of a program execution, without any reductions.

Reduced call graphs. In our approach, we use a more concise "totally reduced" graph representation without thread IDs. Each method is uniquely represented by exactly one node that does not depend on a thread. We introduce edge weights as in [12] for call frequencies: Every edge weight captures the total number of calls between the methods, represented by two connected nodes. Figure 1(b) shows an example for this representation; it is the reduced version of the call graph in Figure 1(a).

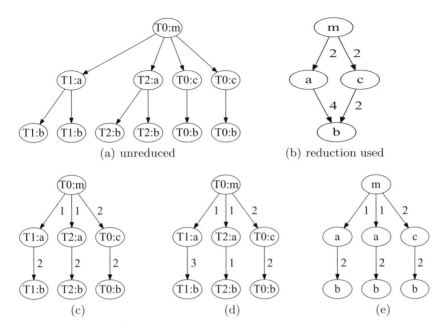

Fig. 1. Example graphs illustrating alternative choices for call-graph representations

3.2 Discussion and Comparison of Alternative Representations

Including temporal relationships may cause too much overhead. For the localization of defects in multithreaded software, it seems to be natural to encode temporal information in call graphs, e.g., to tackle race conditions. The call graphs as the one in Figure 1(a) do not encode any order of execution of the different threads and methods. One straight-forward approach to include such information could use temporal edges as in [18]. The problem with this idea, however, is that the overhead to obtain such information is large and requires sophisticated tracing techniques. Furthermore, it may significantly influence program behavior – possibly making a failure disappear. We therefore employ a more lightweight approach without temporal information encoded in the graphs.

Uncompressed graphs become too large. Call graphs directly derived from program execution – such as the one in Figure 1(a) – become very large in practice. Even for a small program, the number of method calls can become so large that mining algorithms would not scale. Therefore, a compression is necessary. Figure 1(c) represents the "total reduction" of Figure 1(a), merging all nodes having the same node label. This reduction encodes in the edge weights a part of the information that was previously contained in the graph structure.

Thread IDs differ between program runs. Figure 1(c) illustrates a call-graph representation that contains the thread IDs in the node labels. This is awkward, as threads are allocated dynamically by the runtime environment or the operating system; various correct executions could lead to threads with different IDs for the same method call, even for a program using the same parameters and input data. We therefore would not be able to compare several program executions based on the node labels. Omitting this information would result in the graph shown in Figure 1(e), which is directly derived from the one in Figure 1(c).

The effects of replicated tasks and varying thread interleavings must be addressed. Graphs such as the ones in Figure 1(e), (c), and (d) can lead to two problems: (1) They might contain a high degree of redundancy that does not help finding defects. For example, a program using thread pools could have a large number of threads with similar calls due to the execution of replicated tasks (and therefore similar method calls). This typically produces a call graph with several identical and large subtrees, which contain no meaningful information for defect localization. (2) The call frequencies (i.e., the edge weights) might not be useful for defect localization, too. Different execution schedules of the same program can lead to graphs with widely differing edge weights. This can disturb data-mining analyses, as such differences are not related to infections. As an example, think of method a in Figure 1(c) as the `run()` method, calling the worker task method b, which takes work from a task pool. Sometimes, thread 1 and thread 2 would both call method b twice, as in Figure 1(c). In other cases as in Figure 1(d), depending on the scheduling, thread 1 could call method b three times, while thread 2 would only call it once or vice versa.

Based on the observations discussed so far, we decided to use a graph representation that avoids repeated substructures. Furthermore, our representation is robust with respect to thread scheduling. In addition, for graphs such as the one in Figure 1(e), we merge all nodes referring to the same method to a single node. This leads to the representation introduced in Figure 1(b). This representation is robust in the sense that different schedules do not influence the graph structure. The downside of this representation is that graph structures from different executions rarely differ. This makes a structural analysis of the call graphs as in other approaches (e.g., [12]) less promising. To compensate this effect, we encode additional information in the edge weights, which has turned out to be helpful for discovering defective behavior.

3.3 Obtaining the Call Graphs

To generate call graphs for multithreaded applications, we employ AspectJ [17] and use it to weave in tracing functionality into a program. AspectJ has been shown in earlier work to be well-suited for program-trace generation and infection detection in multithreaded programs [7]. AspectJ introduces additional overhead and execution slowdowns; we observed a typical increase in execution time between 50% and 100% for the programs used in our evaluation (see Section 5).

4 Defect Localization in Multithreaded Programs

We first present an overview of the defect-localization procedure and then more details on our data-mining-based technique.

4.1 Overview

Algorithm 1 works with a set T of traces obtained from program executions. A trace is an unreduced call graph where every individual method invocation leads to a new edge and a new node (see Figure 1(a)). Using a test oracle, our algorithm assigns a class (*correct* or *failing*) to every trace $t_j \in T$. Then, the algorithm reduces every t_j to obtain a new call graph, which is assigned to a class of either correct or failing executions. Based on these graphs, the last step calculates for every method m_i its likelihood of being defective. The likelihood is used to rank the order of potentially defective methods shown to the software developer.

Algorithm 1. Overview of call-graph-based defect localization

Input: a set of program traces $t_j \in T$
Output: a method ranking based on each method's likelihood of being defective $P(m_i)$
1: $G = \emptyset$ // initialize a set of reduced graphs
2: **for all** traces $t_j \in T$ **do**
3:   check if t_j was a correct execution and assign a *class* $\in \{correct, failing\}$ to t_j
4:   $G = G \cup \{reduce(t)\}$
5: **end for**
6: calculate $P(m_i)$ for all methods m_i in G

We employ a *test oracle* to decide whether a program execution is correct or not (Line 3 in Algorithm 1). Such oracles are specific for the examined program, and their purpose is to decide if a certain execution manifests any observable problems (i.e., a *failure*). An observable problem can be a wrong output or other erroneous behavior such as a race condition. In this paper, we assume that some kind of test oracle is available.

4.2 Data-Mining-Based Defectiveness-Likelihood Calculation

We now focus on the calculation of the likelihoods of a method being defective (Line 6 in Algorithm 1). The goal is to find out which methods in program's call graph discriminate best between correct and failing executions. We analyze the edge weights of the call graphs to derive such probabilities and create a feature table containing all edges as columns and all program executions (represented by their reduced call graphs) as rows (see Table 1).

Table 1. Example of a feature table

	$a \to b$	$b \to c$	$a \to d$	$\cdots$	Class
g_1	445	445	7	$\cdots$	*failing*
g_2	128	256	0	$\cdots$	*correct*
$\cdots$	$\cdots$	$\cdots$	$\cdots$	$\cdots$	$\cdots$

For illustration, the first column in Table 1 corresponds to the edge from method a to method b, the second column to the edge from b to c, and the third column represents an edge from a to d. The last column contains the class (*correct* or *failing*). The rows correspond to reduced call graphs $g_1, ..., g_n \in G$, which are derived from program executions. If a certain edge is not contained in a call graph, the respective cell is 0. For example, graph g_2 does not possess edge $a \to d$.

Using this table, we analyze the edge weights. We employ a standard feature-selection algorithm to calculate the discriminativeness of the columns of the table and thus of the different edges. In particular, we use the *information-gain-ratio* measure (*GainRatio*, see Definition 1) from the Weka machine-learning suite [27]. This measure is frequently used in data analysis, in particular in decision-tree induction [24,27]. *GainRatio* reaches 1, its highest value, when an attribute discriminates perfectly between classes; at 0, its lowest value, an attribute does not contribute at all to the discrimination of classes.

Definition 1. *The* information-gain ratio *(GainRatio) [24] is a measure based on* information gain *(InfoGain) [24] and ultimately on* entropy *(Info):*

$$Info(D) := -\sum_{i=1}^{|\mathbb{D}_C|} \frac{|D_i|}{|D|} \cdot \log_2(\frac{|D_i|}{|D|})$$

$$InfoGain(A, D) := Info(D) - \sum_{j=1}^{|\mathbb{D}_A|} \frac{|D_j|}{|D|} \cdot Info(D_j)$$

$$SplitInfo(A, D) := -\sum_{j=1}^{|\mathbb{D}_A|} \frac{|D_j|}{|D|} \cdot \log_2(\frac{|D_j|}{|D|})$$

$$GainRatio(A, D) := \frac{InfoGain(A, D)}{SplitInfo(A, D)}$$

where D is a dataset, C is the class of tuples in D, A is an attribute in D, and $\mathbb{D}_C$ and $\mathbb{D}_A$ denote the sets of values reached by C and A, respectively.

Besides *GainRatio*, we could choose from a number of different feature-selection algorithms, but we know from our previous work (see Section 2) that those based on *entropy* are well suited for defect localization. Compared to *InfoGain*, which could be used as well, *GainRatio* is robust regarding imbalanced class distributions because it normalizes the *InfoGain* by its *SplitInfo* [24].

So far, we have derived defect likelihoods for every column in the table, i.e., for edges. However, we are interested in likelihoods for methods m_i. As a method can call several other methods, we assign every column to the calling method. We then calculate the method likelihood $P(m_i)$ as the maximum of the gain-ratio values of the columns assigned to method m_i. We use the maximum because it refers to a method's most suspicious invocation. Other invocations are less important, as they might not be related to a defect. However, the information which specific invocation within method m_i is most suspicious (the column with the highest likelihood) can be important for a software developer to find and fix the defect. We therefore report this additional information to the user.

5 Experimental Evaluation

We now present the experimental results to validate our approach. At first, we describe the benchmark programs and their defects, the experimental setting, and the metrics used to interpret the results. Section 8 presents some comparisons to related techniques.

5.1 Benchmark Programs and Defects

Our benchmark contains a range of different multithreaded programs. The benchmark covers a broad range of tasks, from basic sorting algorithms and various client-server settings to memory allocators, which are fundamental constructs in many programs [5]. As our prototype is implemented in AspectJ, all benchmark programs are in Java. Most of these programs have been used in previous studies and were developed in student assignments [14]. We slightly modified some of the programs; for example, in the *GarageManager* application, we replaced different `println()` statements with methods containing code simulating the assignment of work to different tasks. Furthermore, we included two typical client-server open-source applications in our benchmark. These programs are larger and represent an important class of real applications. Table 2 lists all programs along with their size in terms of methods and normalized lines of code (LOC)[1].

Table 2. Programs considered (#M/#T is the number of methods/threads)

Program	#M	LOC	#T	Source	Description
AllocationVector (Test)	6	133	2	[14]	Allocation of memory
GarageManager	30	475	4	[14]	Simulation of a garage
Liveness (BugGen)	8	120	100	[14]	Client-server simulation
MergeSort	11	201	4	[14]	Recursive sorting implementation
ThreadTest	12	101	50	[14]	CPU benchmark (random divisions)
Tornado	122	632	100	[1]	HTTP Server
Weblech	88	802	10	[2]	Website download/mirror tool

The benchmark programs are seeded with known defects to provide examples for different defect patterns. In the two open-source programs, we manually inserted typical synchronization defects. All defects are representative for common multithreaded programming errors (e.g., forgotten synchronization for some variable) and are occasional. The defects cover a broad range of error patterns,

---
[1] We always use the sum of non-blank and non-comment LOC inside method bodies.

such as atomicity violations/race conditions (on one or several correlated variables), deadlocks, but also other kinds of programming errors (e.g., originating from non-parallel constructs) that can influence parallel program behavior.

We categorize the defect patterns in the programs of our evaluation as follows (according to the classification in [15]):

1. *AllocationVector*; defect pattern: **"two-stage access"**. Two steps of finding and allocating blocks for memory access are not executed atomically, even though the individual steps are synchronized. Thus, two threads might allocate the same memory and cause incorrect interference.
2. *GarageManager*; defect pattern: **"blocking critical section"**. The defect itself is a combination of an incorrectly calculated value in some rare cases due to a forgotten switch case. When this situation occurs, no task is assigned to a particular thread, while a global variable is treated as if work had been assigned. Thus, fewer than the maximum number of threads are active. This makes the program deadlock. We illustrate this program in more detail in Section 6.
3. *Liveness*; defect pattern: similar to the **"orphaned thread"** pattern. When the maximum number of clients is reached, the next requesting client is added to a stack. Although this data structure and a global counter are synchronized, it can happen that the server becomes available while the client is added to the stack. In this case, the client will never resume and will not finish its task.
4. *MergeSort*; defect pattern: **"two-stage access"**. Although methods working on global thread counters are synchronized, the variables themselves are not, which might lead to atomicity violations. In particular, threads ask how many subthreads they are allowed to generate. When two threads apply at the same time, more threads than allowed are generated. This can lead to situations in which parts of the data are not sorted.
5. *ThreadTest*; defect pattern: **"blocking critical section"**. The generation of new threads and checking a global variable for the maximum number of currently available threads is not done correctly in case of exceptions, which occur randomly due to divisions by zero. This leads to a deadlock when all threads encounter this situation. We consider an execution as failing when at least one thread encounters this problem, due to lowered performance.
6. *Tornado*; defect pattern: **"no lock"**. Synchronization statements are removed in one method. This leads to a race condition and ultimately to unanswered HTTP requests.
7. *Weblech*; defect pattern: **"no lock"**. Removed synchronization statements as in *Tornado*, resulting in Web pages that are not downloaded.

For the *Weblech* program, we have two versions: *Weblech.orig* and *Weblech.inj*. In *Weblech.inj*, we introduced a defect in method `run()` by removing all `synchronized` statements (Listing 1 shows an excerpt of this method with one such statement), aiming to simulate a typical programming error. During our experiments, we realized that the original non-injected version (*Weblech.orig*) led to failures in very rare cases, too (the failure occurred in only 5 out of 5,000 executions; we used a sample of the correct executions in the experiments). Thus, *Weblech.inj* contains the original defect besides the injected defects. With our tool, we were able to localize the real defect by investigating two methods only. The result is that two global unsynchronized variables (`downloadsInProgress` and `running`) are modified in `run()`, occasionally causing race conditions. To fix the defect in order to produce a defect-free reference, we added the `volatile` keyword to the variable declaration in the class header.

```
while (queueSize() > 0 || downloadsInProgress > 0) {
    synchronized (queue) {
        nextURL = queue.getNextInQueue();
        downloadsInProgress++; }
}
running--;
```

Listing 1. Method `void weblech.spider.run()` (shortened to a minimum)

5.2 Experimental Setting

Number of executions. Our defect-localization technique requires that we execute every program several times and that we ensure that there is a sufficiently high number of examples for correct and failing executions. This is necessary since we focus on occasional bugs (see Section 2), i.e., failures whose occurrence depends on input data, random components or non-deterministic thread interleavings. Furthermore, we tried to achieve stable results, i.e., analyzing more executions would not lead to significant changes. We used this criterion to determine the number of required executions, in addition to obtaining enough correct and failing cases. Table 3 lists the number of correct and failing executions for each benchmark program.

Varying execution traces. In order to obtain different execution traces from the same program, we rely on the original test cases that are provided in the benchmark suite (e.g., *MergeSort* comes with a generator creating random arrays as input data). Some programs have an internal random component as part of the program logic, i.e., they automatically lead to varying executions (e.g., *GarageManager* simulates varying processes in a garage). Other programs produce different executions due to different thread interleavings that can occasionally lead to observable failures. For the two open-source programs, we constructed typical test cases ourselves; for the *Tornado* web server, we start a number of scripts simultaneously downloading files from the server. For *Weblech*, we download a number of files from a (defect-free) web server.

Test oracles. We use individual test oracles that come with every benchmark program. For the two open-source programs, we compose test oracles that automatically compare the actual output of a program with the expected one. For example, we compare the files downloaded with *Weblech* with the original ones in the pre-configured list.

Testing environment. We run all experiments on a standard HP workstation with an AMD Athlon 64 X2 dual-core processor 4800+. We employed a standard Sun Java 6 virtual machine on Microsoft Windows XP.

5.3 Accuracy Measures for Defect-Localization Results

First of all, the locations of the actual defects are known, so the report of a method containing a defect can be directly compared to see if this is true or not. If there is more than one location which can be altered to fix a defect, we refer to the position of the first of such methods in the ranking. For cases as in *Weblech.orig* where the defect can be fixed outside a method body (e.g., in the class header), one can still identify methods that can be altered to fix the erroneous behavior.

Our experiments produce ordered lists of methods. In order to evaluate the accuracy of the results, we report the position of the defective method in such a list. This ranking position corresponds to the number of methods a software developer has to review in order to find the defect. If two or more methods have the same likelihood, we use a second static ranking criterion: We sort the methods with the same likelihood by decreasing LOC size. Previous research has shown that the LOC size frequently positively correlates with the likelihood of a method being defective [21]. In order to estimate the effort to find a defect, we compare the ranking position with the total number of methods in a program. In addition to the ranking, we also provide more fine-grained information, such as the suspected call within a method.

Another quality criterion is the comparison of our method with the expected value for manual defect localization; in the manual approach, one would expect to find the defect after reviewing about half of the program methods.

As method sizes can vary significantly, it is sometimes more appropriate to consider the LOC rather than only the number of involved methods. We therefore provide the percentage of LOC to review as an addition to the ranking position. This is calculated as the ratio of methods that has to be considered in the program, i.e., the sum of LOC of all methods having a ranking position smaller than or equal to the position reported in the table, divided by the total LOC (see Table 2).

5.4 Results

Table 3 shows encouraging results: In all five benchmark programs, the defective method is ranked first. The ranking position is lower only in the two large programs. However, taking the size of these programs into account, the quality of defect localizations is within the same range (see column "LOC to Review").

Overall, the average ranking position for methods containing the defects is 3.3. Nevertheless, as Table 2 shows, a developer only has to review just 7.1% of all methods to find the defects or 23.6% of the normalized source code, which is low. In other words, a developer has to consider in the worst case less than a quarter of the source code of our programs in order to find a defect. This reduces the

Table 3. Defect-localization results

Program	Executions		Defect Localization	
	#correct	#failing	Ranking Pos.	%LOC to Review
AllocationVector	383	117	1	17.3%
GarageManager	74	26	1	14.2%
Liveness	149	53	1	44.2%
MergeSort	668	332	1	25.9%
ThreadTest	207	193	1	18.8%
Tornado	362	8	14	23.3%
Weblech.orig	494	5	2	23.3%
Weblech.inj	985	15	5	21.8%

percentage of methods (code) to review by a factor of seven (code: more than by half) when compared to an average expected amount of 50% of methods (code) to review. Note that these are maximum values: (1) The methods ranked highest are frequently good hints for the defect, even if the defective method itself is ranked lower; (2) usually not all lines of a method need to be reviewed, in particular due to our report which call within a method is most suspicious.

6 A Detailed Example

We now illustrate a typical defect and the process of its localization with our approach using excerpts form the *GarageManager* program [14]:

The defect. In our example, the calculation of the `taskNumber` variable can produce a negative value, which is read in method `GoToWork()` (see Listing 2) to calculate its modulo-8 value, which is then fed into a `switch-case` block. This block, however, expects values between 0 and 7. Negative values can result when `Java` calculates the modulo operation on a negative number. There are two alternative positions where a developer can modify the code to fix the bug: (1) The `switch-case` block, by adding negative cases or a default case; (2) The parts of the source code where `taskNumber` is calculated (method `SetTaskToWorker()`).

```
switch (taskNumber % 8) {
  case 0: WorkingOn("fix gears", 2000);      break;
  case 1: WorkingOn("change tires", 1400);   break;
  // similar for case 2 to 6...
  case 7: WorkingOn("work on breaks", 2200); break; }
```

Listing 2. Method `void GoToWork()` (shortened).

From the defect to an infection. We now look at the call graph from a failing execution in more detail, shown in Figure 2. The call of `run()` generates five threads: Four "worker" threads calling methods `WaitForManager()`, `GoToWork()` and `PrintCard()` and one "manager" thread calling the remaining methods. In `WorkingOn()` (a defective method), the program state becomes infected: Three

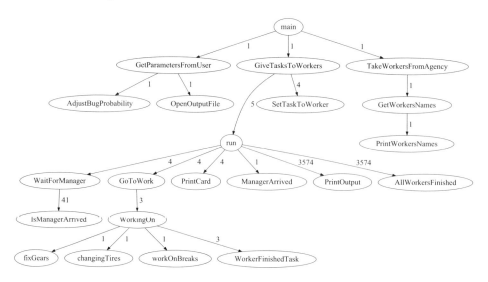

Fig. 2. Call graph from a failing *GarageManager* execution

threads evaluate their switch statement to 0, 1 and 7, but the fourth thread has a negative value, thus causing the thread not to call any further methods.

From an infection to a failure. The aforementioned infection causes the fourth thread not to call `WorkerFinishedTask()`. This method decreases a variable of the global `status` object. This object is queried by `AllWorkersFinished()` in method `run()` (see Listing 3). `AllWorkersFinished()` will never be `true`, as `status` will always indicate that only three out of four "worker" threads have finished their tasks. This causes an infinite loop in `run()` (we manually stopped the loop after 3,574 iterations). In other words, the infection has caused a deadlock, an observable program behavior, which we consider a failure.

```
status.ManagerArrived();
boolean tasksNotFinished = true, printedOutput = false;
while (tasksNotFinished) {
  printedOutput = PrintOutput(printedOutput);
    synchronized (status) {
    if (status.AllWorkersFinished())
      tasksNotFinished = false;
    else
       yield(); }
}
```

Listing 3. Method `void run()` (shortened cutout).

Localizing the defect. In our experiments, our approach found the three methods `GoToWork()`, `WorkingOn()` and `run()` (ordered by increasing ranking position) to be most likely defective. Thus, the defect was pinpointed directly. The high likelihood for `WorkingOn()` is due to a follow-up infection, as it is always called from `GoToWork()`. The `run()` method has a high likelihood as well, caused by the huge number of method calls in the infinite loop (compared to correct executions). Both methods are inherently connected to the defect.

7 Related Work

Defect localization techniques and race detectors are typically classified into *static* and *dynamic* techniques. Dynamic race detectors instrument programs and analyze run-time behavior of every thread access to memory. They introduce significant overhead, possibly influencing the program under test in a way that a race condition disappears. Static race detectors investigate the source code only but produce typically large numbers of false-positive warnings. Hybrid approaches [22] and implementations such as the IBM MulticoreSDK [23] try to combine the best of both worlds.

FindBugs [4] is a static code-analysis tool. It statically checks Java code for certain patterns of defect-prone artifacts. Although it supports a limited number of defect-prone multithreading-related behaviors, it was not designed for detecting multithreading defects. However, FindBugs complements our approach.

Tarantula [16] is a dynamic technique using tracing and visualization. To localize defects, it utilizes a ranking of basic blocks which are executed more often in failing program executions. Though this technique is rather simple, it produces good defect-localization results in the single-threaded case. However, it was not designed for multithreaded programs and causes significant overhead due to its fine-grained tracing. Spectrum-based fault localization techniques as employed in this tool are presented more generally in [3], though with a focus on sequential programs.

The approach of [8] is similar to ours, but instead compares method sequence sets (not call graphs) to avoid the thread interleaving problem, however, it produces a more coarse-grain class ranking instead of a method ranking.

ConTest [15] executes a multithreaded Java program several times and influences thread schedules by inserting different statements (e.g., `sleep()`) into a program. Chess [20] works for C# and has a modified scheduler to exhaustively try out different thread interleavings. Given such a technique, a *delta-debugging* strategy [28] might be used to automatically localize a defect. However, [26] has shown that approaches building on varying thread interleavings and delta debugging do not scale for large software projects. Instead, [26] proposes a featureselection strategy which builds on an approach such as ConTest or Chess and identifies problematic program locations, to avoid scalability problems. In contrast to our approach, the aforementioned tools focus on finding synchronization errors due to wrong usage of parallel constructs, which is a subset of the errors that are detectable by our approach.

8 Result Comparisons with Related Work

Our experiments with the MulticoreSDK applied to all program versions from our evaluation (see Section 5.1) reveal that it is not able find any of the defects.

From the eight versions, the MulticoreSDK incorrectly classified seven versions as defect-free, while producing a false-positive warning for the eighth version.

We also applied FindBugs to all program versions. The result is that it does not directly pinpoint any of the defects. At the same time, FindBugs produces a number of false-positive warnings: On average, there are 5.4 warnings per program version, distributed over 4.3 different methods. Although the warnings do not pinpoint the defective lines and might therefore be misleading, the defective methods from six out of eight versions are included in the warnings. To find these six defects, a developer would have to consider the source code of all methods that are affected by warnings, which in our case amounts to 35.3% of the code.

9 Conclusions

Debugging multithreaded software is difficult and time-consuming, so any progress in tool support will help reduce costs. Most of the existing parallel debugging tools have concentrated on parallel programming errors such race conditions, but there are several defect patterns that are not in the focus of these tools. In this paper, we have presented a novel defect-localization technique for multithreaded programs to address this problem. We have shown that mining call graphs is an effective approach to detect a wider range of errors with the same tool, including race conditions, deadlocks and errors originating from the wrong usage of non-parallel language constructs. Our case study with different multithreaded programs shows that the defective method can be pinpointed straight away in five of the eight cases, and that on average only 7.1% of all program methods have to be investigated to find a defect. This promises significant reductions in the time developers need for debugging.

Acknowledgments

We thank Alexander Bieleš who helped us with the implementation and the experiments and Shmuel Ur who provided us with the defect benchmark [14].

References

1. Tornado HTTP Server, http://tornado.sourceforge.net/
2. WebLech URL Spider, http://weblech.sourceforge.net/
3. Abreu, R., Zoeteweij, P., van Gemund, A.J.: Spectrum-Based Multiple Fault Localization. In: Proc. ASE (2009)
4. Ayewah, N., Hovemeyer, D., Morgenthaler, J.D., Penix, J., Pugh, W.: Using Static Analysis to Find Bugs. IEEE Softw. 25(5), 22–29 (2008)
5. Berger, E.D., McKinley, K.S., Blumofe, R.D., Wilson, R.P.: Hoard: A Scalable Memory Allocator for Multithreaded Applications. SIGPLAN Not. 35(11), 117–128 (2000)
6. Cheng, H., Lo, D., Zhou, Y., Wang, X., Yan, X.: Identifying Bug Signatures Using Discriminative Graph Mining. In: Proc. ISSTA (2009)
7. Copty, S., Ur, S.: Multi-threaded Testing with AOP Is Easy, and It Finds Bugs! In: Cunha, J.C., Medeiros, P.D. (eds.) Euro-Par 2005. LNCS, vol. 3648, pp. 740–749. Springer, Heidelberg (2005)

8. Dallmeier, V., Lindig, C., Zeller, A.: Lightweight Defect Localization for Java. In: Black, A.P. (ed.) ECOOP 2005. LNCS, vol. 3586, pp. 528–550. Springer, Heidelberg (2005)
9. Di Fatta, G., Leue, S., Stegantova, E.: Discriminative Pattern Mining in Software Fault Detection. In: Proc. Int. Workshop on Software Quality Assurance (2006)
10. Edelstein, O., Farchi, E., Nir, Y., Ratsaby, G., Ur, S.: Multithreaded Java Program Test Generation. IBM Syst. J. 41(1), 111–125 (2002)
11. Eichinger, F., Böhm, K.: Software-Bug Localization with Graph Mining. In: Aggarwal, C.C., Wang, H. (eds.) Managing and Mining Graph Data. Springer, Heidelberg (2010)
12. Eichinger, F., Böhm, K., Huber, M.: Mining Edge-Weighted Call Graphs to Localise Software Bugs. In: Daelemans, W., Goethals, B., Morik, K. (eds.) ECML PKDD 2008, Part I. LNCS (LNAI), vol. 5211, pp. 333–348. Springer, Heidelberg (2008)
13. Engler, D., Ashcraft, K.: RacerX: Effective, Static Detection of Race Conditions and Deadlocks. In: Proc. Symposium on Operating Systems Principles (SOSP) (2003)
14. Eytani, Y., Ur, S.: Compiling a Benchmark of Documented Multi-Threaded Bugs. In: Proc. Int. Parallel and Distributed Processing Symposium (IPDPS) (2004)
15. Farchi, E., Nir, Y., Ur, S.: Concurrent Bug Patterns and How to Test Them. In: Proc. Int. Parallel and Distributed Processing Symposium (IPDPS) (2003)
16. Jones, J.A., Harrold, M.J., Stasko, J.: Visualization of Test Information to Assist Fault Localization. In: Proc. ICSE (2002)
17. Kiczales, G., Hilsdale, E., Hugunin, J., Kersten, M., Palm, J., Griswold, W.G.: An Overview of AspectJ. In: Knudsen, J.L. (ed.) ECOOP 2001. LNCS, vol. 2072, p. 327. Springer, Heidelberg (2001)
18. Liu, C., Yan, X., Yu, H., Han, J., Yu, P.S.: Mining Behavior Graphs for "Backtrace" of Noncrashing Bugs. In: Proc. Int. Conf. on Data Mining (SDM) (2005)
19. Lu, S., Park, S., Seo, E., Zhou, Y.: Learning from Mistakes – A Comprehensive Study on Real World Concurrency Bug Characteristics. SIGARCH Comput. Archit. News 36(1), 329–339 (2008)
20. Musuvathi, M., Qadeer, S., Ball, T.: CHESS: A Systematic Testing Tool for Concurrent Software. Technical Report MSR-TR-2007-149, Microsoft Research
21. Nagappan, N., Ball, T., Zeller, A.: Mining Metrics to Predict Component Failures. In: Proc. ICSE (2006)
22. O'Callahan, R., Choi, J.-D.: Hybrid Dynamic Data Race Detection. SIGPLAN Not. 38(10), 167–178 (2003)
23. Qi, Y., Das, R., Luo, Z.D., Trotter, M.: MulticoreSDK: A Practical and Efficient Data Race Detector for Real-World Applications. In: Proc. Workshop on Parallel and Distributed Systems (2009)
24. Quinlan, J.R.: C4.5: Programs for Machine Learning. Morgan Kaufmann, San Francisco (1993)
25. Savage, S., Burrows, M., Nelson, G., Sobalvarro, P., Anderson, T.: Eraser: A Dynamic Data Race Detector for Multi-Threaded Programs. In: Proc. Symposium on Operating systems principles (SOSP) (1997)
26. Tzoref, R., Ur, S., Yom-Tov, E.: Instrumenting Where it Hurts – An Automatic Concurrent Debugging Technique. In: Proc. ISSTA (2007)
27. Witten, I.H., Frank, E.: Data Mining: Practical Machine Learning Tools and Techniques with Java Implementations. Morgan Kaufmann, San Francisco (2005)
28. Zeller, A.: Why Programs Fail: A Guide to Systematic Debugging. Morgan Kaufmann, San Francisco (2009)

Filtering Test Models to Support Incremental Testing

Antti Jääskeläinen

Tampere University of Technology, Department of Software Systems
P.O. Box 553, FI-33101 Tampere, Finland
antti.m.jaaskelainen@tut.fi

Abstract. Model-based testing can be hampered by the fact that a model depicting the system as designed does not necessarily correspond to the product as it is during development. Tests generated from such a model may be impossible to execute due to unimplemented features and already known errors. This paper presents a solution in which parts of the model can be filtered out and the remainder used to generate tests for the implemented portion of the product. In this way model-based testing can be used to gradually test the implementation as it becomes available. This is particularly important in incremental testing commonly used in industry.

Keywords: Model-Based Testing, Test Modeling, Model Filtering, Model Transformation, Strong Connectivity.

1 Introduction

Traditionally software test automation has focused on automating the execution of tests. A newer approach, model-based testing, allows the automation of the creation of tests by generating them from a formal model which depicts the expected functionality of the system under test (SUT). An excellent approach in theory, widespread deployment of model-based testing is nonetheless hindered by a number of practical issues.

One such issue is fitting model-based testing into the product life cycle. The error-detection capability of model-based testing is based on the correspondence between the model and the SUT; a difference between the two indicates an error in one or the other. However, testing should begin before a fully functional SUT is available, which means that this correspondence is in practice broken.

The problem first appears during the early implementation of the product. The test model can be created based on the design plans, and is likely to be ready long before all the features of the SUT have been fully implemented, since modeling is a good method of static testing. In this case, the tests generated from the model may span the whole system under development, even though the SUT only contains limited functionality. Developing and updating the model alongside the product is possible but impractical; it should be possible to model the whole system before it is fully implemented. How, then, can we use a model of the complete system to generate tests just for the current implementation?

A similar situation is encountered when the testing pays off and an error is found. Fixing the error may take some time, especially if it is particularly complicated or not very serious. Testing, of course, should be continued immediately. But how can we ensure that new generated tests do not stumble on the same, already known issue?

In these cases, the problem is that the model contains functionality that cannot be executed on the SUT, yet we need to generate actually executable tests. The magnitude of the problem depends on how the tests are generated. If the process is cheap, it may be possible to generate an overabundance of tests and discard the unfeasible ones. However, if test generation is complicated and costly, it will be necessary to ensure that as little effort as possible is wasted on unproductive tests.

This paper presents a solution based on *filtering* the test model in such a way that unimplemented or faulty functionality is effectively removed. The remainder of the model can then be used to generate tests for the implemented functionality. As new features are implemented they can be allowed into the model and test generation; as erroneous functionality is uncovered it can be filtered out until fixed. Using this method, a complete test model can be used to generate tests as soon as the product is mature enough for automatic test execution. The challenge is to ensure that the filtered model remains suitable for test generation.

The rest of the paper is structured as follows: Section 2 provides an overall presentation on our approach to model-based testing. Section 3 explains our filtering methodology in detail, and Section 4 presents a case study based on it. Finally, Section 5 concludes the paper.

2 Background

Model-based testing is a testing methodology which automates the generation of tests. This is done with the help of a *test model*, which describes the behavior desired in the tests. Depending on the approach, this may mean the behavior of the SUT or its user, or both combined.

There are two ways to execute the generated tests. In *off-line testing* the model is first used to create the test cases, which are then executed just as if they had been designed manually. In the alternate approach, *online testing*, the tests are executed as they are being generated. The latter method is especially well suited for testing nondeterministic systems, since the results of the execution can be continuously fed back into test generation, which can then adapt to the behavior of the SUT.

Our research focuses on online testing based on behavioral models. The formalism in our models is labeled state transition system (LSTS), a state machine with labeled states and transitions. LSTS is a simple formalism and other behavioral models can be easily converted into it, which allows us to create models also in other formalisms, if need be. The formal definition of LSTS is the following:

Definition 1 (LSTS)

A labeled state transition system, abbreviated LSTS, is defined as a sextuple $(S, \Sigma, \Delta, \hat{s}, \Pi, val)$ *where S is the set of states, Σ is the set of actions (transition labels), $\Delta \subseteq S \times \Sigma \times S$ is the set of transitions, $\hat{s} \in S$ is the initial state, Π is the set of attributes (state labels) and $val : S \longrightarrow 2^\Pi$ is the attribute evaluation function, whose value $val(s)$ is the set of attributes in effect in state s.*

Creating a single model to depict the whole SUT is virtually impossible for any practical system. Therefore we create several *model components*, each depicting a specific aspect of the SUT, and combine these into a test model in a process called *parallel composition*. We use a parallel composition method developed in [7], generalized from CSP (Communicating Sequential Processes) [11]. It is based on a rule set which explicitly specifies which actions are executed synchronously. The formal definition is as follows:

Definition 2 (Parallel composition $\|_R$)

$\|_R (L_1, \ldots, L_n)$ *is the parallel composition of LSTSs* $L_1, \ldots, L_n$, $L_i = (S_i, \Sigma_i, \Delta_i, \hat{s}_i, \Pi_i, val_i)$*, according to rules R, such that $\forall i, j; 1 \leq i < j \leq n : \Pi_i \cap \Pi_j = \emptyset$. Let Σ_R be a set of resulting actions and $\sqrt{}$ a "pass" symbol such that $\forall i; 1 \leq i \leq n : \sqrt{} \notin \Sigma_i$. The rule set $R \subseteq (\Sigma_1 \cup \{\sqrt{}\}) \times \cdots \times (\Sigma_n \cup \{\sqrt{}\}) \times \Sigma_R$. Now $\|_R (L_1, \ldots, L_n) = repa((S, \Sigma, \Delta, \hat{s}, \Pi, val))$, where*

- $S = S_1 \times \cdots \times S_n$
- $\Sigma = \Sigma_R$
- $((s_1, \ldots, s_n), a, (s'_1, \ldots, s'_n)) \in \Delta$ if and only if there is $(a_1, \ldots, a_n, a) \in R$ such that for every i $(1 \leq i \leq n)$ either
  - $(s_i, a_i, s'_i) \in \Delta_i$ or
  - $a_i = \sqrt{}$ and $s_i = s'_i$
- $\hat{s} = (\hat{s}_1, \ldots, \hat{s}_n)$
- $\Pi = \Pi_1 \cup \cdots \cup \Pi_n$
- $val((s_1, \ldots, s_n)) = val_1(s_1) \cup \cdots \cup val_n(s_n)$
- *repa is a function restricting LSTS to contain only the states which are reachable from the initial state $\hat{s}$.*

The parallel composition allows us to use a relatively small number of simple model components to create a huge test model. In practice, the test model may well be too large to calculate in its entirety, so the parallel composition is usually performed *on the fly* for the needed portion of the model. The available model components comprise a *model library* [6], from which individual components can be composed into a suitable test model.

The model components are divided into two tiers corresponding to the concepts of action words and keywords [1,4]. *Action words* define user actions, such as those commonly used in use case definitions. Accordingly, the upper tier models based on action words, called *action machines*, describe the functionality of the SUT. Action words and action machines are independent of implementation, and can often be reused in testing other similar systems.

Keywords describe UI events, such as pressing keys or a text appearing on a display. The lower tier models, *refinement machines*, use keywords to define implementations for the action words in the action machines. Refinement machines are specific to implementation, so every different type of SUT requires its own.

The execution of a keyword returns a Boolean value, which tells whether the SUT executed the keyword successfully or not. Usually a certain value is expected, and a different result indicates an error. However, in online testing of nondeterministic systems it may be reasonable to accept either value, since the exact state of the SUT may not be known. This is modeled by adding a separate transition for successful and unsuccessful execution. The actions of such transitions are *negations* of each other. These *branching keywords* allow the implementations of action words to adapt to the state of the SUT. If the nondeterminism affects the execution of the test beyond a single action word, a similar *branching action word* is needed. Such action words can be used to direct an online test into an entirely different direction depending on the state of the SUT. Branching actions do not fit well into the linear sequences of off-line testing, though, and the unpredictability especially at the action word level makes the generation of online tests somewhat more difficult.

Tests are generated with guidance algorithms based on coverage requirements. A *coverage requirement* [8] defines the goal of the test, such as executing all actions in the model or a sequence of actions corresponding to a use case. A *guidance algorithm* is a heuristics whose task is to decide how the test will proceed. A straightforward algorithm may simply seek to fulfill the coverage requirement as quickly as possible. Others may perform additional tasks on the side, such as continuously switching between different applications in order to exercise concurrency features; yet another may be completely random.

Facilitating such diverse goals and methods places some requirements for the test model. The most important of these is that the model must be *strongly connected*, that is, all states must be reachable from all other states. A test model that is not strongly connected poses great difficulties for test generation, since the execution of any transition may render portions of the model unreachable for the remainder of the test run. Coverage requirements can no longer be combined freely, since their combination may be impossible to execute even if they are individually executable. Finally, online test generation becomes effectively impossible, because the only way to ensure that the whole test can be executed is to calculate it out entirely before beginning the execution and making potentially irreversible choices.

If strong connectivity is for some reason broken, it must be restored by limiting the model to the maximal strongly connected portion of the model containing the initial state, which we will call the *initial strong component*. Unfortunately, finding the initial strong component can be difficult if the model is too large to calculate in its entirety. In particular, strong connectivity of model components does not in itself guarantee strong connectivity in the composed test model.

Ensuring the strong connectivity and general viability of the models is in the end up to the *test modeler*, who is responsible for the creation and maintenance of the models. The *test designers*, who are responsible for the actual test runs, should be able to use the models for test generation without needing to worry about their internal structure. Such distribution of concerns relieves most of the testing personnel from the need of specialized modeling expertise [9].

3 Filtering

In this section we present our filtering method. First we go through some basic requirements for the method, and then present a solution based on those. After that, we examine implementation issues concerning the filtering process, especially regarding strong connectivity. Following is some analysis of the algorithm used in implementation, and finally an example of its use.

3.1 Basic Criteria

A method for filtering out unwanted functionality from the models should fulfill the following criteria:

1. The execution of faulty or unimplemented transitions can be prevented.
2. The model should not be restricted more than necessary.
3. The model must remain strongly connected.
4. Filtering may not require modeling expertise or familiarity with the models.
5. The manual effort involved in the process may not be excessive.
6. Filtering must be performed without modifications to the models themselves.

The first three criteria define the desired result for the filtering process. Criterion 1 is the very goal of the filtering process. Criterion 2 is likewise obviously necessary, since we want to keep testing the SUT as extensively as possible. Criterion 3 ensures that the process does not break the basic requirement placed on the test model. As a consequence, the filtering cannot be performed by just *banning* (refusing to execute) problematic transitions or actions, since such a strategy might effectively lead to deadlocks or otherwise break the strong connectivity necessary for test generation.

The next two criteria are procedural requirements. Criterion 4 requires that the filtering process can be performed with no manual involvement with the models. Ideally, the process would be carried out by test designers, who may not be familiar with the models or the formal methods involved [9]. Since the process may need to be carried out often and repeatedly, Criterion 5 states that it may not require much manual effort.

Finally, Criterion 6 is an implementation requirement. Modifying the models for filtering purposes would require extensive tool support, so that individual changes could be made and rolled back as needed, all without breaking the models. Enabling such a feature might also place additional requirements on the structure of the models.

3.2 Methodology

There are a number of potential methods by which the tester might perform the filtering of banned functionality. Most of these require additional actions in order to keep the model strongly connected, as per Criterion 3; however, with properly designed models such actions can be automated. The examined methods are:

1. Ban the execution of specific transitions of the composed test model.
2. Ban the execution of specific transitions within model components.
3. Ban the execution of specific actions.
4. Remove model components from the composition.

Actions are general labels for the events of the SUT, whereas transitions represent the SUT moving from a specific state to another through such an event; therefore, banning an individual action corresponds to banning all of the transitions labeled with it. Likewise, banning a transition from a model component may correspond to banning several transitions from the composed test model.

Method 1 fulfills all of the specified criteria except Criterion 5, where it fails spectacularly. An individual faulty transition in a model component is likely to correspond to many transitions in the test model. Even if the problem is a concurrency issue and appears only with a specific combination of applications, it is unlikely to be limited to a situation where all of the tested applications are in exactly specific states. As such, the method is thoroughly impractical.

Method 2 is more promising, since removing the faulty transition from a model component will remove all of its instances from the test model. This method is no longer minimal (Criterion 2): in case of a concurrency issue, this method may remove more functionality than is strictly necessary. However, it does not greatly limit continued testing; furthermore, a more specific method based on multiple components at once would likely require a deeper understanding of the models, violating Criterion 4. Another problem is that transitions do not have inherent identifiers, although they can be uniquely identified by their source state and action. States are only identified with numbers, whose use would at the very least require some inspection of the model components.

In practice, Method 3 works very much the same as Method 2. It may restrict the models more, but only if the model component uses the same action in multiple places, only one of which actually fails. Unlike transitions, actions are clearly labeled and test designers will work with them in any case, so they can be easily used also for this purpose.

Finally, Method 4 is also easy to use. In fact, it might well be worth implementing for other purposes such as limiting the size of the test model. However, removing whole components from the model goes against Criterion 2, since it could drastically reduce the amount of functionality available for testing. It does have one additional benefit: it is relatively easy to design the models so that the removal of a component leaves the rest of the test model strongly connected.

Of these four, Method 3, based on banning actions, appears to be the best. It does not restrict the models much more than is necessary and is quite easy to use. It does require some additional effort in order to retain the strong connectivity of the models, though.

In contrast, Methods 1 and 2 involve serious procedural issues and in practice do not leave much more of the model available. On the other hand, Method 4 is considerably more restrictive than necessary. However, as mentioned, it may be worth implementing anyway for other reasons, in which case it can be also used to filter models where suitable.

3.3 Banning Actions

There are three implementation issues to take care of. First, we need a means to obtain a test model with individual actions removed without altering the original models, as per Method 3 and Criterion 6. Second, we must devise a method for restoring the strong connectivity of the test model (Criterion 3), since removing individual actions may break it. Third, we must take into account the branching actions, whose both branches must be retained or removed together.

The simplest way to obtain a modified test model is to create a modified copy of the rules of parallel composition such that banned actions will not show up in the test model. This method is simple to implement and limits modifications to one place. Alternatively, modified copies of the model components could be created with banned actions removed, and then composed as usual. However, such an approach would require modifications in several places, and modifying a model component is liable to be more difficult than removing rules from a list.

Ensuring the strong connectivity of the test model is more difficult. It is obviously not possible to design all models so that any actions could be removed without breaking strong connectivity. As for automation, in a general case it is not possible to determine whether a test model is strongly connected without calculating it entirely, which may be impossible due to the potential size of the model. As a solution, our filtering algorithm seeks to deduce the initial strong component from the model components and the rule set, but without calculating the parallel composition. The result is an upper bound for the initial strong component, that is, a limited portion of the original model which contains the initial strong component. The algorithm is based on the following principles:

1. an action must be banned if it labels a transition which leads away from the initial strong component of a model component
2. an action may be banned if it does not label any transition within the initial strong component of a model component
3. an action may be banned if there remain no rules which allow its execution
4. a rule may be removed if any of its component actions is banned

The first principle is the most important: leaving the initial strongly connected component of a model component cannot be allowed, since there would be no way back, and the strong connectivity of the test model would be broken. In contrast, the other three principles ban actions and remove rules which could not be executed in the test model anyway. Actions outside the initial strong components are effectively unreachable, an action without rules does not appear in the composed test model, and a rule without all of its actions can never be applied. Therefore, these three do not limit the models needlessly. They are also not useful in themselves, but may allow greater application of the first principle.

Based on these principles, we have developed Algorithm 1 and implemented it as a part of the TEMA open source toolset [10]. The lines from 1 to 11 set the initial values for the data structures, as well as marking for handling the initially banned actions and removed rules. The loop on line 12 additionally marks for handling those actions for which there are no rules. The three main parts of the algorithm are within the loop on line 16. First, the loop on line 18 handles banned actions, removing any rule which requires them. Second, the loop on line 24 handles rules in a similar way, banning all actions for which there are no rules left. Third, the loop on line 32 calculates the initial strong components of the model components and marks for handling those actions which lead outside the component or cannot be reached within it. These three are repeated until no more actions can be banned or rules removed. The calculation of the strong components, which can be performed for example by Tarjan's algorithm [13], is the most time-consuming part of the algorithm. It is therefore only performed when no other method for progress is available.

The algorithm returns both a set of removed rules and one of banned actions; either can be used to perform the actual filtering. The list of banned actions is also useful to the modeler, since it can be used to estimate the effects of filtering. This is important because the algorithm does not necessarily yield the exact initial strong component but only an upper bound for it. The rest will be up to the modeler, who should design the models so that the bound is in fact exact, and there is no way out of the initial strong component.

The nature of the algorithm makes it easy to define not only an initial set of banned actions, but also one of removed rules. This may be occasionally useful, for example to remove some kinds of actions across the model components.

Specific model semantics may require some changes or additions to the basic algorithm. Branching actions are such a case: if one branch gets banned, the other one must, too. To take this into account, we modify the algorithm such that every time an action is marked to be handled, we check for other branches and mark them also. It might also be useful to allow the modeler to define similar dependencies on a case-by-case basis, where strong connectivity demands it; we have yet to implement such a method, however.

3.4 Analysis

Following is a brief analysis of the time requirements of Algorithm 1. For an arbitrary model component $m \in M$, we will mark $m = (S_m, \Sigma_m, \Delta_m, \hat{s}_m, \Pi_m, val_m)$. All set operations used in the algorithm (addition and removal of elements, check for membership or emptiness) can be performed in amortized constant time.

The handling of each rule requires $O(|M|)$ time: it may get marked for handling by each action it refers to, and may have to mark for handling each of those actions. For all rules, this gives $O(|R||M|)$. In addition to this, the handling of each action takes only constant time, yielding $O(\sum_{m \in M} |\Sigma_m|)$. Calculating the strong components of a single model $m \in M$ with Tarjan's algorithm

Algorithm 1. The filtering algorithm for the set of model components M composed with the rules R, with the rules $remove \in R$ initially removed and the actions $ban(m) \in \Sigma_m$ of model components $m \in M$ initially banned

$banned\_actions, unhandled\_actions, removed\_rules := \emptyset$
$unhandled\_rules := remove$
$changed\_models := M$
for all model components $m \in M$ **do**
5:     **for all** actions $a \in ban(m)$ **do**
        add (m, a) to $unhandled\_actions$
    for all actions a of m **do**
        $remaining\_rules(m, a) := \emptyset$
for all rules $r \in R$ **do**
10:     **for all** actions a of model components m in r **do**
        add r to $remaining\_rules(m, a)$
for all model components $m \in M$ **do**
    for all actions a of m **do**
        if $remaining\_rules(m, a) = \emptyset$ **then**
15:             add (m, a) to $unhandled\_actions$
while $unhandled\_actions \neq \emptyset$ or $unhandled\_rules \neq \emptyset$ **do**
    while $unhandled\_actions \neq \emptyset$ or $unhandled\_rules \neq \emptyset$ **do**
        for all model-action pairs $(m, a) \in unhandled\_actions$ **do**
            for all rules $r \in remaining\_rules(m, a)$ **do**
20:                 **if** $r \notin removed\_rules$ **then**
                    add r to $unhandled\_rules$
            add (m, a) to $banned\_actions$
        $unhandled\_actions := \emptyset$
        for all rules $r \in unhandled\_rules$ **do**
25:             **for all** actions a of model components m in r **do**
                remove r from $remaining\_rules(m, a)$
                if $remaining\_rules(m, a) = \emptyset$ and $(m, a) \notin banned\_actions$ **then**
                    add (m, a) to $unhandled\_actions$
                    add m to $changed\_models$
30:             add r to $removed\_rules$
        $unhandled\_rules := \emptyset$
    while $changed\_models \neq \emptyset$ and $unhandled\_actions = \emptyset$ **do**
        $m :=$ any element from $changed\_models$
        remove m from $changed\_models$
35:         $reachables := \emptyset$
        $isc :=$ the initial strong component of m with banned actions removed
        for all transitions (s, a, s') of m **do**
            if s within isc **then**
                add a to $reachables$
40:             **if** s' not within isc and $(m, a) \notin banned\_actions$ **then**
                add (m, a) to $unhandled\_actions$
                add m to $changed\_models$
        for all actions a of m **do**
            if $a \notin reachables$ and $(m, a) \notin banned\_actions$ **then**
45:                 add (m, a) to $unhandled\_actions$
                add m to $changed\_models$
return $removed\_rules, banned\_actions$

takes $\Theta(|S_m| + |\Delta_m|)$ time. However, since we are only interested in the initial strong component, effectively $|S_m| \leq |\Delta_m| + 1$, resulting in $\Theta(|\Delta_m|)$. The subsequent handling requires $\Theta(|\Delta_m| + |\Sigma_m|) = \Theta(max(|\Delta_m|, |\Sigma_m|))$. The calculation is carried out for each model only after new actions have been banned; since all unreachable actions get banned on the first (compulsory) time, the calculation will be performed at most $min(|\Sigma_m|, |\Delta_m|) + 1$ times. The result is $O(\sum_{m \in M} min(|\Sigma_m|, |\Delta_m|) max(|\Delta_m|, |\Sigma_m|)) = O(\sum_{m \in M} |\Sigma_m||\Delta_m|)$.

Putting the above figures together, we get $O(|R||M| + \sum_{m \in M} |\Sigma_m||\Delta_m|)$. This means linear dependence on the number of rules times the size of a single rule, plus quadratic dependence on what is essentially the sizes of the model components. The first term is quite reasonable, since the same time is required to simply write out the rules. The second term, while not insignificant, is still perfectly manageable if individual model components are kept small enough.

3.5 Example

We will now present an example of Algorithm 1 with the models in Figure 1, combined with the rules $R = \{(a, \sqrt{}, a), (b, \sqrt{}, b), (c, c, c), (d, \sqrt{}, d), (e, e, e)\}$. Let us assume that the implementation of action d of Model 1 is faulty and initially ban $(1, d)$.

Since the action $(1, d)$ is banned, we remove the rule $(d, \sqrt{}, d)$ which refers to it. After that, we must calculate strong connectivity; we shall do it for Model 1 (calculating the strong connectivity for Model 2 would not yield anything new anyway). We notice that in Model 1 the action c leads out of the initial strong

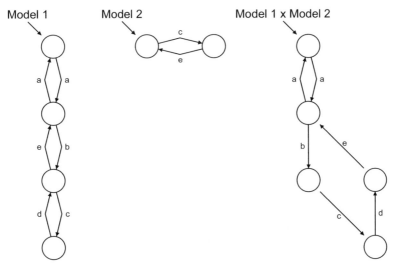

Fig. 1. Two example model components and their composition with the rules $R = \{(a, \sqrt{}, a), (b, \sqrt{}, b), (c, c, c), (d, \sqrt{}, d), (e, e, e)\}$

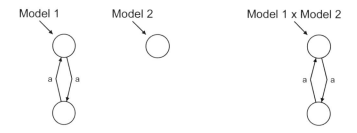

Fig. 2. Filtered versions of the example model components and their composition with the filtered rules $R = \{(a, \sqrt{}, a)\}$

component and ban $(1, c)$. Consequently, we also remove (c, c, c) and then, because there are no longer any rules for it, $(2, c)$.

Again we must calculate strong connectivity. This time, we do not learn anything from calculating it for Model 1, but in Model 2 we notice that $(2, e)$ is unreachable and ban it. Following that, we remove (e, e, e) and ban $(1, e)$. We note that now the action b breaks the strong connectivity of Model 1, and ban $(1, b)$ and remove $(b, \sqrt{}, b)$. Finally, Model 2 has changed since our last connectivity calculation for it, so we perform one, but learn nothing new. At this point the algorithm returns the results and terminates.

In the end, we have banned the actions b, c, d and e from Model 1; banned the actions c and e from Model 2; and removed the rules $(b, \sqrt{}, b)$, (c, c, c), $(d, \sqrt{}, d)$ and (e, e, e). All that is left of the model components is a two-a loop in Model 1, which is also exactly what will show up in the test model composed with the single remaining rule $(a, \sqrt{}, a)$, as seen in Figure 3.5. Looking at the original composed model in Figure 1, it is easy to see that this is what should happen with the action d banned.

3.6 Other Composition Methods

If the algorithm is to be used with a different method of parallel composition, it will be necessary to create a rule set that implements corresponding functionality. For example, the basic parallel composition where actions of the same name are always executed synchronously would correspond to the rules

$$R = \{(\sigma_1, \ldots, \sigma_n, \sigma_R) \in (\Sigma_1 \cup \{\sqrt{}\}) \times \cdots \times (\Sigma_n \cup \{\sqrt{}\}) \times (\Sigma_1 \cup \cdots \cup \Sigma_n) \mid$$
$$\forall i; 1 \leq i \leq n : (\sigma_R \in \Sigma_i \rightarrow \sigma_i = \sigma_R) \wedge (\sigma_R \notin \Sigma_i \rightarrow \sigma_i = \sqrt{})\}$$

Although the rule set is needed for the execution of the algorithm, it is not necessary to actually implement rule-based parallel composition. The list of banned actions the algorithm returns can be used to perform filtering within the model components, and these can then be combined with the original method of composition.

4 Case Study

As a case study, we will examine the process of modifying models from an existing model library to conform to the requirements of filtering. The purpose is to ensure that test models composed from the library can be relied on to remain strongly connected when arbitrary actions are filtered out; afterward, filtering can be performed automatically. First, we will present the model library and how its model components might in practice be filtered. We will then examine the actual modifications made to the models of one application in the library, and finally analyze the results.

4.1 Setup

The model library we will examine has been designed for the testing of smartphone applications [5]. The latest version contains models for eight applications such as Contacts and Messaging, over four different phone models, on different platforms such as S60 and Android. The model components in the library have been designed to yield a usable test model even if only some of them are included in the composition, as long as specified dependencies are met. However, they have not been designed to withstand the arbitrary removal of actions gracefully.

In this case study we will focus on the models of the Contacts application. It consists of six action machines and a corresponding number of refinement machines, and has about 330 states altogether. As such it is one of the smaller applications in the library, and simple enough to be a comprehensible example.

When examining the effects of filtering, we can safely limit ourselves to banning action words in the action machines, since they represent the (potentially unavailable) functionality of the SUT. The task is performed by banning action words one at a time and examining the results with the help of the filtering algorithm. From the results we can determine whether the composed test model would remain strongly connected or not.

4.2 Modifications

An initial execution of the algorithm with no actions banned yields a list of a few unimplemented actions; these appear in the action machines but have no implementation. Such actions would not appear in the test model anyway, so they can be safely banned. We then proceed to banning individual action words, and find two problematic situations.

The first problem we encounter is in the model component depicting the functionality of the list of contacts (Figure 3). The only action word in the model, *awVerifyContactsExist*, is a branching action word used to find out whether there are any contacts in the application (the negative branch is prefixed with a '∼'). This action can only be executed if we are unsure of the current situation regarding contacts; the preceding synchronization actions check from other model components whether we know anything about the existence of contacts.

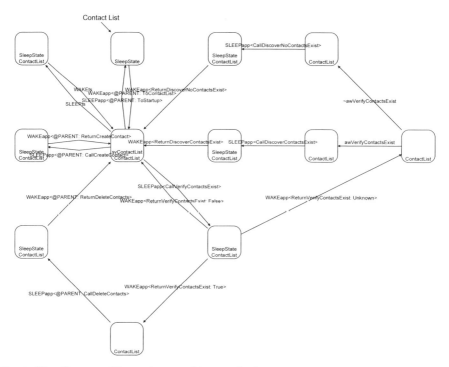

Fig. 3. The Contacts List action machine, with the action word *awVerifyContactsExist* on the right

The filter algorithm quite intuitively suggests that if the action word is banned, the action *WAKEapp<ReturnVerifyContactsExist: Unknown>* should also be banned to preserve strong connectivity. However, that would actually cause a deadlock elsewhere in situations where the existence of contacts really is unknown. The solution here is to add a transition with a new comment action from the state on the right between the synchronization and the action word back to the central state on the middle left. A comment action can be executed with no effect to the other model components or the SUT, allowing us to bypass the verification of contacts' existence. Now the synchronizing action no longer needs to be removed with the action word, and strong connectivity is preserved.

The second problem spot is also related to the way the models keep track of the number of contacts. The existence of contacts is abstracted into three categories: contacts exist, contacts do not exist, and unknown, with unknown used as the initial value. The problem shows up in the model component responsible for the deletion of contacts (Figure 4), if we ban one of the actions *awToggleContact*, *awAttemptDelete* or *awDelete*.

The immediate result of the ban is that contacts can no longer be removed individually (or at all for *awDelete*). However, the individual removal of contacts is the only way that the existence of contacts, once known, can become unknown again. This means that their existence cannot ever be allowed to become known,

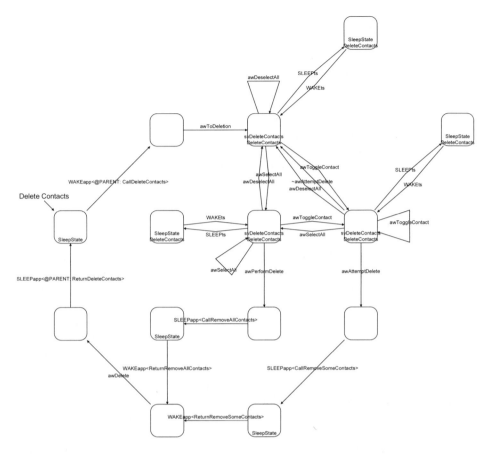

Fig. 4. The Delete Contacts action machine, with the action words *awToggleContact* and *awAttemptDelete* at the right side of the octagon, and *awDelete* at the bottom left. *awAttemptDelete* fails if no contacts are selected.

which results in banning every action related to their creation and handling. The test model becomes next to useless, though is does remain strongly connected. Despite the apparent complexity of the problem, the solution is simple: modify the models so that the knowledge of the existence of contacts can be 'forgotten', moving us back into the unknown state.

4.3 Results

All in all, the Contact models withstood the banning of action words fairly well. The first described problem is likely typical, with complex synchronizations between the model components resulting in a deadlock whose existence the filtering algorithm cannot deduce. The second problem shows that broken strong connectivity is not the only potential issue; one should also consider whether connectivity could be preserved with lesser limitations.

The filtering algorithm was very useful in finding the problematic situations in the models. While the first problem would have been easy enough to spot in manual inspection, the second was more obscure and might have been easily missed. Using the algorithm to calculate the effects of removing actions was also much faster than manual examination would have been.

Making the necessary modifications to the models clearly requires some modeling expertise. This is not a serious issue, since they would usually be made by the original modeler, as part of the normal modeling process. In this case the whole modification process took less than an hour, and was performed manually apart from using the filtering algorithm. Thus, there should not be any significant increase in the modeling effort.

5 Discussion

Using model-based testing in the early phases of product implementation can be difficult, because the product does not yet correspond to the model depicting the entire system. The problem can be solved by altering the model so that unimplemented or faulty functionality is removed and no tests are generated for it. This way the model can be matched to the product throughout its implementation.

Model transformations [2] can be used to modify the test models as needed; their use to keep the test models up to date during development is described in [12]. The use of parallel composition to limit the model to specific scenarios is mentioned in [3,14], although no mention is made of ensuring the viability of the resulting models. All in all, there does not appear to be much previous work on restricting the functionality of test models and the consequences thereof.

The basic method presented in our paper is very simple, based on banning the actions corresponding to unexecutable functionality in the models or removing the rules acting on them in the parallel composition. The greatest challenge is ensuring that the model remains conducive to test generation; specifically that it remains strongly connected. The algorithm presented in the paper seeks to estimate the initial strong component of the model as well as possible without actually calculating the composed test model. The rest is left up to the modeler.

Our case study showed that modifying existing models to withstand filtering without losing strong connectivity is feasible; by extension, so is designing models to match the same requirement from the first. The filtering algorithm proved very useful in the task, since it can be used to show the effects of banning specific actions and thus reveal problematic structures in the models.

The filtering algorithm takes advantage of the explicit set of synchronization rules used by our method of parallel composition. It can also be used with other parallel composition methods, if a suitable rule set is created to describe the synchronizations. The practical issues related to this are left for future work. Likewise for the future are left the methods for filtering non-behavioral models and test data.

Acknowledgements. The author wishes to thank Mika Katara, Shahar Maoz and Heikki Virtanen for their comments. Funding from Tekes, Nokia, Ixonos, Symbio, Cybercom Plenware, F-Secure, Qentinel, Prove Expertise, as well as the Academy of Finland (grant number 121012), is gratefully acknowledged.

References

1. Buwalda, H.: Action figures. STQE Magazine (March/April 2003)
2. Czarnecki, K., Helsen, S.: Classification of model transformation approaches. In: OOPSLA 2003 Workshop on Generative Techniques in the Context of Model-Driven Architecture, pp. 324–339. Springer, Heidelberg (2003)
3. Ernits, J., Roo, R., Jacky, J., Veanes, M.: Model-based testing of web applications using NModel. In: TestCom/FATES, pp. 211–216. Springer, Heidelberg (2009)
4. Fewster, M., Graham, D.: Software Test Automation: Effective use of test execution tools. Addison-Wesley, Reading (1999)
5. Jääskeläinen, A., Katara, M., Kervinen, A., Maunumaa, M., Pääkkönen, T., Takala, T., Virtanen, H.: Automatic GUI test generation for smart phone applications - an evaluation. In: Proc. of the Software Engineering in Practice track of the 31st International Conference on Software Engineering (ICSE 2009), companion volume, pp. 112–122. IEEE Computer Society, Los Alamitos (2009)
6. Jääskeläinen, A., Kervinen, A., Katara, M.: Creating a test model library for GUI testing of smartphone applications. In: Proc. 8th International Conference on Quality Software (QSIC 2008) (short paper), pp. 276–282. IEEE Computer Society, Los Alamitos (August 2008)
7. Karsisto, K.: A new parallel composition operator for verification tools. Doctoral dissertation, Tampere University of Technology (number 420 in publications) (2003)
8. Katara, M., Kervinen, A.: Making model-based testing more agile: a use case driven approach. In: Bin, E., Ziv, A., Ur, S. (eds.) HVC 2006. LNCS, vol. 4383, pp. 219–234. Springer, Heidelberg (2007)
9. Katara, M., Kervinen, A., Maunumaa, M., Pääkkönen, T., Satama, M.: Towards deploying model-based testing with a domain-specific modeling approach. In: Proc. TAIC PART – Testing: Academic & Industrial Conference 2006, pp. 81–89. IEEE CS, Los Alamitos (August 2006)
10. Practise research group: TEMA project home page, http://practise.cs.tut.fi/project.php?project=tema (Cited April 2010)
11. Roscoe, A.W.: The Theory and Practice of Concurrency. Prentice Hall, Englewood Cliffs (1998)
12. Rumpe, B.: Model-based testing of object-oriented systems. In: de Boer, F.S., Bonsangue, M.M., Graf, S., de Roever, W.-P. (eds.) FMCO 2002. LNCS, vol. 2852, pp. 380–402. Springer, Heidelberg (2003)
13. Tarjan, R.: Depth-first search and linear graph algorithms. SIAM Journal on Computing 1(2), 146–160 (1972)
14. Veanes, M., Schulte, W.: Protocol modeling with model program composition. In: Suzuki, K., Higashino, T., Yasumoto, K., El-Fakih, K. (eds.) FORTE 2008. LNCS, vol. 5048, pp. 324–339. Springer, Heidelberg (2008)

Does Testing Help to Reduce the Number of Potentially Faulty Statements in Debugging?

Mihai Nica, Simona Nica, and Franz Wotawa*

Institute for Software Technology, Graz University of Technology
Inffeldgasse 16b/II, 8010 Graz, Austria
{mnica,snica,wotawa}@ist.tugraz.at
http://www.ist.tugraz.at

Abstract. Tools for automated fault localization usually generate too many bug candidates depending on the underlying technique. Hence, further information is required in order to further restrict the bug candidates. Approaches that rely on specific knowledge of the program to be debugged like variable values at specific position in the source code, are not easily accessible for users especially in case of software maintenance. In order to avoid this problem we suggest to integrate testing for restricting the number of bug candidates. In particular, we suggest to compute possible corrections of the program and from this, distinguishing test cases. A distinguishing test case is a test that reveals different output values for two given program variants, given the same input values. Besides the formal definitions and algorithms, we present the first empirical results of our approach. The use of mutations and distinguishing test cases substantially reduces the number of bug candidates.

Keywords: Automated debugging, distinguishing test cases, test case generation.

1 Introduction

Debugging, i.e., detecting, locating, and correcting a bug, in a program is considered a hard and time consuming task. This holds especially in case of software maintenance where the programmer has little knowledge of the program's structure and behavior. Today's research activities mainly focus on the fault detection part of debugging. Automated verification and testing methods based on models of the system and specification knowledge have been proposed. Little effort has been spent in automated fault localization and even less in fault correction. There has been also no research activity bringing together testing and fault localization and correction, except the fact that test cases are used for debugging. However, to the best of our knowledge there is no work that analyzes the impact of test suites on the obtained debugging results.

In this paper, we contribute to the test case generation problem in order to improve the obtained results of automated debugging based on a model of the program. In particular we show how test cases can be generated to distinguish potential diagnosis candidates. A potential diagnosis candidate, or diagnosis candidate for short, is a statement

---
* Authors are listed in alphabetical order.

that can explain why the test cases fail. A diagnosis candidate needs not to be the real bug. But the real bug should be included in the list of diagnosis candidates delivered by an automated debugger.

We now consider the following code snippet to illustrate our combined debugging and testing approach. We use this small program to avoid introducing too much technical overhead and to focus on the underlying idea.

```
    ...
1.  i = 2 * x;
2.  j = 2 * y;
3.  o1 = i + j;
4.  o2 = i * i;
    ...
```

We cannot say anything about the correctness of such a code fragment without any additional specification knowledge. Let us assume that we also have the following test case specifying expected outputs for the given inputs: x = 1, y = 2, o1 = 8, o2 = 4. Obviously, the program computes the outputs o1 = 6 and o2 = 4, which contradicts the given test case. Therefore, we know that there is a bug in the program and we have to localize and correct it. At this stage we might use different approaches for computing potential fault locations. If using the data and control dependencies of the program, we might traverse the dependencies from the faulty outputs to the inputs backward. In our example, we are able to identify statements 1, 2, and 3 as potential candidates.

A different way to locate bugs is to consider statements as equations and to introduce correctness assumptions. If the test case together with the assumptions and the equations are consistent, the assumptions stating incorrectness of statements can be used as potential diagnosis candidates. Consider for example Statement 1 to be faulty and all other statements to be correct. As a consequence, Statement 1 does not determine a value for variable i. However, from Statement 4 and the test case we can conclude that i has to be 2 (if assuming only positive integers). Hence, we are able to compute a value for o1 again, which contradicts the given test case. Therefore, the assumption that Statement 1 is a diagnosis candidate cannot be correct. Note that even when assuming that i might be -2, we are able to derive a contradiction. It is also worth noting that the described approach for generating diagnosis candidates can be fully automated.

We are able to apply this technique for making and checking correctness assumptions for all statements and finally obtain statements 2 and 3 as diagnosis candidates. For larger programs we might receive a lot of potential diagnosis candidates and the question of how to reduce their number becomes very important. One solution is to ask the user about the expected value of intermediate variables like i or j for specific test cases. Such an approach requires more or less executing the program stepwise. Moreover, especially in the case of software maintenance where a programmer is not very familiar with the program answering questions about values of intermediate variables, this can hardly be done. Therefore, we suggest an approach that computes test cases, which allow to distinguish the behavior of diagnosis candidates. More specifically, we are searching for inputs that reveal a different behavior of diagnoses candidates. Such test cases are called distinguishing test cases [1]. In case no such distinguishing test case can be computed, the diagnosis candidates are, from the perspective of their input output behavior, equally good.

What prevents us from applying the approach of distinguishing test cases to distinguish diagnosis candidates is the fact that the fault localization approaches only give us information about the incorrectness and correctness of some statements but not about the correct behavior of potentially faulty statements. Hence, computing test cases is hardly possible. In order to solve this problem we borrow the idea of mutation or genetic-based debugging [2,3]. Mutants, i.e., variants of the original program, are computed and tested against a test suite. The mutants that pass all test cases are potential diagnosis candidates. Computing mutants for all statements and testing them against the test suite is very time consuming and some techniques for focusing on relevant parts of the program have been suggested. In our case we are able to use the diagnosis candidates for focusing on relevant parts of the program. Hence, when finding a mutant for a diagnosis candidate that passes all test cases, we do not only localize the bug but also state a potential correction.

For our example program we might obtain two mutations m_1, m_2 for statements 2 and 3, e.g.: $m_1 = 2$. `j=3*y` and $m_2 = 3$. `o1=i+j+2`. Obviously there are more mutations available but for illustrating the distinguishing test cases we only use these two now. A distinguishing test case for these mutants is `x = 1, y = 1`. Mutant m_1 computes the value 5 and mutant m_2 the value 6 for the output variable `o1`. If we know the correct value of `o1`, we are able to distinguish the two mutants. From this example we conclude that we are able to distinguish diagnosis candidates using distinguishing test cases. What remains an open research issue is to provide empirical evidence that the approach is feasible and provides a reduction of diagnosis candidates when applied to general programs.

In this paper, we introduce and discuss the approach and tackle the research question regarding the approach's practicability with some exceptions. The programs used for the empirical evaluation are small programs and they mainly implement algebraic computations. Moreover, we do not handle object-oriented constructs. However, we do not claim to answer the research question completely. We claim that the approach can be used for typical programs comprising language constructs like conditionals, assignments, and loops. The structures of the used programs are similar to those of larger programs or at least we do not see why there should be any big differences. Another argument is that the approach is mainly for debugging at the level of methods comprising a smaller amount of statements where our approach is definitely feasible.

The paper is organized as follows. We first introduce the basic definitions. These include the definition of test cases and stating the debugging problem. Since the debugging approach is based on a model of the program, we introduce a constraint representation of programs that serves our purpose in the next section. This model can be used for debugging as well as for computing distinguishing test cases. In the section afterwards, we introduce the diagnosis algorithm using constraints and mutations. This section is followed by the presentation and discussion of the obtained empirical results. Finally, we discuss related research and conclude the paper.

2 Basic Definitions

In order to be self contained we briefly introduce the basic definitions. This includes the definition of test cases and test suites, the debugging problem, as well as the definition of mutations. The paper deals with debugging based on models of programs, which are written in a programming language. In this paper we assume an imperative, sequential assignment language $\mathcal{L}$ with syntax and semantics similar to Java ignoring all object-oriented constructs and method calls. We further restrict the data domain of the language to integers and booleans. In Figure 1 we state an example program, which serves as running example. The program implements the division of two integer numbers where a bug is introduced in Line 1.

```
1.      tmp = (a + 1); // ERROR correct version is tmp = a
2.      if (b == 0) {
3.          result = -1;
        } else {
4.          result = 0;
5.          while (tmp > 0) {
6.              result = result + 1;
7.              tmp = tmp - b;
        }}
```

Fig. 1. A program for dividing two natural numbers

In order to state the debugging problem, we assume a program $\Pi \in \mathcal{L}$ that does not behave as expected. In the context of this paper such a program Π is faulty when there exist input values from which the program computes output values differing from the expected values. The input and correct output values are provided to the program by means of a test case. For defining test cases we introduce variable environments (or environments for short). An environment is a set of pairs (x, v) where x is a variable and v its value. In an environment there is only one pair for a variable. We are now able to define test cases formally as follows:

Definition 1 (Test case). *A test case for a program $\Pi \in \mathcal{L}$ is a tuple (I, O) where I is the input variable environment specifying the values of all input variables used in Π, and O the output variable environment not necessarily specifying values for all output variables.*

For example a (failing) test case for the program from Fig. 1 is $I_\Pi : \{a = 2; b = 1\}$ and $O_\Pi : \{result = 2\}$.

A test case is a *failing test case* if and only if the output environment computed from the program Π when executed on input I is not consistent with the expected environment O, i.e., when $\mathbf{exec}(\Pi, I) \not\supseteq O$. Otherwise, we say that the test case is a *passing test case*. If a test case is a failing (passing) test case, we also say that the program fails (passes) executing the test case. For the program from Fig. 1 the test case (I_Π, O_Π) is a failing test case. For input I_Π the program will return $result = 3$ which contradicts the expected output $O_\Pi : \{result = 2\}$.

Definition 2 (Test suite). *A test suite TS for a program $\Pi \in \mathcal{L}$ is a set of test cases of Π.*

A program is said to be correct with respect to TS if and only if the program passes all test cases. Otherwise, we say that the program is incorrect or faulty. This definition of correctness is similar to the input output conformance relation (IOCO) from Tretmans [4].

We are now able to state the debugging problem.

Definition 3 (Debugging problem). *Let $\Pi \in \mathcal{L}$ be a program and TS its test suite. If $T \in TS$ is a failing test case of Π, then (Π, T) is a debugging problem.*

A solution to the debugging problem is the identification and correction of a part of the program responsible for the detected misbehavior. We call such a program part an explanation. There are many approaches that are capable of returning explanations including [5,6,7,2,8] and [9,10] among others. In this paper, we follow the debugging approach based on constraints, i.e., [9,10]. In particular, the approach makes use of the program's constraint representation to compute possible fault candidates. So, debugging is reduced to solving the corresponding constraint satisfaction problem (CSP).

Definition 4 (Constraint Satisfaction Problem (CSP)). *A constraint satisfaction problem is a tuple (V, D, CO) where V is a set of variables defined over a set of domains D connected to each other by a set of arithmetic and boolean relations, called constraints CO. A solution for a CSP represents a valid instantiation of the variables V with values from D such that none of the constraints from CO is violated.*

Note that the variables used in a CSP are not necessarily variables used in a program. We discuss the representation of programs as a CSP in the next section. Afterwards we introduce an algorithm for computing bug candidates from debugging problems. This algorithm only states statements as potential explanations for a failing test cases. No information regarding how to correct the program is given. Hence, we have to extend the approach to deliver also repair suggestions. This is done by mutating program fragments. In the context of our paper we define program mutation as follows.

Definition 5 (Mutant). *Given a program Π and a statement $S_\Pi \in \Pi$. Further let S'_Π be a statement that results from S_Π when applying changes like modifying the operator or a variable. We call the program Π', which we obtain when replacing S_Π with S'_Π, the mutant of program Π with respect to statement S_Π.*

Another important issue in the theory of program mutation is the identification of a test case able to outline the semantical difference between a program and its mutant. We call such a test case a *distinguishing test case*.

Definition 6 (Distinguishing test case). *Given a program $\Pi \in \mathcal{L}$ and one of its mutant Π', a distinguishing test case for program Π and its mutant Π' is a tuple $(I, \emptyset)$ such that for the input value I the output value of program Π differs from the output value of program Π'.*

In the next section we discuss the conversion of programs into their corresponding constraint representation.

3 CSP Representation of Programs

Before converting a program $\Pi \in \mathcal{L}$ into its corresponding constraint representation we have to apply some intermediate transformation steps. These transformations are necessary for removing its imperative behavior, i.e., making it a declarative one, as required by the constraint programming paradigm.

Our three step algorithm for converting a program and encoding its debugging problem into a CSP, is as follows:

1. *Loop elimination* $\Pi_{LF} = LR(\Pi)$: We define loop-elimination as a recursive function where n is the number of iterations:

$$LF(\text{while } C \{B\}, n) = \begin{cases} \text{if } C\{B \; LF(\text{while } C \{B\}, n-1)\} & \text{if } n = 0 \\ \epsilon & \text{otherwise} \end{cases}$$

   We replace each loop-structure by a number of nested if-statements, i.e., number of iterations. The number of iterations n, is given by the test case. The two-iterations version of the program from Figure 1 is given in Figure 2.

```
1.      tmp = (a + 1); // ERROR correct version is tmp = a
2.      if (b == 0) {
3.          result = -1;
        } else {
4.          result = 0;
5.          if (tmp > 0) {    // first iteration
6.              result = result + 1;
7.              tmp = tmp - b;
8.              if (tmp > 0) { //second iteration
9.                  result = result + 1;
10.                 tmp = tmp - b;
            }}}
```

Fig. 2. Two iteration unrolling for the program from Figure 1

2. *SSA conversion* $\Pi_{SSA} = SSA(\Pi_{LF})$: The static single assignment (SSA) form is an intermediate representation of a program with the property that no two left-side variable share the same name. This property of the SSA form allows for an easy conversion into a CSP. It is beyond our scope to detail the program-to-SSA conversion. However, to be self-contained we only explain the necessary rules needed for converting our running example into its SSA representation. For more details regarding the SSA-conversion see for example [11].
   – We convert **assignments** by adding an index to a variable each time the variable is defined, i.e., occurs at the left side of an assignment. If a variable is redefined, we increase its unique index by one such that the SSA-form property holds. The index of a referenced variable, i.e., a variable occurring at the right side of an assignment, equals to the index of the last definition of the variable.

- We split the conversion of **conditional structures** into three steps: (1) the entry condition is saved in an auxiliary variable, (2) each assignment statement is converted following the above rule, and (3) for each conditional statement and variable defined in the sub-block of the statement, we introduce an evaluation function

$$\Phi(\mathtt{v_{then}}, \mathtt{v_{else}}, \mathtt{cond}) \stackrel{def}{=} \begin{cases} \mathtt{v_{then}} & \text{if } \mathtt{cond} = true \\ \mathtt{v_{else}} & \text{otherwise} \end{cases}$$

which returns the statement conditional-exit value, e.g., $\mathtt{v_{after}} = \Phi(\mathtt{v_{then}}, \mathtt{v_{else}}, \mathtt{cond})$.

The SSA representation of the program from Figure 2 is given in Figure 3.

```
1.  tmp_1=(a_0+1);
2.  cond_0=b_0==0;
3.  result_1=-1;
4.  result_2=0;
5.  cond_1=(!cond_0 ∧ tmp_1>0);
6.  result_3=result_2+1;
7.  tmp_2=tmp_1-b_0;
8.  cond_2=(cond_1 ∧ tmp_2>0);
9.  result_4=(result_3+1);
10. tmp_3=tmp_2-b_0;
11. result_5=Φ(result_3,result_4,cond_2);
12. tmp_4=Φ(tmp_2,tmp_3,cond_2);
13. result_6=ϕ (result_2,result_5,cond_1);
14. tmp_5=Φ(tmp_1,tmp_4,cond_1);
15. result_7=Φ(result_6,result_1,cond_0);
16. tmp_6=Φ(tmp_5,tmp_1,cond_0);
```

Fig. 3. The SSA form corresponding to the program from Figure 2

3. *Constraint conversion* $CON = CC(\Pi_{SSA})$: This last step of the conversion process transforms the SSA statements to the corresponding constraints, including also the encoding of the debugging problem. For this purpose we introduce a special boolean variable $AB(S)$ for a statement S, that states the incorrectness of a statement S. The constraint model of a statement comprises corresponding constraints or-connected with $AB(S)$. Let $S \in \Pi_{SSA}$ and let C_S be the constraint encoding statement S in the constraint programing language. Note that ϕ functions cannot be incorrect. Hence, no AB variable is defined for statements using ϕ. We model S in CON as follows:

$$CON \cup \begin{cases} AB(S) \vee C_S & \text{if } S \text{ does not contain } \phi \\ C_S & \text{otherwise} \end{cases}$$

Hence the CSP representation of a program Π is given by the tuple $(V_{\pi_{SSA}}, D_{SSA}, CON)$, where $V_{\pi_{SSA}}$ represents all variables of the SSA representation Π_{SSA} of program Π, defined over the domains $D_{SSA} = \{Integer, boolean\}$.

Debugging of a program requires the existence of a failing test case. This means that in addition to the set of constraints CON, we must add an extra set of constraint encoding a failing test case (I, O). For all $(x, v) \in I$ the constraint $x\_0 = v$ is added to the constraint system. For all $(y, w) \in O$ the constraint $y\_\iota = w$ is added where ι is the greatest index of variable y in the SSA form. Let CON_{TC} denote the constraints resulted from converting the given test case. Then, the CSP corresponding to the debugging problem of a program Π is now represented by the tuple $(V_{\pi_{SSA}}, D_{SSA}, CON \cup CON_{TC})$.

In our implementation we model the CSP to represent the debugging problem in the language of the MINION constraint solver [12]. MINION is an out of the box, open source constraint solver. Its syntax requires a little effort in modeling the constraints than other constraint solvers, e.g., it does not support different operators on the same constraint. Because of this drawback sometimes complex constraints have to be split into two or three more simpler constraints. However, because of this characteristic, MINION, unlike other constraint solver toolkits, does not have to perform an intermediate transformation of the input constraint system. For example the MINION representation of statement 1 from Fig. 3 is in Fig. 4 given by statements 1 and 2, whereas the MINION constraints corresponding to line 5 of the program from Fig. 3 are represented by: 7, 8, 9. Statements 24, 25 of the MINION representation correspond to the Φ function given in statement 13 from Fig. 3. The failing test case is given by the lines 32 to 34.

After explaining the conversion of debugging problems into CSP, in the following section we discuss the debugging algorithm and its extension with mutations and distinguishing test cases.

```
1.  watched-or({element(ab,0,1), sumleq([a_0,1], tmp_1)})
2.  watched-or({element(ab,0,1), sumgeq([a_0,1], tmp_1)})
     ......
7.  reify(eq(cond_0,0),not_cond_0)
8.  watched-or({element(ab,4,1), reify(ineq(0,tmp_1,-1 ), cond_aux3)})
9.  watched-or({element(ab,4,1), reify(watchsumgeq([not_cond_0, cond_aux3], 2),cond_1)})
10. watched-or({element(ab,5,1), sumleq([result_2,1], result_3)})
11. watched-or({element(ab,5,1), sumgeq([result_2,1], result_3)})
     ......
24. watched-or({eq(cond_1,0), eq(result_6, result_5)})
25. watched-or({eq(cond_1,1), eq(result_6, result_2)})
     ......
28. watched-or({eq(cond_0,0), eq(result_7, result_1)})
29. watched-or({eq(cond_0,1), eq(result_7, result_6)})
     ......
32. eq(a_0, 0)
33. eq(b_0, -250)
34. eq(result_7, 0)
```

Fig. 4. The constraint representation of the program from Figure 3

4 Debugging

The debugging approach presented in the paper comprises 3 steps. The first step comprises the computation of bug candidates, i.e., program statement that might cause the revealed misbehavior, from the constraint representation of a program $\Pi \in \mathcal{L}$. In the second step, for each candidate a set of mutants is computed that would lead to a new program passing all previously failing test cases. If no such mutant can be found the bug candidate is removed from the list of potential candidates. In the third step, distinguishing test cases are computed that allow choice between two randomly selected bug candidates. The third step can be executed several times to further reduce the number of bug candidates. In this section, we explain each of the debugging steps starting from the computation of candidates using the CSP representation to the computation and use of distinguishing test cases.

Let CON_Π be the constraint representation of a program Π and CON_T the constraint representation of a failing test case T. The debugging problem formulated as a CSP comprises CON_Π together with CON_T. Note that in CON_Π assumptions about correctness or incorrectness of statements are given, which are represented by a variable AB assigned to each statement. The algorithm for computing bug candidates calls the CSP solver using the constraints and asks for a return value of AB as a solution. The size of the solution corresponds to the size of the bug, i.e., the number of statements that must be changed together in order to explain the misbehavior. We assume that single statement bugs are more likely than bugs comprising more statements. Hence, we ask the constraint solver for smaller solutions first. If no solution of a particular size is found, the algorithm increases the size of the solutions to be searched for and iterates calling the constraint solver. This is done until either a solution is found or the maximum size of a bug, which is equivalent to the number of statements in Π, is reached.

Algorithm CSP_Debugging (CON_Π, CON_T)
Inputs: A constraint representation CON_Π of a program Π, and a constraint representation CON_T of a failing test case T.
Outputs: A set of minimal bug candidates.

1. Let i be 1.
2. While i smaller or equal to the number of statements in Π do:
   (a) Call the constraint solver using CON_Π, CON_T to search for solutions regarding the AB variables, where only i statements are allowed simultaneously to be incorrect.
   (b) If the constraint solver returns a non-empty set of solution, then return this set as result and leave the algorithm.
   (c) Otherwise, let i be $i + 1$.
3. Return the empty set as result.

For example, for the constraint system from Fig. 4 the constraint solver MINION finds 5 possible explanations for the failing test case $I : (a\_0 = 0, b\_0 = -250), O : (result\_7 = 0)$ in less the 0.1s. This result is very satisfactory, especially with respect to computation time. However, further steps might be performed in order to reduce the size of the bug candidates. For this purpose we suggest to use mutations.

Assume a faulty program Π and a failing test case (I, O). Let D_{AB} be the set of bug candidates obtained when calling **CSP_Debugging** on the constraint representation of Π and (I, O). The following algorithm makes use of program mutations for further restricting D_{AB}.

Algorithm Filter_TestCase (D_{AB}, Π, T)
Inputs: A set of bug candidates D_{AB}, the faulty program Π, and the failing test case T.
Outputs: A set of mutants Mut_Π of program Π.

1. Let Mut_Π be the empty set.
2. For all elements $d \in D_{AB}$ do:
   (a) Generate all mutants of program Π with respect to the statements stored in d and store them in V_{Mut}.
   (b) Add every program $\Pi' \in V_{Mut}$ passing test case T to Mut_Π.
3. Return Mut_Π.

The **Filter_TestCase** algorithm returns for the faulty program Π a set of repair possibilities Mut_Π. Due to the usage of the debugging algorithm **CSP_Debugging**, we compute the repair only for the resulting bug candidates set D_{AB}. A mutant is part of Mut_Π, i.e., a repair, if and only if it is able to pass the failing test case T. Hence, we expect that the number of bug candidates can be reduced. Moreover, since mutation is only applied for bug candidates we do not need to compute all possible mutations even in the case when they cannot explain the revealed misbehavior.

The number of repair possibilities for a statement of the D_{AB} set is strongly tied to the capabilities of the used mutation operators and the used mutation tool. Because of this fact this part of the approach is as good as the available capability of the used mutation tool. Note that after applying the **Filter_TestCase** algorithm, in our experiments we were able to eliminate between 20% and 60% of the bug candidates, because of the inability of the suggested repair to pass the test case. Hence, filtering based on mutations was very successful.

The last step of our algorithm comprises the integration of distinguishing test cases to further reduce the bug candidate set. Let Mut_Π be the set of mutants for a program Π obtained after applying the **Filter_TestCase** algorithm. And let CON_{Mut_Π} be the constraint representation of the programs from Mut_Π.

Algorithm TestCase_Generator Mut_Π, CON_{Mut_Π}
Inputs: A set of valid repair possibilities, Mut_Π, for a faulty program Π and their constraint representation CON_{Mut_Π}.
Outputs: A subset of Mut_Π.

1. Let $Tested$ be empty.
2. If there exists mutants $\Pi', \Pi'' \in Mut_\Pi$ with $(\Pi', \Pi'') \notin Tested$, add (Π', Π'') to $Tested$ and proceed with the algorithm. Otherwise, return Mut_Π
3. Let $CON_{\Pi'}$ and $CON_{\Pi''} \in CON_{Mut_\Pi}$ be the constraint representation of programs Π' and Π'' respectively.
4. Let CON_{TC} be the constraints encoding $Input_{\Pi'} = Input_{\Pi''} = I \wedge Output_{\Pi'} \neq Output_{\Pi''}$
5. Solve the CSP: $CON_{\Pi'} \cup CON_{\Pi''} \cup CON_{TC}$ using a constraint solver.
6. Let O be the correct output for the original program Π on input I (derived from user interaction or specifications).
7. If $Output_{\Pi'} = O \wedge Output_{\Pi''} \neq O$, then delete Π'' from Mut_Π.
8. If $Output_{\Pi''} = O \wedge Output_{\Pi'} \neq O$, then delete Π' from Mut_Π.

9. If $Output_{\Pi'} \neq O \wedge Output_{\Pi''} \neq O$, delete Π' and Π'' from Mut_Π.
10. If (CSP has no solution) go to step 1.
11. For all $\Pi' \in Mut_\Pi$ do:
    (a) If Π' fails on generated test case (I, O) delete Π' from Mut_Π.
12. Return Mut_Π.

The above algorithm searches for two mutants, distinguished via a test case. The algorithm in the current form is restricted to search for only one pair of such mutants but can be easily changed in order to compute several different pairs where a distinguishing test case is available. The only disadvantage of this algorithm is that Step 6 requires an interaction with an oracle. If no automated oracle is available user interactions are required and prevent the approach from being completely automated. To solve the constraint system resulted at step 5 we use the MINION constraint solver. Another particularity of this approach is that, for the CSP to be solvable, the name of the variables of the two mutants should differ. This is however an encoding problem which can be easily overcome by encapsulating in the name of each variable the name of the mutant file. When using the above approach for the example from 2 we are able to reduce the conflict set to one element, which was also the correct one. For more information regarding distinguishing test cases and their computation using MINION, we refer the interested reader to [1].

To obtain the program's set of mutants relative to the set of fault candidates we relay on the JAVA mutation tool MuJava [13]. MuJava is a Java based mutation tool, which was originally developed by Offut, Ma, and Kwon. Its main three characteristics are:

1. Generation of mutants for a given program.
2. Analysis of the generated mutants.
3. Running of provided test cases.

Due to the new implemented add-ons, the tool supports a command line version for the mutation analysis framework, which offers an easy integration of the tool in the testing or debugging process.

Offutt proved that the computational cost for generating and executing a large number of mutants can be expensive, and thus he proposed a selective mutation operator set that is used by the MuJava tool. It works with both types of mutation operators:

– Method level mutation operators (also called traditional), which modify the statements inside the body of a method;
– Class level mutation operators, which try to simulate faults specific to the object oriented paradigm (for example faults regarding the inheritance or polymorphism).

For our experiments we take into account only the traditional mutation operators. Moreover, we further restrict the mutation operators to mutations on expressions comprising deletion, replacement, and insertion of primitive operators (arithmetic operators, relational operators, conditional operators, etc.). Mutation by deletion of operands or statements was proved to be inefficient [14]. Because of the selected tools there are currently some limitations of our implementation. If the bug is on the left side of an assignment we cannot correct it. Another limitation is with respect to constants. If the bug is due to an initialization, MuJava is not able to generate any mutants. Missing statements are another limitation of the approach. We currently do not consider bugs because of missing statements. Finally, there is a limitation regarding multiple bugs in one statement. In this case the MuJava tool is not able to mutate more than one variable or operator per statement and mutant, i.e., each mutant contains only one change when compared with the original program.

5 Empirical Results

We tested our approach against a set of faulty programs. In each program we manually injected one single fault. All the faults are found at the right side of the assignment and with the exception of the *tcsa03* program all faults are functional faults. We used as test oracle the original bug free version of each faulty program. Using the output values of the original bug-free program we were able to decide which of the mutants are to be eliminated after computing the distinguishing test cases. In the real life situation we cannot benefit from the existence of such a program. Therefore, we must relay on the user or a given formal specification to determine the correct output for a given input.

The process of mutant generation, program to CSP conversion, and the computation of the conflict set is fully automated. However the generation of the distinguishing test cases was performed manually.

In order to obtain the empirical results, we applied the following process. For each program we first performed the conversion into its constraint representation. Then we computed the fault candidates. For each fault candidate, i.e., faulty statement, we computed all its possible mutants. We eliminated from the generated set of mutants all mutants which were not able to pass the error revealing test case. In addition, we tested the number of oracle-interactions required to obtain the minimal set of faulty components. By an oracle-interaction we understand repeating the **TestCase_Generator** algorithm until no other distinguishing test case can be generated, i.e., each time we applied the algorithm we asked the oracle, i.e., the original fault free program in our case, to provide the correct output for the generated test case. This is represented in the table by the **#UI** column which states the number of user-interactions to obtain the number of fault candidates $|\text{Diag}_{TC}|$.

The results of the empirical study are given in Table 1. In most of the cases we were able to eliminate more than half of the initial fault candidates set. Reducing the diagnosis candidates by eliminating those candidates where no mutant that passes the original test suite can be found, is very effective. The use of distinguishing test cases further reduces the number of fault candidates. Thus finally, only one diagnosis candidate remains, which was always the correct one. When using larger programs like *tcas* a reduction to one diagnosis candidate was not possible. However, even in this case the approach lead to a reduction of more than 60 percent regarding the computed diagnosis candidates.

Another factor, which influences the quality of the obtained results, is the way of choosing the mutant pairs for computing distinguishing test cases. There is no way to predict if a certain pair of mutants will produce the best or worst distinguishing test case. Therefore, we randomly selected the pair of mutants when carrying out the

Table 1. Each program **Name**, has associated a number of iterations **It**, the number of inputs **Inputs**, number of outputs **Outputs**, the size of its SSA representation given as lines of codeLOC_{SSA}, the number of MINION constraints $|CO|$, the number of MINION variables over which the constraint system is defined Var_{CO}, the size of the conflict set resulted after applying $Filter\_TestCase$ algorithm, $|Diag_{filt}|$, the number of calls to the $TestCasegenerator$ algorithm, **#UI** to obtain the number of fault candidates $|Diag_{TC}|$.

Name	It	Var_Π	LOC_Π	Inputs	Outputs	LOC_{SSA}	$|CO|$	Var_{CO}	$|Diag|$	$|Diag_{filt}|$	#UI	$|Diag_{TC}|$
DivATC_V1	2	5	21	2	1	32	33	29	3	2	1	2
DivATC_V2	2	5	21	2	1	32	33	29	5	3	1	1
DivATC_V3	2	5	21	2	1	32	33	29	3	2	1	2
DivATC_V4	2	5	21	2	1	32	33	29	4	4	1/2	3(1)/1
GcdATC_V1	2	6	35	2	1	49	61	46	2	2	1	1
GcdATC_V2	2	6	35	2	1	49	61	46	10	3	1/2/3/4/5	3/3/2/2/1
GcdATC_V3	2	6	35	2	1	49	61	46	2	2	1	1
MultATC_V1	2	5	16	2	1	26	24	19	2	2	1	1
MultATC_V2	2	5	16	2	1	26	24	19	2	2	1	1
MultATC_V3	2	5	16	2	1	26	24	19	2	2	1	1
MultATC_V4	2	5	16	2	1	26	24	19	5	2	1	1
MultV2ATC_V1	2	6	20	2	1	49	67	46	6	2	1	1
MultV2ATC_V2	2	6	20	2	1	49	67	46	2	1	1	1
MultV2ATC_V3	2	6	20	2	1	49	67	46	6	1	1	1
SumATC_V1	2	5	18	2	1	27	24	20	2	2	1	1
SumATC_V2	2	5	18	2	1	27	24	20	3	2	1	1
SumATC_V3	2	5	18	2	1	27	24	20	5	2	1	1
SumPowers_V1	2	11	36	3	1	72	87	70	16	6	1/2/3/4	4/4/2/2
SumPowers_V2	2	11	36	3	1	72	87	70	11	6	1/2	2/1
SumPowers_V3	2	11	36	3	1	72	87	70	11	1	1	1
tcas08	1	48	125	12	1	125	98	132	27	13	1/2/3/4	11/11/11/10
tcas03	1	48	125	12	1	125	98	132	27	13	1/2/3/4	13/12/9/9

empirical evaluation. For example, we observed that after trying out all mutant pairs for the *DivATC_V4* program the best distinguishing test case would lead to 1 element in the conflict set contrary to 3 as given in Table 1.

It is also worth noting that computing the diagnosis candidates and the distinguishing test cases using the CSP solver MINION was very fast. For all examples, the necessary time never exceeded 0.3 seconds using a Pentium 4 Dual core 2 GHz with 4 GB of RAM computer. Hence, for smaller programs or program parts that can be separately analyzed like methods, the proposed approach is feasible.

6 Related Research

Our work is mainly based on model-based diagnosis [15] and its application to debugging [8,5,16]. In contrast to previous work we are not using logic-based models of programs but a constraint representation and a general constraint solver. The most similar work in this respect is [9,10,11,17]. Instead of focusing only on constraint-based debugging, we combine fault localization with mutations and testing.

In [2] and more recently [3] the authors describe the application of mutations and genetics programming to software debugging. In order to avoid computing too many mutants the authors use focusing techniques based on dependencies and spectrum-based methods respectively. The use of mutations is similar to our work. The difference is that we are using constraint-based debugging for focusing and integration of testing for reducing the size of the conflict set, which, to the best of our knowledge, has not been introduced before.

Other more recent approaches of debugging include delta debugging [18], spectrum-based debugging [19,7,20], and slicing based methods like [21,22,23,24]. The focus of our approach is on generating automated tests for distinguishing diagnosis candidates and thus to further make automated debugging more accessible and useful in practice.

7 Conclusion

In this paper we presented an approach for restricting the number of potential diagnosis candidates by providing distinguishing test cases. A distinguishing test case for two diagnosis candidates is characterized by a set of inputs that reveal different executions for both diagnosis candidates such that they can be distinguished with respect to their output behavior. Just using the distinguishing test case alone we are not able to decide which diagnosis candidates to remove or if we should eliminate both from the list of candidates. This can only be done after consulting a test oracle, e.g., the user or a formal specification, for the expected output of the distinguishing test case. Candidates where the computed output is not equivalent to the expected one can be eliminated. The advantage of this approach is that only the input-output behavior of a program is used for distinguishing diagnosis candidates. Moreover, the approach computes additional test cases based on their discriminating power for distinguishing diagnosis candidates. Usually, test cases are generated for fulfilling coverage criteria like statement coverage or branch coverage.

Beside the theoretical contribution we present first empirical results of the proposed approach. The results indicate that the approach allows a substantial reduction of the diagnosis candidates. For smaller programs we were able to reduce the diagnosis candidates to the real bug. Obviously, this was not always the case. For larger programs more diagnosis candidates remain. This has been somehow expected because programs cannot be usually corrected only by replacing one statement with another. Instead the right repair actions might comprise changes at different positions in the program. In future work we want to extend the empirical study. This includes to use more and larger programs as well as example programs comprising multiple faults.

References

1. Wotawa, F., Nica, M., Aichernig, B.K.: Generating distinguishing tests using the minion constraint solver. In: CSTVA 2010: Proceedings of the 2nd Workshop on Constraints for Testing, Verification and Analysis. IEEE, Los Alamitos (2010)
2. Weimer, W., Nguyen, T.V., Goues, C.L., Forrest, S.: Automatically finding patches using genetic programming. In: ACM/IEEE International Conference on Software Engineering (ICSE), pp. 512–521 (2009)
3. Debroy, V., Wong, W.E.: Using mutation to automatically suggest fixes for faulty programs. In: Third International Conference on Software Testing, Verification and Validation (ICST 2010). IEEE, Los Alamitos (2010)
4. Tretmans, J.: Test generation with inputs, outputs and repetitive quiescence. Software - Concepts and Tools 17(3), 103–120 (1996)
5. Wotawa, F., Peischl, B.: Automated source level error localization in hardware designs. IEEE Design and Test of Computers 23(1), 8–19 (2006)
6. Mayer, W., Abreu, R., Stumptner, M., van Gemund, A.J.: Prioritising model-based debugging diagnostic reports. In: Proceedings of the International Workshop on Principles of Diagnosis (DX) (2009)
7. Abreu, R., Zoeteweij, P., van Gemund, A.J.: On the accuracy of spectrum-based fault localization. In: Proceedings TAIC PART 2007, pp. 89–98. IEEE, Los Alamitos (2006)
8. Mayer, W.: Static and hybrid analysis in model-based debugging. PhD Thesis, School of Computer and Information Science, University of South Australia (2007)
9. Ceballos, R., Gasca, R.M., Valle, C.D., Borrego, D.: Diagnosing errors in dbc programs using constraint programming. In: Marín, R., Onaindía, E., Bugarín, A., Santos, J. (eds.) CAEPIA 2005. LNCS (LNAI), vol. 4177, pp. 200–210. Springer, Heidelberg (2006)
10. Nica, M., Weber, J., Wotawa, F.: How to debug sequential code by means of constraint representation. In: 19th International Workshop on Principles of Diagnosis (DX 2008) (2008)
11. Wotawa, F., Nica, M.: On the compilation of programs into their equivalent constraint representation. Informatika 32, 359–371 (2008)
12. Gent, I.P., Jefferson, C., Miguel, I.: Minion: A fast, scalable, constraint solver. In: 17th European Conference on Artificial Intelligence, ECAI 2006 (2006)
13. Ma, Y.S., Offutt, J., Kwon, Y.R.: Mujava: An automated class mutation system. Software Testing, Verification and Reliability 15, 97–133 (2005)
14. Offutt, A.J., Lee, A., Rothermel, G., Untch, R., Zapf, C.: An experimental determination of sufficient mutation operators. ACM Transactions on Software Engineering Methodology 5, 99–118 (1996)
15. Reiter, R.: A theory of diagnosis from first principles. Artificial Intelligence 32(1), 57–95 (1987)

16. Mayer, W., Stumptner, M.: Model-based debugging using multiple abstract models. In: Proceedings of the 5th International Workshop on Automated and Algorithmic Debugging, AADEBUG 2003, pp. 55–70 (2003)
17. Ceballos, R., Nica, M., Weber, J., Wotawa, F.: On the complexity of program debugging using constraints for modeling the program's syntax and semantics. In: Proc. Conference of the Spanish Association for Artificial Intelligence (CAEPIA), Seville, Spain (2009)
18. Zeller, A., Hildebrandt, R.: Simplifying and isolating failure-inducing input. IEEE Transactions on Software Engineering 28(2) (2002)
19. Jones, J.A., Harrold, M.J.: Empirical evaluation of the tarantula automatic fault-localization technique. In: Proceedings ASE 2005, pp. 273–282. ACM Press, New York (2005)
20. Abreu, R., Zoeteweij, P., van Gemund, A.J.: Spectrum-based multiple fault localization. In: Proc. IEEE/ACM International Conference on Automated Software Engineering (ASE), pp. 88–99 (2009)
21. Kusumoto, S., Nishimatsu, A., Nishie, K., Inoue, K.: Experimental evaluation of program slicing for fault localization. Empirical Software Engineering 7, 49–76 (2002)
22. Binkley, D., Harman, M.: A survey of empirical results on program slicing. In: Zelkowitz, M. (ed.) Advances in Software Engineering – Advances in Computers, vol. 62, pp. 106–172. Academic Press Inc., London (2004), citeseer.ist.psu.edu/661032.html
23. Zhang, X., He, H., Gupta, N., Gupta, R.: Experimental evaluation of using dynamic slices for fault localization. In: Sixth International Symposium on Automated & Analysis-Driven Debugging (AADEBUG), pp. 33–42 (2005)
24. Wotawa, F.: Bridging the gap between slicing and model-based diagnosis. In: Proc. of the 20th Intl. Conference on Software Engineering and Knowledge Engineering (SEKE), Knowledge Systems Institute Graduate School, pp. 836–841 (2008)

Linguistic Security Testing for Text Communication Protocols

Ben W.Y. Kam and Thomas R. Dean

School of Computing, Queen's University, Kingston, Canada
Electrical and Computer Engineering, Queen's University, Kingston, Canada

Abstract. We introduce a new Syntax-based Security Testing (SST) framework that uses a protocol specification to perform security testing on text-based communication protocols. A protocol specification of a particular text-based protocol under-tested represents its syntactic grammar and static constraints. The specification is used to generate test cases by mutating valid messages, breaking the syntactic and constraints of the protocol. The framework is demonstrated using a toy Web application and the open source application KOrganizer.

Keywords: security testing, mutation testing, text-based communication protocol.

1 Introduction

Despite widespread knowledge of classes of security bugs [20, 23], vulnerabilities continue to occur. Security faults have serious consequences, such as the theft of information or the complete failure of systems. This paper describes a framework for testing that applies transformation techniques from the program comprehension literature to generating test cases specific to the security of the system. Our general approach is similar to previous research on binary protocols [1, 21, 22, 26], but the flexibility of text based protocols such as iCalendar [7] or HTTP [9] raises new challenges.

In our approach, we describe the protocol using a context free grammar with XML markup to specify additional lexical, syntactic and context sensitive constraints. From this augmented grammar we automatically generate a markup engine that transfers the markup to captured valid test data. The markup is used to mutate the test data (Protocol Data Unit) to check for security vulnerabilities. Therefore, our mutation testing differs from the conventional mutation testing approach which mutates the program. We demonstrate the framework against applications using the HTTP and iCalendar protocols, discovering a previously unknown vulnerability in the Qt library in the process.

In next section, we discuss the goals of this paper. SST framework overviews and SST components anatomy will be illustrated in Section 3 and 4 respectively. Section 5 states the SST low/middle levels concrete architectures. Section 6 reports experiments in SST and follows with the related work. Finally, the conclusion and future work will be drawn in the last section.

2 Goals and History

Binary protocols such as OSPF [19] are protocols in which the data exchanged is transmitted in a similar representation to that used in memory. For example, the integer value 4 is transmitted as the binary value 0x04 (8 bits) or the value 0x00000004 (32 bits). In text based protocols such as HTTP, use ASCII or UNICODE, and the value 4 may be transmitted as the ASCII character '4' 0x34. While binary protocols provide some flexibility in lengths of fields, the number and order of fields in the messages is fixed. Syntactic mutations to messages such as deleting a field have little meaning, as the next sequence bytes in the message will be interpreted by the system under test as the new value for the field. Binary protocols also tend to have limited support for the nesting of structures. Text based protocols have a flexible syntax, often allowing extra spaces and newline characters, and when MIME [4] or XML [5] are used as part of the encoding, allow flexible ordering and deletion of fields. Thus the syntax and lexical properties of the protocol become valid concerns for security and robustness testing.

Our previous versions of Protocol Tester [1, 21, 22, 26] handled binary protocols by translating them to a textual form, mutating them using program transformation techniques and then translating back to the binary format. The protocols were described using a context dependent grammar, and XML markup that specified constraints such as the types of fields or the relation between the length of one field and the value of another. These markups are used by a test planner to insert a different set of XML markup tags into the captured message sequences to guide the mutation. While the tags used to guide the mutation are flexible and expandable, the set of tags available for use in the protocol specification was hard coded into the tool set, requiring code modification when they were extended.

Thus the goal of SST is a lightweight framework capable of handling the more complex mutations for text protocols and at the same time supporting an easily extensible markup system for specifying constraints in the protocol description. More detailed markup information will be discussed in section 4. As specified by Beizer "data validation is the first line of defense against a hostile world", all input data should conform to its grammar and the best input format should be defined as a formal language [3].

3 SST Framework Overviews

The SST framework is similar to the structure of Protocol Tester, and consists of a total of five modules: Capture, Markup, Mutate, Replay, and Oracle. Fig. 1 shows the five components of the SST framework. The protocol dependent module **Capture** is responsible for capturing and decoding the network traffic between the client and the server. Capturing is done by a sniffing component (Sniffer), which in the case of web applications is a modified version of the Firefox browser allowing us to capture encrypted messages (https) in unencrypted form. If the captured response messages are compressed or encoded a decoding component is be invoked translate them to plain text. The Capture module also creates a manifest file. The manifest file specifies the protocol, the server addresses, port numbers and the information of proxy servers for each message. This allows SST to test systems spanning multiple servers.

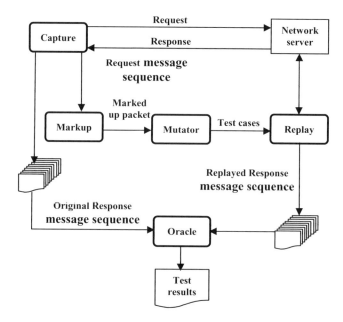

Fig. 1. SST overview

The **Markup** module uses the protocol description file to insert markup into the captured messages. This markup is then used by the **Mutator** module to generate the test cases. Both of these modules are protocol independent.

The **Replay** module uses the manifest file generated by the capture module to transmit the test cases to the server(s). When the mutated message is not the first message in a sequence, the original versions of the previous messages in the sequence are sent. The current version of the module is largely protocol independent, with a custom component handling HTTP cookies and session information. In the future this will be made protocol independent by adapting the approach for specifying state dependent messages used in Protocol Tester [26].

4 Protocol Specification and Markup

SST uses a protocol specification to mutate captured messages to generate the test cases. We distinguish between three levels of protocols in the specification. At the lowest level we have the base format of the captured messages. Since we are interested in text protocols, this is the lowest level above the TCP/IP stream protocol, such as the HTTP protocol. This lowest level protocol may also serve as a container for other protocols. For example, SOAP [10] can be used to encode remote procedure calls within the HTTP protocol. At the highest level we have the application protocol which assigns application specific meaning to messages, such as the messages related to shopping carts. In this paper we discuss the specification of the low and middle level protocols.

```
% partial HTTP grammar
define program
    [request-message]
end define
define request-message
    [request-line][repeat headers_message]
    [CRLF][opt message_body]
end define
define request-line
    [method][space][request-uri][space]
    [http-version][CRLF]
end define
```

Fig. 2. The partial low level HTTP protocol

```
Include "http.grm"
redefine entity_header
    ...
    | [SOAPAction]
end redefine
define SOAPAction
    [soap_uri][soap_message]
end define
define soap_message
    [xml_declaration][open_soap_envelope]
    [soap_header] [soap_body][close_soap_envelope]
end define
```

Fig. 3. The middle level XML SOAP protocol specification

4.1 Syntax Specification

The protocol specification is created based on the syntax specification of the protocol. We use the TXL [6] language to specify the syntax of the protocols. Figure 2 shows a partial grammar for the HTTP protocol. The non-terminal `program` specifies the goal symbol of the grammar. Square brackets are used to indicate the use of another non-terminal, the keyword `repeat` indicates multiple instances of a non-terminal and the keyword `opt` indicates that an element is optional. So in the figure, a `request_message` consists of a `request_line`, followed by multiple `headers_message`, a `CRLF` and an optional `message_body`.

Middle level protocols are specified by extending the lower level protocols. For example in Figure 3, the SOAP protocol is defined by first including the HTTP grammar (the `include` statement) and then extending the entity_header non-terminal (the `redefine` statement). The `entity_header` non-terminal was previously defined in the HTTP grammar.

4.2 Grammar Markup

The syntax of the protocol is extended using XML markup to specify constraints. In the SST framework, the meaning of these constraints is open ended, as they are simply markers to signal the location where the mutators should operate on the messages. SST also supports the specification of linked tags. That is, a markup tag that can be used to specify a relationship between two separate elements of a message.

The grammar is used to place the markup tags at the appropriate locations in the captured messages. To specify the use of markup, the tester places the XML tags in the grammar surrounding the grammar elements that represent the sections of the message that the tester wishes to mutate. Figure 4 shows an example. In this example, the request-line definition has been marked with both the `enumeratedLiteral` and `caseSensitive` tags. These indicate that the method of the request line is one

```
define request_line
    <enumeratedLiteral>< caseSensitive >[method]</ caseSensitive ></enumeratedLiteral>
        [space] [request_uri] [space] [http_version] [CRLF]
end define
```

Fig. 4. Markup tags in the protocol grammar

of a limited set of literal values, and is case sensitive. When multiple tags are used, they must be properly nested. From the grammar, SST generates a program that inserts the markup into the appropriate place in the captured messages.

Figure 5 shows a snippet of the result of running the generated insert markup program against a captured HTTP post request message. The request line has been wrapped in the figure, but in the marked up message, it is a single line. As can be seen from the figure, the XML markup has been inserted surrounding the literal POST which is matched by the `method` non-terminal.

Figure 6 shows an example of a relationship tag. Relationship tags are identified by presence of the `id` and `root` attributes. In this case all of the markups with the same tag name are considered related to each other in some way. In this particular case we are indicating that the value given in the `Content-Length` mime header gives the length of the message body. Unlike the similar constraint in Protocol Tester, this tag is not used as part of the parsing process, but used to indicate the relationship so that the length mutator may make appropriate changes. Since the grammar may match more than one instance in a given message, the `id` attribute is used to identify each instance that was recognized. The % character is replaced with a unique integer as each instance is matched. The root attribute of the tag identifies the root non-terminal in which multiple instances of the tag are considered the same. The markup program starts by identifying each instance of the non-terminal given by the root attribute and assigns each instance of the tag within that non-termial the same id.

Figure 7 shows the instantiation of the length tag from figure 6 in a captured message. The length tag with the length role has been added to the `Content-Length` header, while the length tag with the `value` role has been added to the message

```
<enumeratedLiteral><caseSensitive>POST</caseSensitive></enumeratedLiteral>/return.asp HTTP/1.1
Host: 192.168.1.105
...
```

Fig. 5. Nested Markups on the method POST

```
define Content_Length
    'Content-Length : [space] <length id="%" root="request_message" role="length"> [number]
        </length>'
end define
define message_body
    <length id="%" root="request_message" role="value">
    [repeat token_or_key]
    </length>
end define
```

Fig. 6. Length linked tag in the grammar

```
...
Content-Length: <length id="1" root="request_message" role="length">48</length>
...
<length id="1" root="request_message" role="value">FirstName=John&LastName=Smith&DOB=10%2F15%2F1980</length>
```

Fig. 7. Length linked tag in captured message

body. There is no limit to the number of roles for a markup tag that can be specified, all will be inserted into the captured message by the generated markup program.

4.3 Markup Tags

As mentioned in the last section, each markup is implemented by its own mutator. The generated insert markup engine simply moves the markup from the grammar to appropriate parts of the captured messages. Thus the set of mutator tags is entirely open ended. We demonstrate the framework with an initial set of markup tags and mutators that illustrate the different purposes they serve and the types of mutators that can be created.

Table 1 shows these initial markup tags for which mutators have been created. The first of these, the enumeratedLiteral tag illustrates a tag in which the mutator is generated from the grammar specification. It is used to indicate that the purpose of the non-terminal is to generate one of a list of literal values. While this can be inferred from an analysis of the grammar, the use of the tag allows the tester to indicate which of these non-terminals should be tested. A separate program analyzes the grammar, and for each instance of the enumeratedLiteral tag, genererates a mutator that will alternate the values based on the values given in the grammar. In the example in Figure 4, the method non-terminal was marked with this tag. The method non-terminal recognizes the set of HTTP methods: GET, POST, OPTIONS, HEAD, PUT, DELETE, TRACE and CONNECT. The generated mutator will modify the method in the message shown in figure 5 from POST to each of the other alternatives. Similar mutators can be generated based on common syntax vulnerabilities such as missing termination tags.

Table 1. The categorization of markup tags

Types	Tags	Purpose
Syntactic	enumeratedLiteral	Change to another terminal provided from grammar to alter the original semantics
Lexical	caseSensitive	Change the terminal letters from upper case to lower case or vice
	charSpecific	Change the terminal character
	dateSpecific	Change the terminal date format
	syntaxSpecific	Alter the terminal characters
	valueLimitation	Change the terminal value to common boundary values
	stringSpecific	Replace a string values with common alternate strings
Relational	length	Indicates that the number marked by the length role gives the number of characters in the value role.
Custom	jpeg	The content identified by the tag is an embedded jpeg image (e.g. file upload).

Lexical tags are used when the lexical constraints are stricter than the lexical tokens used in the grammar, or we want to substitute particular values for the tokens. Our initial set of tags deals with changes to the case of the token, changes to individual characters (for example, substituting "," and ":" for "." in the HTTP version of the request line), deletion of arbitrary literals such as mime headers, and changing values of integers and strings. The current mutators for integer and string values targets buffer overflows, but other mutations are easily introduced.

We have only implemented one relationship tag, the length tag, but another candidate tag is a mime type tag that links the Content-type header to the message body allowing mutators to recognize specific content types for mutation. We have implemented one custom tag that is inserted when embedded jpeg images are recognized (image gallery web applications, for example). In this case, the mutator extracts the embedded jpeg image, invokes an external binary mutator and then inserts the resulting mutated images back into the request messages.

The markup can be specified by the tester in one of two ways, it can be manually inserted directly into the protocol grammar, or alternatively, it can be specified separately from the grammar. Fig 8 shows the use of the Grammar Merge Program that merges a markup specification into a Generalized Protocol Grammar. The markup specification contains alternate versions of grammar definitions from the generalized grammar that includes the markups. It may also contain additional definitions that are used in the alternate grammar definitions. Fig 9 shows an example of such a file. The example shows a definition of http_version that parses the version number as two numbers separated by a period, and the period has been annotated with the charSpecific tag. The original definition of http_version, might use a single floating point number. Thus this approach allows us to write a more general protocol

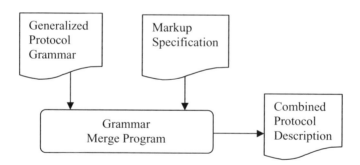

Fig. 8. Merging a markup specification into a generalized protocol grammar

```
define http_version
    HTTP / [number] <charSpecific> [period] </charSpecific> [number]
end define

define period
    `.`
end define
```

Fig. 9. A markup specification file

define http_version
   [**repeat** not_CRLF_Token_or_Key]
end define

define Token_or_Key
   [token] | [key]
end define

define not_CRLF_Token_or_Key
   [**not** CRLF] [Token_or_Key]
end define

Fig. 10. Generalized grammar

grammar and then specialize it for alternate testing strategies. In particular, when crafting a grammar for a new protocol, we could use agile parsing techniques [8] such as robust parsing and island grammars to adopt a minimal grammar specification and then extend each part of the grammar in separate markup files to be tested independently. Figure 10 shows an example of such an approach for the http_version non-terminal. In this variation, the http version is any sequence of tokens or keywords that is not a carriage return followed by a linefeed. The not keyword in TXL means that the particular non-terminal cannot be parsed at this point in the input.

This approach has several advantages. First there is no need to implement the grammar for the entire protocol, only the portions which are to be tested. Second, if the generalized grammar is written exactly to the protocol specification, parts may be difficult to mark. Thus the markup specification can provide alternate parses making the markup tag placement easier. It also allows several testers to operate in parallel, each using separate markup specifications on different parts of the generalized grammar. Lastly, it is difficult to get a generalized grammar that will be suitable for all testing. The markup specification can modify the grammar appropriately for each test.

Figure 11 shows the process diagram of this portion of SST. The combined protocol description is used to generate an insert markup program. The insert markup program in turn is used to parse and insert markup into each of the captured messages. The marked messages are then passed to mutators which run independently to produce the test cases.

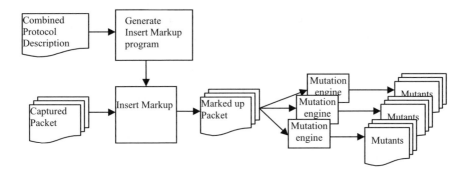

Fig. 11. Markup and mutate process

5 Replay and Oracle

The replay module consists of four components, an injector, a transporter, a realtime update module and a decoder. The process flow of this component is shown in Fig 12.

The injector is the primary component responsible for overall control of the replay process. It fetches each of the mutants from the test suite, and uses the transporter to send the test case to the server. The transporter is responsible for communicating with the server. It handles monitoring the connection for the response, and handling timeouts if the server crashes. The real-time update component is used if the protocol has state dependent elements. For example, some web applications use session cookies, or encode session identifiers into the URLs.

The realtime update component monitors the response messages and modifies the appropriate elements of the request messages. The current real-time update component is protocol independent using a regular expression matching engine to locate the elements in the response and request messages. However the program that generates the configuration file for this component is HTTP specific. In the future, the approach can be made protocol independent by adopting the approach used by Zang et al [26].

The Injector is also responsible for maintaining the state of the database on the test server. If needed, the injector will reinitialize the database, typically restoring it from a snapshot prepared for the test.

The decoder component handles any compression or encoding of the response packets, storing the response sequence in clear text so that the Oracle can compare against the original set of responses.

The current oracle contains two phases addressing this task. The first phase is to check whether the injector has completed each test run. This means all the packets in a test run have been sent to the server. In some situations, the injector will stop the test run after the mutated packet has been sent. This may be because the server is unable to respond to any more requests after receiving the mutated packet. If the test run passes the preliminary check, then the oracle will start a detailed analysis.

A detailed analysis is the second phase and consists of two stages. The first one compares each character of the original response message to the response message received from the mutated request message. If they are identical, it means the response message received from the mutated request message is well-formed. However, if they are not identical, the current oracle cannot make the verdict that the response message received from the mutated request message is well-formed. The oracle will generate the report and the tester needs to analyze this report to make the final decision.

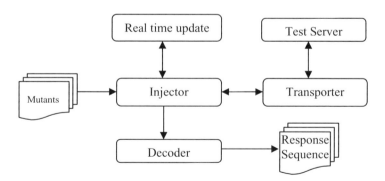

Fig. 12. Replay process structure

6 Experiments

We have tested our approach by conducting two experiments on two separate protocols. The first experiment is designed to show the correctness of the SST framework. The second experiment on the iCalendar protocol demonstrates the protocol independence of SST, and exposes a new vulnerability in the open source application kOrganizer.

6.1 Toy Web Applications

Several toy web applications were constructed that contained vulnerabilities for six tags. These servers were used to validate the functionality of the framework before attempting to find new, unknown errors in other applications. A total of six small tests were conducted to demonstrate six different mutated packets that were sent to the toy server successfully causing a web application, database and/or web server to run with anomalous behavior.

One of the test cases uses the `caseSensitive` tag to change the method of the request message "POST" to "post". In the first test, IIS accepted the request message and stored the posted message to the database. This experiment was retested using the Apache2 server. The mutated message was correctly rejected by the Apache2 server. All of the planted vulnerabilities were discovered by the framework.

6.2 kOrganizer

The second experiment applied the framework to the open source kOrganizer. In this case the capture module was not a modified firefox browser, but iCalendar files generated by kOrganizer and Apple's iCal. Instead of using an injector as the replay component, we use a xmacroplay [25] to script the opening of the mutated iCalendar files (kOrganizer cannot be given an iCalendar file on the command line). The oracle is also simple since we are looking for a catastrophic failure of kOrganizer (i.e. kOrganizer crashes). Thus our test is a script that copies each mutated iCalendar file to a specified directory, opens a new instance of kOrganizer and runs an xmacroplay script to instruct kOrganizer to open the file and exit. If the exit status is abnormal, or the kOrganizer process is still running (i.e. it has deadlocked), then an error is reported. The test case is then manually inspected to determine if the failure represents an exploitable vulnerability. There was an inherent inefficiency as xmacroplay must include multiple worst case delays to ensure that the appropriate dialog box has been rendered by kOrganizer before a mouse or keyboard event is sent.

In this experiment, the caseSensitive, charSpecific, dateSpecific, syntaxSpecific, valueLimitation, and the stringSpecific tags were used to generate a total of 1026 test cases from a single iCalendar file. The total running time was 244188 seconds (67.83 hours). Table 2 and Table 3 show the experimental setup information and testing data, respectively. Of the 1026 test cases, one error was logged (test case 559). This test case was one of those generated by the stringSpecific mutator to insert multiple string values. This particular case changed the description field to a 16 Megabyte string, causing a segmentation violation (SIGSEGV). Examining the code revealed that the vulnerability was actually in the Qt interface library used to build KDE applications.

Table 2. The Second experimental setup information

Computer	Operating system	Memory	kOrganizer
AMD3300+	Ubuntu 8.10	512M	4.1.4

Table 3. The data of the experiment two

Create 1026 Mutants	9.069s
Remove tags	45.742s
Test driver runtime	244188s
Total	244242.811s

7 Related Work

There are many security flaws that can be found in literature about web applications security testing. These flaws are created by violating the fundamental of CIA security requirements. CIA stands for confidentiality, integrity, and availability. Confidentiality holds when only authorized users have the ability to access data. Integrity ensures data cannot be altered by an unauthorized user. Availability requires that data should always be available to legitimate users.

If the CIA security requirements of web application are not met, multiple consequences can result. First, it is possible to cause the web application, database, and/or web server to crash. Second, users' data and/or system information can be stolen and/or modified. Third, computer resources can be wasted by illegal users. Table 4 shows different kinds of security flaws caused by breaking CIA security requirements. A slight change in the content of the packet by breaking the syntax and/or semantics of the grammar will break the CIA. SST provides markup tags to instruct mutation engines explicitly to perform the changes. For example, stringSpecific tag instructs the mutation engine to replace the original string value with a specially crafted string for SQL injection. If the attack is successful, the information could be altered and/or stolen and compromises the confidentiality (C) and/or integrity (I) of the security requirements.

Table 4. Consequence of CIA security requirements violation

CIA security requirements violation	Security flaws
Confidentiality	Information stolen
Confidentiality	Information alternation
Confidentiality	Privacy violations
Confidentiality	Impersonation
Integrity	Web application crash
Integrity	Web server crash
Integrity	Database crash
Integrity	Information alternation
Availability	Wasting computer resources
Availability	Take over the system

There is a great deal of research on security testing of web application. Much of this research focuses on SQL injection, cross-site scripting and command injection. Some research also provides method to generate guards in the applications from the models. User input strings must be passed through the guards for security checking prior to accessing the database. Jing et al [13] use a non-deterministic finite state machine to mutate packets. However their approach, like our previous research is focused on binary protocols. Text is more flexible and less susceptible to value changes.

Martin et al [15, 16] and Mouelhi et al [18] use mutation techniques to evaluate the quality of test cases to evaluate access control policies. In the papers they define a set of mutation operators for access control policies. One of mutation operators defined by Martin et al is the Change-Rule Effect which will toggle the rule decision from permit to deny or vice versa. Another mutation operator from Mouelhi et al is the Type Changing operator which enumerates the rule types. For example, if there are three types of rules (prohibition, permission, and obligation) and the original rule is the permission, then the two mutants created will be prohibition and obligation. While not a mutation of the code, this approach is still a mutation to the application in order to evaluate test cases. SST uses language mutation techniques to change the data that will be executed to the system to generate test cases.

Aitel's block-based network protocols security testing [2] is the most similar to SST. However, the test cases generation obtained by random fuzzing variables only breaks the syntactic constraint of the protocol grammar. SST, in addition to generating random fuzzing values, also provides different types of markup tags to violate syntactic and semantic of the protocol grammar. For example, relational type markup tags break the semantics relationship between terminals.

Jurjens et al and Wimmel et al [14, 24] use the relational calculus and automata to formal model the system's required security requirements. Their security testing only can test application level security. SST not only can test application level security, but also low level and middle communication protocol level security.

Halfond et al [11, 12] propose a combination of static and dynamic analysis for SQL injection protection of web application. For the static part, they build models based on static analysis of the source code that contains all of the possible legitimate SQL queries in a PHP application. Test cases generation is accomplished by injecting additional SQL statements into a query to intentionally violate the model. The dynamic analysis incorporates the comparison of runtime queries with the static model. If the dynamic query violates the model, execution is halted and noted.

Merlo et al [17] use dynamic analysis of legitimate test cases and security scenarios to build static models corresponding to the call site. A query invocation at the call site will be compared to the corresponding model to check whether or not it is a legitimate query. Both approaches focus on SQL injection, and do not address cross-site scripting or command injection. The approach of Merlo et al has the advantage of not relying on the source code and thus is capable of testing SQL-injection by malicious code. Their method can be reused for other languages but an execution environment with appropriate instrumentation is required.

The main contribution of our approach is that it is protocol independent, and can be used to test most text based protocols. The other contribution is that we can easily generate tests for multiple vulnerabilities such as cross-site script injection and command injection. In addition our approach requires only the specification of the protocol and direct access to the database to detect modification of the application data.

8 Conclusion and Future Work

SST is a lightweight framework for generating security and robustness test cases for text based network applications. The protocol is easily expanded by adding markup tags and the mutators to implement each of the tags. We have demonstrated the framework by expressing and testing two applications, each of which uses a different protocol.

There are several ways in which the system can be extended. The first is to add more markup tags and more mutators. There is a lot of inherent flexibility in the system. The current mutators only use attributes in the markup for the relationship type of tag. The only attributes that have special meaning are the id, root and role attributes. Other attributes can be used to pass parameters to the mutators such as range of numeric values or expected maximum lengths for strings. In addition mutators need not only use single tag types, but may perform mutations on multiple tags simultaneously.

The second avenue of exploration is more syntactic dependent mutators. The only one implemented in the SST prototype was enumeratedLiteral. One extension is to identify and insert markup for non-terminals that implement this role by analyzing the grammar. Other grammar based markup can also be added, such as changing the order of or deleting elements of the captured messages.

We have already extended SST to handle higher level application protocols that are built on top of the lower level protocols such as HTTP and SOAP. This involves a domain specific language to automatically generate recognizers to identify messages that are syntactically similar but semantically different, such as the difference between a login request and a list shopping cart request. This allows the grammar to be refined using agile parsing techniques and the tester to insert markup tailored to the semantics of the message such as mutating user names and passwords in login requests.

References

1. AboElFotoh, M., Dean, T.R., Mayor, R.: An Empirical Study of a Language Based Security Testing Technique. In: Proc. 19th IBM Centres for Advanced Studies Conference, Toronto, Canada, pp. 112–121 (November 2009)
2. Aitel, D.: The Advantages of Block-Based Protocol Analysis for Security Testing, http://citeseerx.ist.psu.edu/viewdoc/download?doi=10.1.1.116.1178&rep=rep1&type=pdf (Last accessed, 2010)
3. Beizer, B.: Software testing techniques. Van Nostrand Reinhold Company, New York (1990) ISBN: 0-442-24592-0
4. Borenstein, N., Freed, N.: MIME Part One: Format of Internet Message Bodies. Internet RFC 2045 (1996)
5. Bray, T., Paoli, J., Sperberg-McQueen, C.M., Maler, E., Yergeau, F.: Extensible Markup Language (XML) 1.0 (Fifth Edition). W3C (2008)
6. Cordy, J.R.: The TXL Source Transformation Language. Science of Computer Programming 61(3), 190–210 (2006)
7. Dawson, F., Stenerson, D.: Internet Calendaring and Scheduling Core Object Specification (iCalendar). Lotus, Microsoft, IETF RFC 2445 (1998)
8. Dean, T.R., Cordy, J.R., Malton, A.J., Schneider, K.A.: Agile Parsing in TXL. Journal of Automated Software Engineering, 311–336 (2003)

9. Fielding, R., Irvine, U.C., Gettys, J., Mogul, J., Frystyk, H., Masinter, L., Leach, P., Berners-Lee, T.: Hypertext Transfer Protocol - HTTP/1.1. Compaq/W3C, Compaq, W3C/MIT, Xerox, Microsoft, W3C/MIT, IETF RFC 2616 (1999)
10. Gudgin, M., Hadley, M., Mendelsohn, N., Moreau, J., Frystyk, H., Karmarkar, A., Lafon, Y.: SOAP Version 1.2 Part 1: Messaging Framework (Second Edition). W3C Recommendation (2007)
11. Halfond, W.G.J., Orso, A.: AMNESIA: Analysis and Monitoring for NEutralizing SQL-Injection Attacks. In: Proceedings of the 20th IEEE/ACM International Conference on Automated Software engineering (ASE 2005), pp. 174–183 (2005)
12. Halfond, W.G.J., Orso, A.: Combining static analysis and runtime monitoring to counter SQL-injection attacks. In: Proceedings of the 3rd International ICSE Workshop on Dynamic Analysis (WODA), pp. 105–110. IEEE Computer Society Press, Los Alamitos (2005)
13. Jing, C., Wang, Z., Shi, X., Yin, X., Wu, J.: Mutation Testing of Protocol Messages Based on Extended TTCN-3. In: Proceedings of the 22nd International Conference on Advanced Information Networking and Applications, pp. 667–674 (2008)
14. Jurjens, J., Wimmel, G.: Formally Testing Fail-safety of Electronic Purse Protocols. In: Automated Software Engineering, pp. 408–411. IEEE Computer Society, Los Alamitos (2001)
15. Martin, E., Xie, T.: A fault model and mutation testing of access control policies. In: Proceedings of the 16th International Conference on World Wide Web (WWW 2007), Security, Privacy, Reliability, and Ethics Track, Banff, Alberta, Canada, pp. 667–676 (May 2007)
16. Martin, E., Xie, T., Yu, T.: Defining and measuring policy coverage in testing access control policies. In: Ning, P., Qing, S., Li, N. (eds.) ICICS 2006. LNCS, vol. 4307, pp. 139–158. Springer, Heidelberg (2006)
17. Merlo, E., Letarte, D., Antoniol, G.: Automated Protection of PHP Applications Against SQL-injection Attacks. In: Proceedings of the 11th European Conference on Software Maintenance and Reengineering, pp. 191–202 (2007)
18. Mouelhi, T., Le Traon, Y., Baudry, B.: Mutation analysis for security test qualification. In: Proceedings of the Testing: Academic and Industrial Conference Practice and Research Techniques, pp. 233–242 (2007)
19. Moy, J.: OSPF Version 2. Internet RFC 2328 (1998)
20. OWASP: The Open Web Application Security Project, http://www.owasp.org/ (Last accessed: 2009)
21. Tal, O., Knight, S., Dean, T.R.: Syntax-based Vulnerabilities Testing of Frame-based Network Protocols. In: Proceedings of the Second Annual Conference on Privacy, Security and Trust (2004)
22. Turcotte, Y., Oded, T., Knight, S., Dean, T.R.: Security Vulnerabilities Assessment of the X.509 Protocol by Syntax-Based Testing. In: Proceedings of MILCOM 2004 on Military Communications Conference, pp. 1572–1578 (2004)
23. WASC Projects. Web Application Security Consortium, Threat Classification, http://projects.webappsec.org/Threat-Classification (Last accessed 2008)
24. Wimmel, G., Jurjens, J.: Specification-based Test Generation for Security-Critical Systems Using Mutations. In: George, C.W., Miao, H. (eds.) ICFEM 2002. LNCS, vol. 2495, pp. 471–482. Springer, Heidelberg (2002)
25. Xmacro, http://xmacro.sourceforge.net/ (Last accessed April 29, 2010)
26. Zhang, S., Dean, T.R., Knight, G.S.: Lightweight State Based Mutation Testing for Security. In: Proc. TAICPART-MUTATION 2007, Windsor, UK, pp. 223–232 (2007)

An Open-Source Tool for Automated Generation of Black-Box xUnit Test Code and Its Industrial Evaluation

Christian Wiederseiner[1], Shahnewaz A. Jolly[1], Vahid Garousi[1], and Matt M. Eskandar[2]

[1] Software Quality Engineering Research Group (SoftQual), University of Calgary, Canada
[2] MR Control Systems International Inc., Calgary, Canada
{christian.wiederseiner,sajolly,vgarousi}@ucalgary.ca,
matt.eskandar@mrcsi.com

Abstract. The body of knowledge in the area of black-box unit testing is quite well established, e.g., the concepts of category partitioning, boundary value analysis, and pair-wise testing. However, tool support to apply the existing techniques in large-scale industrial software projects is fairly limited. Although tools such as HexaWise enable testers in automatic generation of all-combination pair-wise test input data, nevertheless converting them to actual test case source code (e.g., in NUnit) is both very tedious and also error prone. To address the above challenge, we have developed an open-source tool, referred to as AutoBBUT, for automated generation of black-box NUnit test cases for the C# .Net platform. Evaluation of the tool in an industrial setting by using it to automatically generate more than 1,962 NUnit test cases (having 15,906 test line of code) in NUnit shows the effectiveness of the tool in saving testers a lot of time and also preventing unwanted defects and/or test *smells* in test code, which can occur due to manual test code development.

Keywords: Open-source tool, automated test code generation, black-box unit testing, Microsoft Visual Studio team test, industrial evaluation, SCADA.

1 Introduction

Software testing is an integral, costly, and time-consuming activity in the software development life cycle. Black-box Unit Testing (BBUT) focuses on testing the functionality of a System Under Test (SUT)'s individual components or units without using knowledge from their source code to ensure that they behave properly and satisfy their defined specification [1].

A key idea of unit testing is that each functional unit needs its own test cases. However, generating test code for each unit under test (UUT) manually is very expensive, especially when there are many possible test cases. Automatic test data generation is essential to support unit testing and as unit testing is achieving more attention, there is a tremendous need to use automated unit test data generation tools more often.

The body of knowledge in the area of BBUT is fairly well established, e.g., the concepts of category partition method, boundary value analysis [1], and n-way testing [2] (e.g., pair-wise testing [3]). However, tool support to apply the existing BBUT techniques in large-scale industrial software projects is quite limited.

There are existing tools to generate pair-wise BBUT test case input data, such as: HexaWise [4] and CTS (Combinatorial Test Services) from IBM [5]. Although such tools help testers in automatic generation of all-combination n-way BBUT test input data, however converting them to actual test case source code (e.g., in JUnit or NUnit [6]) and "writing unit tests can be a tedious and error prone process" [7].

For example, in recent academic-industry software testing collaboration among the authors of this paper, we wanted to apply BBUT to develop NUnit test code to adequately test 89 function blocks (i.e., units) of a commercial large-scale Supervisory Control and Data Acquisition (SCADA) software system (more details in Section 4). In this SUT, there are simple function blocks such as Add and Multiply and also more complex units such as: Send Email, and Generate PDF Reports.

We applied category partition testing, boundary value analysis [1], and pair-wise testing [3] to generate test cases for each unit in this SUT. For example, if one wants to apply category partitioning and boundary value analysis to an input variable of type *Int32* for a SUT unit developed in .Net, one would get at least 7 category partitions (depicted in Figure 1).

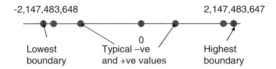

Fig. 1. Category partitioning and boundary value analysis of an input of type Int32 in .Net

If we consider three inputs to the Add functional unit in the above SUT, if we apply strong (multi-dimensional) category partitioning [1] (without pair-wise testing), we would get 7^3= 343 test cases. Let us assume that automating each of these test cases in NUnit, for example, would require at least 4 Test Lines of Code (TLOC), i.e., one line respectively for each of the xUnit popular phases: setup, exercise, verify and tear-down [8]. This would result in 343*4=1,372 TLOC. Even if one uses n-way testing [2] to reduce the number of test cases (e.g., pair-wise testing in the above case), one would get 58 test cases, or 58*4=232 TLOC. Developing that amount of TLOC can be both tedious and error prone (i.e., it is a tester's nightmare to have defects in test code).

Further note that the Add functional unit in our case study SUT is flexible in the number of its inputs, i.e., it can take 2 or more inputs and is supposed to add all of them while correctly triggering overflow and other exceptions. It is easy to imagine how large the test code-base can get in such a complex SUT, especially for functional units such as Send Email with over 7 input variables (e.g., *from_email, to_email, subject, smpt_server, port_number*, etc.).

For instance, we started developing unit test case codes for our SUT in the Visual Studio Team Test environment (a built-in feature in the Microsoft Visual Studio similar to the NUnit framework). Even with the good skill set of our test developers, we soon came to the conclusion that an automated or even a semi-automated tool should be developed to help testers in generating BBUT test code in xUnit frameworks [6].

To address the above goal, we have developed an open-source tool, referred to as *AutoBBUT* [9], for automated generation of BBUT test cases in the .Net C# language for the Visual Studio Team Test platform. The current paper is a *tool* paper describing the above tool. Note that we have made the tool available to practitioner software testers and researchers as open-source on the Google Code [9].

The rest of this article is structured as follows. We discuss in Section 2 the related tools and then motivate the need for the proposed tool. Section 3 presents the AutoB-BUT tool, example usages, and its development details. Evaluation of the tool in an industrial setting is presented in Section 4. Finally, Section 5 concludes the article and discusses the future work.

2 Related Tools and Need for the Proposed Tool

There are several frameworks and tools which enables (semi-) automated generation of unit test code, e.g., Microsoft Pex [10], and JML-JUnit tool [11], JUB (JUnit test case Builder) [12], TestGen4J [13], JCrasher [14], and NModel [15].

Microsoft Pex [10] is a Visual Studio add-in for testing .Net Framework applications. It automatically generates white-box test cases directly from the Visual Studio code editor environment. Using "symbolic code execution", Pex finds input-output values of object-oriented methods, and can potentially produce test suites to achieve high code coverage. Since it uses source code to generate test cases, it cannot be used for BBUT. This tool generates test suites with high block coverage [16] which is not an effective strategy to be followed for test cases. Furthermore, the tool does not seem to scale up when we used it to generate test cases for a sub-system of our industrial partner's .Net-based tool (as discussed above). Microsoft Pex was not able to generate meaningful test cases in this case.

JML-JUnit tool [11] is a tool which uses design-by-contract-based notations specified in methods source code, e.g., pre- and post-conditions, to generate JUnit test code. It requires the contractual information to be specified using the Java Modeling Language (JML) [17]. This tool takes a set of values of each parameter of each method as well as a set of object instances (as receivers of the method call) from the user. Then, the tool executes the test cases for every possible combination of receiver objects, method and parameters [18]. However, in a study, Tan and Edwards have noticed that test cases created by this tool are not that effective in fault detection in terms of mutation score [18].

JUB (JUnit test case Builder) [12] is another automated test code generation tool with white-box test generation support. JUB takes into account object-oriented constructs such as multiple constructors and overloaded methods. It places correct method signatures and exception testing / handling code into test methods source code. It also allows generation of test code for protected and default methods. This tool only generates test cases having 0 for integers and null for other types of input variables [19]. Thus, the tool is not useful in generating effective test cases for our purpose.

TestGen4J [13] automatically generates test cases from Java source or class (compiled) files. Its primary focus is to exercise boundary value testing of the arguments passed to the method. It uses a rules engine, with a user-configurable XML file that defines boundary conditions for the data types.

JCrasher [14] is an automatic robustness testing tool for Java code. JCrasher examines the type information of a set of Java classes and constructs code fragments and creates instances of different types to test the behavior of public methods with random data. JCrasher attempts to detect defects by causing the program under test to "crash", i.e., to throw an unhandled runtime exception.

NModel [15] is a model-based testing and analysis framework similar to the JML-JUnit tool. This framework contains a library for writing model-based programs in C# using a visualization and analysis tool called Model Program Viewer (MPV). A test generation tool called Offline Test Generator (otg), and a test runner tool called Conformance Tester (ct) are also part of the framework. In order to use this technology, the testers should write the model program in C# that references the NModel library. Then, to make sure that the model program functions according to the requirement and to detect the design defects, mpv tool can be used to visualize and analyze the behavior of the model program. Afterward, it is required to write a test harness in C# for executing the tests using the test runner tool ct. Finally, test generator otg can be used to create the tests from the model program in advance or else, ct can be used to generate the test cases on the fly from the model program as the test run executes. If it is required, the testers can write a custom strategy that ct uses in order to maximize test coverage according to defined criteria [20].

We can classify the above tools and our proposed AutoBBUT tool into either white-box (WBUT) or black-box unit testing (BBUT) tools as follows:

- WBUT: Microsoft Pex [10], JML-JUnit [11], JUB [12], and JCrasher [14]
- BBUT: TestGen4J [13], NModel [15], AutoBBUT (this tool) [9]

Since only TestGen4J and NModel closely relate to our proposed AutoBBUT tool in terms of application context (both being BBUT tools) and objective, we compare the three tools more closely next. While TestGen4J is able to apply boundary value testing [1] in a black-box fashion and NModel can generate test cases according to the written model program [20], our tool can additionally apply category partition testing and pair-wise testing [3] as well as we do not need to write model program to define the test case strategy. Furthermore, AutoBBUT has a GUI interface which can increase its usability compared to command line interface of TestGen4J. Also, as we discuss in Section 3, AutoBBUT has automated test oracle support, and its simpler design would make it easily extensible and adaptable to other platforms (e.g., JUnit) and SUTs by other testers.

On a related topic, Wang and Offutt have conducted a recent interesting study [19] to compare three of the above unit-level automated test code generation tools (JCrasher, TestGen4j, and JUB). They applied mutation testing (by using the MuJava tool) to generate traditional (method level) and also object-oriented mutants, and assess the fault detection effectiveness (mutation score) of the test suites generated by the above tools. The study concludes that these tools generate test cases that are very poor at detecting faults. The authors viewed this as a *"depressing* comment" on the state of practice. As users expectations for reliable software continue to grow, and as agile processes and test driven development continue to gain acceptance throughout the industry, unit testing is becoming increasingly important. Wang, Offutt and also we believe that unfortunately, software developers have few choices in high quality test data generation tools.

3 AutoBBUT Tool

The AutoBBUT tool is presented in this section. We present the tools GUI, its features, an example usage of the tool, and its development details.

It should be noted again that the tool is now available to practitioner software testers and researchers as open-source on the Google Code [9]. To help other practitioner and researchers to use, extend and/or adapt our tool to other platforms (e.g., JUnit) and SUTs, we also discuss next the design, and extensibility aspects of this tool.

3.1 GUI and Features

Three snapshots from the Graphical User Interface (GUI) of AutoBBUT are provided in Figure 2. Essentially, the tool takes the list of input variables for a UUT (UUT) and the list of its output variables (under the two GUI tabs, as shown).

Two input parameters (called *A* and *B*) of an Add function block (UUT) of our case study system is shown in Figure 2. In the "output" tab, the tester enters the list of UUT's output parameters along with their types. Some of the features of this tool to support and accelerate the generation of unit test code are as follows.

Automated generation of test input values: Once the user (tester) enters an input type (e.g., parameter *A* of type *Int8* bits), the tool automatically generates test data values for that parameter based on the seven category partitions shown in Figure 1. The boundary values for each data type are constant however the *typical* positive and negative number are generated randomly while being in the valid range of values (e.g., [-128, 127] for the *Int8* bit data type). As per our observations, this saves testers a lot of time by preventing them from having to manually enter these category partitions values and is less error prone. The tester has the flexibility to change the values if s/he desires to.

Support for n-way testing [2]: n-way testing is a widely accepted test technique in which the test space of a SUT is reduced from all combinations of all inputs parameters to combinations of only *n* inputs parameters. For example, when n=2, n-way testing is called pair-wise testing [3]. For the input value *n* for n-way testing, when '0' is chosen in AutoBBUT, the tool generates all combinations of all inputs parameters (i.e., does not apply n-way testing). If n=2, pair-wise (2-way) testing is applied, and so on.

Support for automated test oracle generation: In the "output" tab, the tester has the option of entering test oracle formula to enable automated generation of test oracle (expected outputs). Note that this feature is only available for rather simple mathematical and logic function blocks under test currently. Two examples of oracles for an Absolute and also a Power function block are shown in Figure 2. Technical details of how this test oracle is implemented are provided in Section 3.3.

3.2 Example Usage

One of the 89 function blocks (i.e., units) of the SUT reported in Section IV is the Power function block. The schematic and example usage of this unit is shown in Figure 2. Part of the test suite code generated by AutoBBUT for this unit is shown Figure 3.

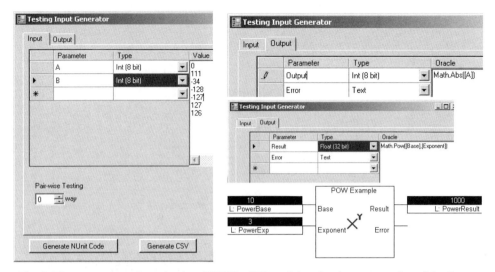

Fig. 2. Three snapshots from the AutoBBUT's GUI, and the visual representation of the Power function block (an example UUT)

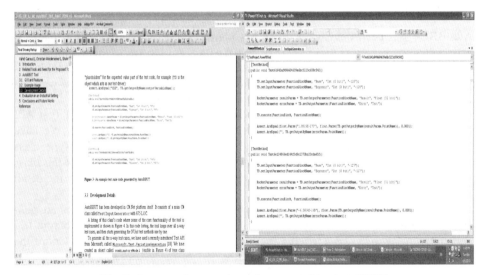

Fig. 3. An example test suite code generated by AutoBBUT

The code syntax is based on the C#'s built-in unit testing framework (very similar to NUnit). Since the test oracle shown in the bottom of Figure 2 is entered for this UUT, AutoBBUT automatically generates all the test source code in this case. This can be a major help for testers in similar cases when the number of test cases is too large. For units under test for which a test oracle is not specified, the tool generates "placeholders" for the expected value part of the test code, for example (TD is the object which acts as our test driver):

```
Assert.AreEqual("XXX", TD.getOutputByName(outputVariableName));
```

Fig. 4. A screenshot of the AutoBBUT source code

3.3 Development Details

AutoBBUT has been developed in C#.Net platform itself. It consists of a main C# class called xUnitTestSuiteGenerator with 875 LOC (as of this writing).

A listing of this class's code where some of the core functionality of the tool is implemented is shown in Figure 4. In this code listing, the tool loops over all n-way test cases, and then starts generating the NUnit test methods one by one.

To generate all the n-way test cases, we have used a recently introduced Test API from Microsoft, called Microsoft.Test.VariationGeneration [21]. We have created an object called combinatoryModel (visible in Figure 4) of type class Model defined in this API. Once the method GenerateVariations of this class is called, the list of all combinatorial test cases is returned (refer to [21] for detail usage scenarios and examples).

Afterwards, test method signatures (starting with public void Test) are generated. The input parameters of the UUT are then fed one by one to the output test code (starting with TD.setInputParameter). The list of output parameters of the UUT is then written to the output test code file.

For the development of automated test oracle generation, we have used a utility available in the .NET framework class library, called System.CodeDom.Compiler. According to the Microsoft MSDN [22]: *"The Compiler namespace contains types for managing the generation and compilation of source code in supported programming languages"*. The test oracle specifications as entered by the tester inside the "Oracle" textbox under the "Output" tab (as shown in Figure 2) are executed at runtime by this library and the expected results are automatically generated. They are then inserted in the output NUnit test code. To do this, we instantiate an object of class Microsoft.CSharp.CSharpCodeProvider defined in this library which let us execute C# code (test oracles in this case) at runtime.

An Open-Source Tool for Automated Generation of Black-Box xUnit Test Code   125

For space constraints, the reader is referred to the online source code repository of our tool [9] for more details on design and development of AutoBBUT tool. AutoBBUT has been designed to be easy to use, extend and adapt by other testers to other platforms (e.g., JUnit) and other SUTs. A lot of effort has been spent to have a clean design for it which makes it easily extensible and adaptable to other platforms (e.g., JUnit) and SUTs by other testers.

4 Evaluation in an Industrial Setting

The authors have been involved in an industry-academia software testing R&D collaboration in which the System Under Test (SUT) is a commercial large-scale Supervisory Control and Data Acquisition (SCADA) software system. The system is called *Rocket Monitoring and Control* and is developed by MR Control Systems International Inc. (www.mrcsi.com), a Canadian control software development firm, founded and led by the last author. The system is developed using Microsoft Visual Studio C#. As discussed in Section 1, the project was actually the main motivation behind developing the AutoBBUT tool.

The *Rocket* SCADA system has a tool called *Automation Engine*, which is an IDE for developing advanced control systems. This tool supports 89 function blocks grouped under 12 categories (see Figure 5), e.g., Math, Logic, and Control. Two example function blocks with example input/output values are shown in Figure 6. For example, the Add function block adds two or more input values and calculates the *Sum* result. The input can be any integer or floating point value, or a text. In the example shown, three integer values (variables pre-fixed with *G*) with values of 1, 3, and 5 have been added together and the system has generated an output integer equal to 9.

During a three month period, we developed the AutoBBUT tool and used it to generate 1,962 NUnit test cases for automated black-box unit testing of 58 out of the 89 function blocks in this system. The remainder of the function blocks are still in final stages of development, and we plan to generate automated test cases for them as their production code become ready/stable in the upcoming months. The total size of the NUnit test suite is currently 15,906 test LOC. Since test case code is automatically generated, each test case method is 8±2 LOC (see the example in Figure 3). Unit test codes were inspected after being generated by the AutoBBUT tool and, if an automated oracle was not chosen, manual expected output values were encoded in the

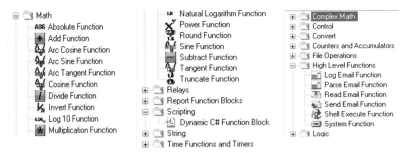

Fig. 5. 89 function blocks grouped under 12 categories are supported in the Automation Engine tool (SUT)

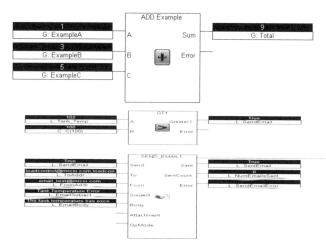

Fig. 6. Two example function blocks in the *Automation Engine* tool

test code. Due to space constraints, we cannot report more examples of NUnit test cases generated by our tool in this article, but many examples can be found in this online URL [23].

For confidentiality reasons, we cannot reveal the pass/fail statistics of our NUnit test suite (1,962 NUnit test cases). However, both the industrial partners and also the research team have been so far very satisfied with the effectiveness of the automated test suite. Since as of this writing, the project developers are still working on the system for the improvement, so after every change, it is required to verify that the system is functioning according to the requirement and the existing test cases can be used for this purpose. If they change the features in such a way that the existing test cases are not useful anymore and new test cases are required, then they can generate a large number of new test cases using this tool within a few minutes.

5 Conclusions and Future Works

AutoBBUT tool has shown so far, in our project, to be very effective and efficient in automated generation of automated test suites which has been useful in revealing the defects of the function blocks and also keeping them as regression test suites for future versions of the SUT. We believe the entire R&D collaboration experience we have had so far has been a true industry-academia success story and we are already expanding our test R&D collaborations to other test techniques, e.g., GUI and performance testing.

As a future work direction, we plan to apply mutation testing and analysis to the test suites generative by our tool to assess their fault detection effectiveness and to compare that effectiveness with those of the test suites generated by other comparable tools (JCrasher, TestGen4j, and JUB). We also plan to compare the effort and time spent in using those tools. Also, the execution time of our tool to automatically generate test case code is very fast, and we plan to compare the associated efficiency to manual coding of xUnit test suites when our tool is used in large-scale projects.

Acknowledgments. This work was supported by the Discovery Grant no. 341511-07 from the Natural Sciences and Engineering Research Council of Canada (NSERC). Vahid Garousi was further supported by the Alberta Ingenuity New Faculty Award no. 200600673.

References

1. Mathur, A.P.: Foundations of Software Testing. Addison-Wesley Professional, Reading (2008)
2. Nie, C., et al.: Automatic Test Generation for n-Way Combinatorial Testing. In: Reussner, R., Mayer, J., Stafford, J.A., Overhage, S., Becker, S., Schroeder, P.J. (eds.) QoSA 2005 and SOQUA 2005. LNCS, vol. 3712, pp. 203–211. Springer, Heidelberg (2005)
3. Tai, K.C., Lie, Y.: A Test Generation Strategy for Pairwise Testing. IEEE Transactions on Software Engineering 28(1), 109–111 (2002)
4. Hunter, J.: HexaWise Tool, http://www.hexawise.com (Last accessed: March 2010)
5. Czerwonka, J.: Pairwise Testing Tools - Combinatorial Test Case Generation, http://www.pairwise.org/tools.asp (Last accessed: March 2010)
6. Hamill, P.: Unit Test Frameworks. O'Reilly, Sebastopol (2004)
7. Tan, R.P., Edwards, S.H.: Experiences Evaluating the Effectiveness of JML-JUnit Testing. In: Special issue on Workshop on Empirical Research in Software Testing, vol. 29(5), pp. 1–4 (2004)
8. Meszaros, G.: Four-Phase Test Pattern, http://www.xunitpatterns.com (Last accessed: March 2010)
9. Wiederseiner, C., Garousi, V., Jolly, S.A.: AutoBBUT - Automated Code Generation for Black-box Unit Testing, http://code.google.com/p/autobbut (Last accessed: April 2010)
10. Tillmann, N., de Halleux, J.: Pex-White Box Test Generation for .NET. In: Conference on Tests and Proofs (2008)
11. Cheon, Y., Kim, M.Y., Perumandla, A.: A Complete Automation of Unit Testing for Java Programs. In: Proc. of Int. Conf. on Software Engineering Research and Experience (2005)
12. JUB (JUnit test case Builder), http://jub.sourceforge.net (Last accessed: March 2010)
13. TestGen4J, http://sourceforge.net/projects/spike-test-gen/ (Last accessed: March 2010)
14. JCrasher, http://code.google.com/p/jcrasher (Last accessed: March 2010)
15. NModel, http://nmodel.codeplex.com (Last accessed: June 2010)
16. Tillmann, N., de Halleux, P.: Code Digging with Pex Code Understanding and Automatic Testing At Your Fingertips. Microsoft Corporation (2008)
17. JML Team, Java Modeling Language, http://www.jmlspecs.org (Last accessed: March 2010)
18. Tan, R.P., Edwards, S.H.: Experiences Evaluating the Effectiveness of JML-JUnit Testing. In: ACM SIGSOFT Software Engineering Notes. ACM, New York (2004)
19. Wang, S., Offutt, J.: Comparison of Unit-Level Automated Test Generation Tools. In: Proc. of IEEE Int. Conf. on Software Testing, Verification, and Validation (2009)
20. Jacky, J., et al.: Model-Based Software Testing and Analysis with C#. Cambridge University Press, Cambridge (2008)

21. Manolov, I.: Introduction to TestApi – Part 4: Combinatorial Variation Generation APIs, http://blogs.msdn.com/ivo_manolov/archive/2009/08/26/9884004.aspx (Last accessed: April 2010)
22. Microsoft MSDN: System. CodeDom.Compiler Namespace, http://msdn.microsoft.com/en-us/library/system.codedom.compiler.aspx (Last accessed: April 2010)
23. Wiederseiner, C., Garousi, V., Jolly, S.A.: Supplementary Project Data-NUnit Test Suite, http://www.softqual.ucalgary.ca/projects/2010/AutoBBUT_TAIC_PART/ (Last accessed: April 2010)

TeCReVis: A Tool for Test Coverage and Test Redundancy Visualization

Negar Koochakzadeh and Vahid Garousi

Software Quality Engineering Research Group (SoftQual)
Department of Electrical and Computer Eng., University of Calgary, Alberta, Canada
{nkoochak,vgarousi}@ucalgary.ca

Abstract. This tool paper presents the feature set, graphical user interface and also the implementation details of a test coverage and test redundancy visualization tool, called *TeCReVis*. The tool is an Eclipse plug-in and supports JUnit test suites helping testers in analyzing the coverage information more effectively in a visual way compared to traditional text-based coverage tools.

Keywords: Test coverage, test visualization, tool development.

1 Introduction

Software testing is the most visible activity in assuring the quality of software systems. Furthermore, maintenance for regression test suites is a critical and costly activity that should be performed in software maintenance. Effective and efficient fault localization, test enhancement and test selection for regression testing are usually challenging for large-scale systems.

Various test adequacy (i.e., coverage) criteria such as statement coverage have been defined in the last few decades to help testers in finding how much (automated) testing has been performed for a System Under Test (SUT). Besides, test results are another source of information that can be used for localizing faults in the system. In large systems with large automated test suites (e.g., in xUnit framework), both the above sources of information are usually huge and very complex to analyze. Thus comprehending such information by human testers in conventional formats (e.g., textual) are very time consuming [13].

To summarize the above types of information and to effectively use them for fault localization and test improvement, several test visualization attempts have been made, e.g., a tool called Tarantula [12]. However, there exists no tool to visually represent coverage information, i.e., which SUT elements (e.g., statements or classes) are covered by which xUnit test methods. Many testing researchers and practitioners believe that visual illustration of test artifacts and test information (such as coverage) would help testers to use and comprehend them effectively [5].

On the other hand, test redundancy detection is an important task in software testing and maintenance. This is because it can reduce test maintenance costs, and also ensure the integrity of test suites. As defined in the software testing literature, a redundant test case is one, which if removed, will not affect the fault detection effectiveness of the test suite [13].

One of the most widely-used approaches for test redundancy detection in the literature is based on coverage information [13]. In a recent previous work [1], we evaluated this approach and the main conclusion was that although coverage-based information can be useful in detecting redundant tests, it may suffer from large number of false-positive errors in some systems, i.e., a test case being identified as redundant while it is really not.

To improve test redundancy detection, we recently proposed a semi-automated tester-assisted methodology to derive a reduced test suite from a given test suite, while keeping the fault detection effectiveness unchanged [3]. The tool implemented in this work is used to create a graph-based illustration of test redundancy information referred as Test Redundancy Graph (TRG). In this tool, visualized redundancy information would be updated along the process in which a human tester can identify a test artifact as redundant.

To the best of our knowledge, there exists no publicly-available tool with the two above features, i.e., visualization of test coverage and test redundancy. Referred to as TeCReVis (Test Coverage and Test Redundancy Visualization), the tool reported in this article is able to automatically create a graph-based illustration of test coverage information referred as Test Coverage Graph (TCG). In this tool, it is possible to change the coverage criteria and the granularity of SUT (e.g., statement, decision, class, or package) and also test artifacts (e.g., test package, class and method in xUnit).

This article is a *tool* paper which describes the feature set and its graphical user interface (Section 2) and also the implementation details (Section 3) of the TeCReVis tool. The tools usage scenarios are presented in Section 4. A summary of similar tools is discussed in Section 5. Finally, conclusions are made in Section 6.

2 TeCReVis' Features and Graphical User Interface

TeCReVis tool is implemented as an Eclipse plug-in by extending an open-source test coverage tool called CodeCover [4]. While our tool supports test suites developed in JUnit, extending it to support other xUnit frameworks (e.g., NUnit) should be relatively easy. By installing this plug-in on Eclipse, it can be used to automatically generate Test Coverage Graphs (TCG) and Test Redundancy Graphs (TRG) of all or subset of the JUnit test suite (details and examples are presented next).

During our discussions with the CodeCover [4] development team, our tool received their attention and TeCReVis was recently adapted by (included in) the CodeCover toolset. The reader can refer to [6] for video demos and further information about TeCReVis and to [4] to download and install it.

2.1 Test Coverage Graph (TCG)

Fig. 1 shows an example TCG created by TeCReVis. Left side and right side of this graph represent test items and SUT items, respectively. Various granularities can be selected for both groups of items (e.g., method, class or package). The edges in the graph are directed edges coming from a test node to a SUT node which is covered by that test artifact. Two numbers on each edge show number of calls and percentage of coverage (according to the selected coverage criterion) of that SUT item by the test artifact.

TeCReVis: A Tool for Test Coverage and Test Redundancy Visualization   131

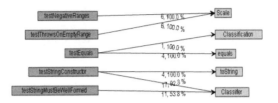

Fig. 1. A TCG created by the TeCReVis tool

To draw the coverage graph in TeCReVis, in the Eclipse environment, the user should select from the *Window* menu, *Show View*, *Other...*, *CodeCover* and then *Coverage Graph*. There are several options for this graph shown in Fig. 2.

Fig. 2. Options in Coverage Graph View of TeCReVis

Option ![] can be used to show/hide the uncovered items and full name of the each node. Option ![] is to change the mode of the graph to move the whole graph or pick and move a specific node. ![] and ![] are to change the granularity of test and SUT respectively. Option ![] can be used to change the coverage criteria.

2.2 Test Redundancy Graph (TRG)

Fig. 3 shows an example TRG created by TeCReVis. Each node in this graph represents a test method. There is an edge from one node to the other when the first node covers some common code artifacts as the second one. The number on each edge represents the ratio of the number of SUT items covered by both test cases to number of SUT items covered by the first test case. At the beginning of the redundancy detection process, redundant candidate tests are shown by yellow nodes (light colors in Fig 3) while others are shown by green (darker colors in Fig. 3). After detecting a test method as redundant by human tester, that test is shown by a red node (darkest colors in Fig. 3) and is not considered in later redundancy calculation.

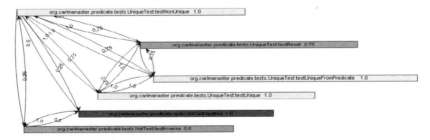

Fig. 3. A TRG created by the TeCReVis tool

To generate TRGs using TeCReVis in the Eclipse environment, the user should select from the *Window* menu, *Show View*, *Other...*, *CodeCover* and then *Redundancy Graph* . There are several options for this graph shown in Fig. 4.

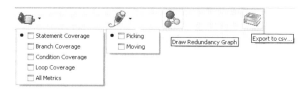

Fig. 4. Options in Redundancy Graph View of TeCReVis

Option ![] can be used to change the coverage criteria. Option ![] is to change the mode of the graph to move the whole graph or pick and move a specific node. ![] is to draw the graph and ![] is for saving the redundancy result into a CSV output file.

In TRG, redundant candidates test cases (JUnit test methods) are shown by yellow nodes. After detecting (confirming) a test method as redundant by human tester in Manual Redundancy View (Fig. 5), that test method is shown by a red node (darker node) in the TRG. The reader can refer to [3] for details and examples on features related to test redundancy analysis and detection.

Name	Statement Red...	Branch Redun...	Condition Red...	Loop R.
Mar 5, 2009 2:06:25 PM				
OperationsTests.AddTest:testAddTwoNumberNotE 0.86	0.5	0.5	NaN	
OperationsTests.AddTest:testAddTwoNumberFirstE 0.83	0.0	0.0	NaN	
OperationsTests.AddTest:testAddTwoNumberSeco 0.86	0.5	0.5	NaN	
OperationsTests.AddTest:testCreateAdd 1.0	NaN	NaN	NaN	

Fig. 5. Manual Redundancy View in TeCReVis

3 Implementation Details

As discussed above, we have implemented TeCReVis in Java as an Eclipse plug-in. We adopted the CodeCover [4] open-source coverage tool and extended it to implement TeCReVis. For the purpose of graph visualization, a Java visualization framework called Jung [5] was used in TeCReVis.

We believe (and hope) that dissemination of the tool's design, technical details and features can help other testing researchers and practitioners build similar (testing) tools. It can also encourage a wider usage of the tool and possibly further extensions of this tool.

3.1 Architecture

There are 5 main package categories in CodeCover: `instrumentation`, `report`, `model`, `metrics` and `eclipse` (see the simplified UML package diagram of this system in Fig. 6). Two first categories (`instrumentation` and `report`) were not modified in TeCReVis, while some parts of three other categories were modified.

TeCReVis: A Tool for Test Coverage and Test Redundancy Visualization   133

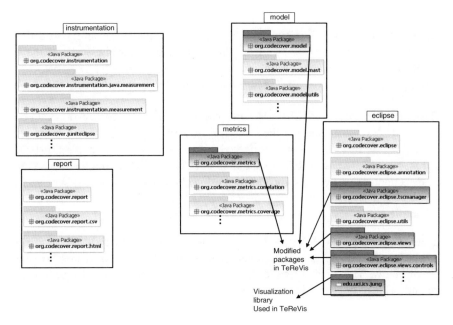

Fig. 6. Simplified package diagram of CodeCover and the modified parts in TeCReVis

Redundancy metrics are calculated in `org.codecover.metrics` package and are stored as attributes in the instances of `TestCase` class in `org.codecover.model` package.

According to the UML package diagram in Fig. 6, most of the changes on CodeCover to create TeCReVis is in the `eclipse` package. The Jung visualization library was attached to this package for visualizing coverage and redundancy information.

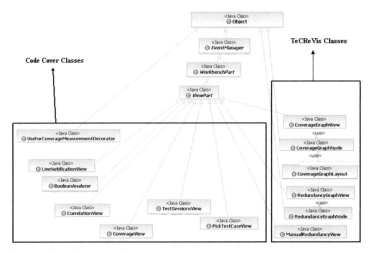

Fig. 7. Class Diagram of package `org.codecover.eclipse.views`

Managing redundancy information is implemented in `org.codecover.eclipse.tsmanager` package. Six new classes were added to `org.codecover.eclipse.views`. The class diagram in Fig. 7 shows the hierarchy of old and new classes in this package. Classes `CoverageGraphNode` and `CoverageGraphLayout` are used (called) by `CoverageGraphView` which draws TCGs.

Class `RedundancyGraphNode` in package `org.codecover.eclipse.views` and one other class called `RedundancyViewerFactory` from `org.codecover.eclipse.views.controls` package are used in `RedundancyGraphView` which draws TRGs. In addition to TCG and TRG, semi-automated redundancy detection/analysis view is implemented using class `ManualRedundancyView`.

3.2 Sample Code

As a sample code in TeCReVis, the source code of a part of `GraphComposite`, a class which is in a composition relationship under the class `CoverageGraphView` is shown below. This piece of code shows how we have used Jung for setting label, shape and color of nodes in drawing TCGs.

```
private final class GraphComposite extends Composite {
    VisualizationComposite<CoverageGraphNode, CoverageGraphLink> vv;
    public GraphComposite(Composite parent, int style, Point size,
    Graph<CoverageGraphNode, CoverageGraphLink> graph,String MouseStyle){
        super(parent, style);
        //Setting Labels for each node:
        Transformer<CoverageGraphNode,String> lableTransformer = new
        Transformer<CoverageGraphNode,String>() {
            public String transform(CoverageGraphNode node) {
                if(node.CompletName) return node.getLable();
                else return node.getShortLable();}};
        vv.getRenderContext().setVertexLabelTransformer(lableTransformer);
        //Changing the Shape of each node:
        final Rectangle rectangle = new Rectangle();
        Transformer<CoverageGraphNode,Shape> vertexTransformer = new
        Transformer<CoverageGraphNode,Shape>() {
            public Shape transform(CoverageGraphNode node) {
                int length;
                if(node.CompletName)length = node.getLable().length()*8;
                else length = node.getShortLable().length()*8;
                rectangle.setSize(length, 16);
                if(node.type == "SUT"){
                    rectangle.setLocation(0,-8);
                    return rectangle;}
                else{
                    rectangle.setLocation(-length,-8);
                    return rectangle;}}};
        vv.getRenderContext().setVertexShapeTransformer(vertexTransformer);
        //Changing the Color of each node:
        Transformer<CoverageGraphNode,Paint> vertexPaint = new
        Transformer<CoverageGraphNode,Paint>() {
            public Paint transform(CoverageGraphNode node) {
                if(node.type == "SUT")return Color.orange;
                else return Color.green;}};
        vv.getRenderContext().setVertexFillPaintTransformer(vertexPaint);
}
```

4 TeCReVis Usage Scenarios

The proposed graph-based test coverage visualization tool can be used in various tasks in software testing and maintenance activities, e.g.:

1. Coverage (test adequacy) improvement
2. Test suite maintenance as the SUT evolves
3. Fault localization
4. Test redundancy detection

For coverage (test adequacy) improvement (usage scenario #1 above), testers need to find uncovered part of the SUT and attempt to cover them by creating new test cases. For this purpose, by using TCG, testers only require to find the SUT nodes with no incoming edges. By double clicking on those nodes, related part of the code is shown by our tool. By only using the conventional code-coverage tools to show the coverage information, multiple files should be inspected manually for this purpose which can take extensive time from human testers to find uncovered parts of the SUT.

As an example of the usage scenario #2 above, consider the following scenario. As a result of SUT evolution, source code modifications can make a number of test methods invalid for regression testing and thus testers need to modify them appropriately. TCG can help testers to find all the tests related to modified part of the system. For this purpose, tester needs to find the modified SUT node in the graph and consider all those tests which are covering these items.

In the usage scenario #3 above by referring to TCGs, testers can find which part of the system is covered more frequently by failing tests. Number of incoming edges to a SUT item and number of the calls shown on each of those edges can be used to find more suspicious fault prone parts of the SUT. Again, by only using the conventional code-coverage tools to show the progress-bar like coverage information, multiple files should be inspected manually which can take extensive effort.

To detect redundant test cases (usage scenario #4 above), testers need to find the tests that cover part of the system which are also covered by other test cases in the test suite. For this purpose, TCG and TRG can be useful to find which parts of the system are covered by each test and compare the covered parts by various test cases with each other. See our recent work in this area for details [2].

Last but not least, from a higher-level perspective, we can qualitatively estimate the cost of test maintenance (entailed by a change in the SUT) by visually analyzing the volume of edges from the test suite domain to the SUT domain.

To assess and evaluate the usefulness and benefit of the TeCReVis in software maintenance and test activities, we have performed an experimental study by having eight grad students as participants on an open-source ATM machine simulation software (available from [7]). We have previously reported the result of these experiments which have confirmed the usefulness of TeCReVis [1-3].

5 Similar Tools

There are existing techniques and tools that address software visualization with the purpose of more effective software comprehension which may lead to reduction in cost of software maintenance. *SeeSoft* and *SeeSys* are two early examples of software visualization tools [7, 8], in which metrics with certain characteristics (e.g., code complexity metrics) are displayed visually.

In addition to software (i.e., SUT) comprehension, test comprehension is critical for reducing the cost of test maintenance. Test (or code) coverage percentage is one of the most important sources of information for test comprehension. There are various code-coverage tools such as CodeCover [4], Emma [9] IBM Rational Pure Coverage

[10] and Clover [11] which show coverage information by progress-bar-like green/red boxes and color the statements according to the test coverage information.

Besides coloring the source code, a visualization technique is used in Clover [11] which is a tree-map that shows all part of the system with different colors according to the covered ratio of each part. Fully covered parts (e.g., method) are shown by green and fully uncovered parts are shown by red. Partially covered parts are shown by a color intensity between red and green.

In addition, there exist works and tools (e.g., Tarantula) that visually present coverage information together with test results [12]. In these tools, SUT's source code is colored differently based on test case results, e.g., statements that are executed primarily by failing test cases are colored red, meaning that they are highly suspicious of having faults.

6 Conclusions

Test coverage and test redundancy information are important sources of information to help testers in fault localization and test enhancement tasks. The TeCReVis tool presented in this article can help testers by visualizing that information. The experiments performed in our recent works [1-3] have confirmed the usefulness of the proposed tool.

References

1. Koochakzadeh, N., Garousi, V., Maurer, F.: Test Redundancy Measurement Based on Coverage Information: Evaluation and Lessons Learned. In: Proc. of Int. Conf. on Soft. Testing, Verification, and Validation (ICST) (2009)
2. Koochakzadeh, N.: A Measurement, Detection, and Visualization Framework for Software Test Redundancy, MSc thesis, University of Calgary (2009)
3. Koochakzadeh, N., Garousi, V.: A Tester-Assisted Methodology for Test Redundancy Detection. Journal on Advances in Software Engineering, Special Issue on Software Test Automation, 1–13 (2010)
4. Scheller, T.: CodeCover, http://codecover.org (Last accessed: April 2010): O'Madadhain, J., Fisher, D., Nelson,T., "Jung, http://codecover.org (Last accessed: February 2010)
5. Whittaker, J.: http://blogs.msdn.com/james_whittaker/archive/2008/09/19/the-future-of-software-testing-part-5.aspx (Last accessed: April 2010)
6. Garousi, V., Koochakzadeh, N.: TeCReVis Home Page, http://www.softqual.ucalgary.ca/sw_tools.html (Last accessed: February 2010)
7. Baker, M.J., Eick, S.G.: Visualizing Software Systems. In: Proc. of Int. Conf. on Software Engineering, pp. 59–67 (1994)
8. Eick, S.G., Steffen, J.L., Sumner, E.E.: Seesoft-A Tool For Visualizing Line Oriented Software Statistics. IEEE Transactions on Software Engineering 18(11), 957–968 (1992)
9. Roubtsov, V.: Emma, http://emma.sourceforge.net (Last accessed: February 2010)
10. IBM: IBM Rational PureCoverage, ftp://ftp.software.ibm.com/software/rational/docs/documentation/manuals/unixsuites/pdf/purecov/purecov.pdf (Last accessed: Febuary 2010)
11. Atlassian Corporation: Clover, http://www.atlassian.com/software/clover (Last accessed: February 2010)
12. Jones, J.A., Harrold, M.J.: Tarantula, http://pleuma.cc.gatech.edu/aristotle/Tools/tarantula/ (Last accessed, Febrauary 2010)
13. Mathur, A.P.: Foundations of Software Testing, 1st edn. Dorling Kindersley, Pearson Education (2008)

A Fault Injection Tool for Testing Web Services Composition

Fayçal Bessayah[1], Ana Cavalli[1], Willian Maja[2],
Eliane Martins[2], and Andre Willik Valenti[2]

[1] IT/TELECOM SudParis - CNRS SAMOVAR, Evry, France
{faycal.bessayah,ana.cavalli}@it-sudparis.eu
[2] IC/UNICAMP, Sao Paulo, Brazil
eliane@ic.unicamp.br
{willian.maja,andre.valenti}@students.ic.unicamp.br

Abstract. Web Services are increasingly becoming the standard for both Web-based commercial application as well as distributed scientific projects. Given the prominence of this technology, test methods and tools are required to ensure that robust systems are deployed. Testing is required not only to uncover existing problems but also to provide users with tools and metrics to compare similar solutions. In this paper, we propose WSInject, a fault injection tool for testing Web Services. WS-Inject is a script-driven fault injector able to inject both interface and communication faults. Unlike other Web Service fault injectors, WSInject allows users to combine several types of fault in one injection statement and is able to handle either single or composed services. We also present the results of preliminary experiments on a case study and show some revealed failures.

Keywords: Testing tools, Fault Injection, Web services.

1 Introduction

Web services are becoming increasingly widespread technology and tend to emerge as a standard paradigm for program-to-program interactions over Internet. The strength of this technology comes probably from its ability to manage communication between heterogeneous applications and systems with a dramatically lower cost. Consequently, Web services have been widely used for building all kind of distributed systems for different areas: business, multimedia, security, etc.

However, these inherent and powerful characteristics of Web services (widely distributed and heterogeneous applications) are paradoxically, also their main weakness points. This is due primarily to the problem of reusing and integrating older and/or third-party service components which may lead to several interoperability, security and/or performance issues.

Testing Web services is, therefore, a very important process which has to be performed, not only during the development of new Web service applications, but also before and after deployment.

Fault injection is a powerful testing technique for assessing system dependability. It consists to introduce deliberate errors in a system and observe its behavior to verify whether it continues to have appropriate functionalities when running in a stressful environment. This technique is usually used to assess error recovery and fault tolerant mechanisms, to perform some dependability measures such as availability, integrity and performance or simply to understand the effects of real faults.

In the case of Web services, faults can be injected at both interface and communication levels. Interface faults affects operations input/output parameters and other SOAP [1] message fields by corrupting data or assigning invalid parameter values. On the other hand, communication faults consider SOAP messages as black boxes. Instead of corrupting carried data, we can delay the forwarding of messages or simulate a connection loss for example.

These two types of faults are very important for testing Web service interactions. They can be used either to perturb communication between a client application and its Web service or between service partners within the same service composition. Furthermore, combining between interface and communication faults could generate more complex errors and permits deeper injection tests.

In this paper, we present WSInject, a Web service fault injector for testing simple and composed Web services. It is a script driven fault injector able to inject both interface and communication faults based on user specifications. Its script language follows the condition-action paradigm and provides a simple and powerful way for composing several types of faults.

We also present an experimental study of our tool based on a set of injection experiments conducted on a case study of Web services.

The remainder of this paper is organized as follows. In the next section we present the related work tackling with fault injection and Web services. Then, in section 3, we describe our fault injection tool and detail its functionalities. In section 4, we depict a set of experiments conducted on a case study and discuss obtained results. Finally, section 5 concludes our paper and introduces to future work.

2 Related Work

Fault injection tools for assessing Web service dependability can be categorized into two main classes. First, we find all network level fault injectors which were not originally developed for Web services but which could be very useful for injecting communication faults. Doctor(integrateD sOftware fault injeCTiOn enviRonment) [12], Orchestra [11] and DEFINE [8] are all good examples of such injectors which fit perfectly on Web services.

However, as communication faults are not enough for testing Web services dependability, other researches focused on providing injection tools able to decode SOAP messages so that they can inject significant interface faults. This constitutes the second fault injector class: Web services fault injectors.

Although there exists several Web service fault injectors able to decode and corrupt SOAP messages (WSBang [2], PUPPET [6], GENESIS [9], etc.), only a very small and limited subset of them can be considered as complete fault

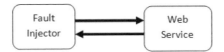

Fig. 1. A client-side fault injection architecture

injectors, in the sens where they could inject both interface and communication faults. In fact, tools like WSBang, PUPPET and GENESIS are more like active testers or client-side injectors than real network level fault injection mechanisms. They all proceed like a client application which consumes the tested Web service (figure 1). They parse the WSDL file provided by the tested service and generate a set of test suites. Each test suite is a set of sequential invocations of the Web service operations. The main difference compared to active testing tools is the fault injection step. Before invoking the tested service, faults are injected inside the SOAP messages to corrupt carried data.

Actually, this kind of tools suffers from two main drawbacks. First, they can only inject interface faults by corrupting data and procedure parameters inside SOAP messages (communication faults such as message delaying for example cannot be performed).

The second problem concerns the type of tests that can be conducted. As such tools proceed by simulating service clients, only simple Web services can be tested. The fault injector needs to consume the tested service. Therefore, it is impossible to use it for testing composed Web services (testing communication between service partners) or to test communication between a service and its original client application (as it will be substituted by the injector itself).

It is important also to highlight other Web service perturbation approaches based on mutation testing. In [13] for example, authors used mutation testing to generate and insert faults on Web service components. The approach consists at creating mutants of the XML schemes of the tested services. Then, test cases (SOAP messages) are generated from those mutants and run against the tested service. Previously, faults are inserted on the service implementations. The goal is to be able to detect those faults by running the generated inputs.

As the above cited tools, the existing mutation testing approaches consider only interface faults by corrupting message structure and parameter values. Also, mutation testing differs from fault injection in the way the faults are injected and also in their testing purpose. In mutation testing, faults are first inserted in the application code and then test cases are generated from a mutation model of the system and run against the faults. The goal here is to detect the seeded faults. In fault injection however, faults are injected during system execution and the goal is to create a hostile environment to be able to study system behavior in stressful environmental conditions.

To address both interface and communication faults, we need to rely on a fault injector which could intercept communication messages exchanged between service partners or between a service and its client application as shown in the schema presented in figure 2.

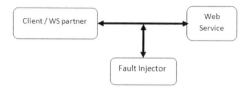

Fig. 2. A network level fault injection architecture

As far as we know, WS-FIT [10], is currently the only Web service fault injector which really fits to this architecture. However, WS-FIT needs to implement a set of *hooks* and *triggers* at the SOAP protocol layers of every machine hosting one or more tested services. This introduces a strong intrusiveness and can, unintentionally, disrupt the communication. Moreover, WS-FIT can only be used in a completely controlled testing environment (because we need to modify the SOAP protocol layers). Therefore, we cannot rely on this tool to test real world Web services i.e. Web services deployed by a third-party and running in their own environment.

For all these reasons, we propose in this paper WSInject: a Web service fault injector able to inject both communication and interface faults while being completely independent from the environments of the tested services.

3 WSInject

WSInject is a script driven fault injector designed specifically to assess SOAP based Web service systems. Its generic architecture is given in figure 3.

We can see in this figure that WSInject relies on a network proxy (*Proxy*) to capture all message exchanges between service partners or between a client

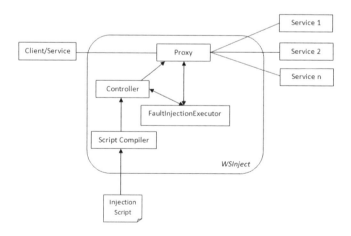

Fig. 3. WSInject architecture

application and a single Web service. This proxy is also used to collect execution traces of all injection processes, telling which messages have been corrupted and which injection operations were applied. These traces may serve later to check whether all injections were well performed or not [7].

The *Controller* is the main component of WSInject. It plays the role of an orchestrator who manages communication between the other components. Thus, according to the content of the injection script (provided by users), the *Controller* tells the *Proxy* which messages must be captured and calls the *FaultInjectionExecutor* to apply the specified injection operations.

Every injection process executed by WSInject is driven by users scripts. Testers must specify all injection operations they want to run using a dedicated script language.

An injection script is in fact a set of condition-action rules specifying the SOAP messages concerned by the injection (the condition) and the injection operations that must be applied on those messages (the actions). An abstract and simplified grammar of this script language is given in figure 4.

```
CampaignDescriptor -> FaultInjectionStatement [CampaignDescriptor]
FaultInjectionStatement -> ConditionSet : FaultList ;
                           [FaultInjectionStatement]
ConditionSet -> Condition [&& ConditionSet]
Condition -> operation(String)| contains(String) | uri(String) |
             isRequest()|isResponse()
FaultList -> Fault [, FaultList]
Fault -> delay(Integer) | multiply(String,Integer) | stringCorrupt
         (String,String) | xPathCorrupt(String, String) | empty()
```

Fig. 4. A simplified grammar of WSInject script language

We can see in this grammar that the basic injection statement is of the form of : *ConditionSet* : *FaultList*;. Conditions are more like selection criteria used to intercept the SOAP messages we want to corrupt. We can define such conditions using one of the following statements:

- *operation("OperationName")* : specifies that we are interested in messages carrying an invocation of operation *"OperationName"*.
- *contains("StringMessagePart")*: specifies that we are interested in messages containing the string *"StringMessagePart"*
- *uri("WS_URI")*: specifies the URI (Uniform Resource Identifier) of the target Web service. All messages addressed to (or coming from) this service would be concerned by the injection.
- *isRequest()/isResponse()*: to specify whether we are interested by corrupting request or response messages.

An important feature provided by our script language is the ability to specify a selection criteria by combining several condition statements. To do, we use the symbol && which defines a logical *and* between the specified conditions. For example, we can specify that we want to intercept all login requests sent by a user *Bob* as follows.

```
operation("LoginRequest") && contains("<username>Bob</username>");
```

Once the selection criteria is specified, we need to define the injection operations that must be performed. This constitutes the "action" part of an injection rule (the *FaultList*). The script language offers several possibilities to specify injection operations. We can categorized them into two main classes following whether they represent interface or communication faults.

3.1 Specification of Interface Faults

For interface faults, we define two main corruption operations: *stringCorrupt* and *xPathCorrupt*. *stringCorrupt("OriginalString","NewString")*, replaces any part of a SOAP message (identified by *OriginalString*) by another part specified as *NewString*. This injection operation can be used either to corrupt data carried by a SOAP message or to modify its structure. For example, we can corrupt login requests of a user *Bob* by specifying the following injection rule.

```
              operation("LoginRequest"):
stringCorrupt("<username>Bob</username>","<username>XXXX</username>");
```

We can also specify a structure corruption statement which inverses opening and closing XML tags as follows.

```
              operation("LoginRequest"):
stringCorrupt("<username>Bob</username>","</username>Bob<username>");
```

Operation *stringCorrupt* requires from the user to know exactly what he wants to corrupt. For example, if the user needs to corrupt the user name, he must know how the user name appears inside the SOAP message (<username>Bob</username>). If there is a single fault in the specified string, operation *stringCorrupt* will fail. Therefore, we propose a second corruption operation named *xPathCorrupt*.

Using *xPathCorrupt*, one needs to know only the parameter name and its location inside the SOAP message. *xPathCorrupt* uses XPath queries to locate the parameter and to modify it. For example, we can specify the injection rule of the previous example as follows.

```
operation("LoginRequest"):xPathCorrupt("//username/text()", "XXXX");
```

We also define two other operations for injecting interface faults: *multiply* and *empty*. *multiply(xPathExpression, n)* replicates a part of a message specified as *xPathExpression* by a number of times n. For example, `multiply("/",2)` duplicates the whole message content, while `multiply("/Envelope/MyNode",3)` triplicates only the *MyNode* XML element.

The *empty()* operation is used to completely remove the SOAP message from its HTTP packet, delivering an HTTP message with no content.

3.2 Specification of Communication Faults

We define two kinds of communication faults: message delaying and connection closing. The operation $delay(n)$ is used to delay the forwarding of a message for n milliseconds. Each time this operation is executed, the intercepted message is kept for n milliseconds before it is delivered.

To simulate a connection loss, WSInject provides the operation *close Connection()* which closes the connection between the client and the current invoked service.

3.3 Injection Composition

Besides the possibility of composing several condition statements in the condition clause, the syntax of an injection rule allows us to compose also a set of injection operations. We can specify, for example, a corruption and a replication of a SOAP message using a unique injection command. For example, if we want to corrupt and replicate login requests of a user *Bob*, we can specify the following injection rule.

```
operation("LoginRequest") && contains("<username>Bob</username>"):
    xPathCorrupt("//username/text()","XXXX"), multiply("/",10);
```

We can also combine between an interface and a communication faults, for example, by corruption and delaying the login request.

```
operation("LoginRequest") && contains("<username>Bob</username>"):
    xPathCorrupt("//username/text()","XXXX"), delay(5000);
```

Note: The comma between injection operations defines a strict sequential order. Therefore, if the first operation cannot be executed, those who follow will not be executed also.

This composition ability provided by our script language (both at condition and injection clauses) allows one to inject complex faults with a minimum set of commands. We can also rely on this technique to combine interface and communication faults like in the example above. This way, we would be able to generate more complex errors and therefore, we could conduct deeper injection experiments.

4 Experimentations and Results

In this section, we present some preliminary results we got after conducting first experimentations using WSInject. The testbed architecture is presented in figure 5. The tested service is the Travel Reservation Service (TRS) from Netbeans 6.5.1 SOA examples [3]. TRS is a simulation of a real-life organization that manages airline, hotel and vehicle reservations using Web service partners. It is composed of three services - *VehicleReservationService (VRS)*, *AirlineReservationService (ARS)* and *HotelReservationService (HRS)*- and one BPEL process

(TRS), which orchestrates partner services to build a travel itinerary. All services composing the TRS were deployed on the GlassFish [4] Web Application server.

SoapUI [5] is a well known test tool for Web services. We used it in our experiments as a client of TRS, sending requests with travel itineraries and activating the BPEL process, which in turn makes reservations with its partner services. The TRS implements also some temporal constraints to regulate the reservation process. Each time the TRS passes the client itinerary to one of its service partners, it waits for a response within the following 20 seconds. In the case of no response, it must send a cancellation message to abort the reservation request.

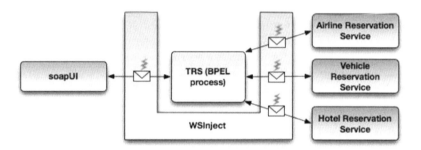

Fig. 5. Testbed Architecture

4.1 Injection Process

SoapUI and GlassFish were configured to make connections through WSInject's proxy component. We conducted two injection campaigns. One for interface faults and the other for communication faults. For interface faults, we corrupted integer and string values of the SOAP messages. Two experiments were conducted: one only for integer values and one only for string values. Each experiment consisted of 10 runs and each run consisted of corrupting all integer or string values from SOAP messages. We also executed 10 runs of structure corruption injections. We considered three types of structure corruption: (i) duplicating SOAP messages, (ii) deleting SOAP messages and (iii) inversing opening and closing XML tags.

For communication faults, we performed one experiment for each type of faults: message delaying and connection closing. For each experiment we conducted 8 runs (2 runs for each service). For example, we executed two runs of delaying faults between the client and the TRS (the BPEL process) and two other runs between TRS-ARS, TRS-VRS and TRS-HRS. Therefore, we had in all, 24 runs of communication faults.

4.2 Result Analysis

Interface faults. Corruption of integer values produced normal responses from the Web services composition. This was not the expected result, since invalid data were sent to the service composition. For example, when sending a negative value for credit card expiration date, the TRS should have complained about these incorrect values, but it did not. This demonstrates that faults have gone undetected, meaning they would probably be propagated to a database in a real system.

Structure corruption faults which consisted at inversing opening and closing XML tags, were however, all detected by target services which had immediately rejected all malformed SOAP messages.

Deletion of SOAP messages causes internal server error. Each time we run operation *empty* between TRS and one of its service partners, the client receives an HTTP 500 error code which notifies a connection close due to an internal server error.

SOAP message duplication faults did not affect the TRS system. Whenever we duplicate a SOAP request, the destination service partner addresses only the first SOAP envelope and ignores the rest of the packet (the duplicated part).

Communication faults. For message delaying, we noticed that when we apply operation *delay* on a request to delay its forwarding for more than 20 seconds (for example when delaying invocation of operation *reserveVehicle* provided by the VRS), the TRS system hangs until the Glassfish server timeout is reached (2 minutes). On the other hand, when we delay the forwarding of the response message (reservation confirmation returned by the VRS for instance), we receive an error message from the sun-bpel-engine indicating that there has been an instantiation error when sending the cancellation message. This shows a bug in the implementation of the cancellation process.

The *closeConnection*() operation was used to simulate a connection loss between system partners. Each time we executed this operation between the TRS and one of its partners, the connection between all the other services and between the TRS and the client was also closed. This is due probably to the fact that the whole tested composition was deployed on the same server.

5 Conclusion

We presented, in this paper, a fault injection tool for testing Web services. Its architecture as well as its simple and powerful script language make it suitable for testing both single and composed services. Particularly, we shown that WSInject can easily inject interface and communication faults and even combine a set of faults in a single injection statement. We also conducted preliminary experiments on a case study from Netbeans and were able to detect some important implementation faults.

As future work, we are currently working on improving WSInject to support new and more powerful injection operations. We are also studying the possibility to deploy it as a Web service and make it easily available for the testing community to be able to perform larger and deeper experiments.

References

1. W3C recommendation, http://www.w3.org/TR/soap/
2. WSBang, https://www.isecpartners.com/wsbang.html
3. NetbBeans IDE, http://netbeans.org/
4. GlassFish, https://glassfish.dev.java.net/
5. SoapUI, http://www.soapui.org/
6. Angelis, G.D., Bertolino, A., Polini, A.: A qos test-bed generator for web services. In: Baresi, L., Fraternali, P., Houben, G.-J. (eds.) ICWE 2007. LNCS, vol. 4607, pp. 17–31. Springer, Heidelberg (2007)
7. Bessayah, F., Cavalli, A., Martins, E.: A formal approach for specification and verification of fault injection process. In: ICIS 2009: Proceedings of the 2nd International Conference on Interaction Sciences, pp. 883–890. ACM, New York (2009)
8. Kao, W.L., Iyer, R.K.: Define: A distributed fault injection and monitoring environment. In: Proceedings of IEEE Fault-Tolerant Parallel and Distributed Systems (IEEE-FTPDS 1994), pp. 252–259 (1994)
9. Truong, H.L., Juszczyk, L., Dustdar, S.: Genesis - a framework for automatic generation and steering of testbeds of complexweb services. In: Proceedings of the 13th IEEE International Conference on Engineering of Complex Computer Systems(ICECCS 2008), pp. 131–140 (2008)
10. Xu, J., Looker, N., Munro, M.: Ws-fit: A tool for dependability analysis of web services. In: Proceedings of the 28th Annual International Computer Software and Applications Conference (2004)
11. Jahanian, F., Dawson, S., Mitton, T.: Orchestra: A probing and fault injection environment for testing protocol implementations. In: Proceedings of IEEE International computer performance and dependability symposium, Urbana-Champaign, IL (1996)
12. Shin, K.G., Han, S., Rosenberg, H.A.: Doctor: An integrated software fault injection environment for distributed realtime systems. In: Proceedings of IEEE International computer performance and dependability symposium, Erlangen, Germany (1995)
13. Offutt, J., Xu, W., Luo, J.: Testing web services by xml perturbation. In: The 16th IEEE International Symposium on Software Reliability Engineering (ISSRE 2005) (2005)

Synthesis of On-Line Planning Tester for Non-deterministic EFSM Models

Marko Kääramees, Jüri Vain, and Kullo Raiend

Tallinn University of Technology
marko.kaaramees@ttu.ee

Abstract. We describe a method and algorithm for model-based construction of an on-line reactive planning tester (RPT) for black-box testing of state based systems specified by non-deterministic extended finite state machine (EFSM) models. The key idea of RPT lies in off-line preprocessing of the System Under Test (SUT) model to prepare the data for efficient on-line reactive test planning. A test purpose is attributed to the transitions of the SUT model by a set of Boolean conditions called traps. The result of the off-line analysis is a set of constraints used in on-line testing for guiding the SUT towards taking the moves represented by trap-labelled transitions in SUT model and generating required data for inputs. We demonstrate the results on a simple example and discuss the practical experiences of using the proposed method.

1 Introduction

It is common that the specification of a System Under Test (SUT) has a lot of freedom for accommodating different implementations. Such freedom is conveniently captured in a non-deterministic model for conformance testing of the SUT. Non-determinism can also result from unspecified inputs and abstraction of unimportant details. Testing a black-box system having a non-deterministic behaviour poses a problem that the test sets cannot be generated beforehand, but the inputs must be generated on-line according to the actual behaviour of the SUT to cover all the test goals.

Contemporary model-based on-line test generators tend to use computationally cheap but far from optimal planning strategies to avoid costly computation at run time. Typical examples of such strategies are random choice and anti-ant [1]. Even the state of art dynamic testing methods don't use stronger planning methods than anti-ant or heuristic search [2,3]. Exhaustive planning during on-line testing of non-deterministic systems looks out of reach because of the low scalability of the methods with regard to the size of a real-life SUT model. Reactive planning was introduced first by Williams and Nayak [4] as a FSM model based control strategy for NASA autonomous space probes. The key idea of Reactive Planning Tester (RPT) relies on performing off-line computations on the SUT model and preparing the guiding data for efficient on-line test planning.

Reactive planning tester proposed in [5] and studied in [6] for industrial scale testing applications was targeted to fill the gap between the computationally cheap and exhaustive planning strategies.

In this paper we extend the method of generating RPT [5] to SUT modelled by non-deterministic Extended Finite State Machine (EFSM) with variables having finite domains and observable outputs. The task is to generate test path selection criteria and related data constraints off-line while leaving the concrete data selection by constraint solving for the RPT on-line test execution phase. As established by some earlier benchmarking experiments the state of the art SMT and constraint solvers satisfy our need for that purpose.

A test purpose is expressed as a set of "traps"[7]. By trap we mean a condition attributed to each transition of the SUT model. The traps are used for guiding the testing process and measuring the feasibility of test runs. We present a way of constructing a tester that at run-time selects a suboptimal test path from trap to trap by finding the shortest path to the nearest unvisited trap.

We start describing the proposed method by introducing the notation and illustrating the method on a simple double-counter example to give an intuition. Then we explain the activities performed in the on-line phase to give a motivation why all the different constraints and parameters are needed. This is followed by a description of the method for off-line generation of the data for the RPT tester. In conclusion we propose the practical use of the RPT for systems with high degree of non-determinism, deep nested control loops, and requiring bounded response time of the tester.

2 Tester Generation

We model the SUT using EFSM formalism consisting of states, transitions and variables where a transition is defined with the source and target states, guard, input, output and update function with the formal definition given e.g. in [5]. The set of variables consists of two mutually exclusive subsets of input and state variables. Variables must be of finite domain. The guards can contain variables from both subsets. The state variables are altered by update functions and the input variables get their values from the environment.

The goal of the test is specified as a set of traps to cover. A trap tr is a pair (t_{tr}, P_{tr}) where t_{tr} is a transition and P_{tr} is a predicate defined on the variables. Defining traps in this way allows to express many different coverage criteria, e.g. all transitions or state variable border conditions. To avoid multi-level indexing a notation $guard_{tr}$ means the guard of the transition t_{tr} associated to the trap. By a set $Path(t, tr)$ we mean a set of all transition sequences $< t, ..., t_{tr} >$ from transition t to the transition of trap tr, where all the transitions are feasible for the model and P_{tr} is satisfied in the source state of t_{tr}. Covering a trap tr means finding a path in $Path(t_i, tr)$ for transitions t_i leaving from initial states.

The testing process is divided into the computationally expensive off-line phase where the SUT model is analysed and the computationally efficient on-line phase where the instances of test data used for guiding testing process are generated. The result of the off-line process is a set of constraints and expected gain measures to make the decisions on-line. More specifically, for every pair of a transition t and trap tr the following is generated: (i) a constraint $C_{t,tr}$ being a sufficient reachability condition for the shortest path of the set $Path(t, tr)$ and its length $L_{t,tr}$; (ii) the weakest possible constraint $C^*_{t,tr}$ that is a sufficient reachability condition for any path in $Path(t, tr)$ and the length $L^*_{t,tr}$ of the longest such path in $Path(t, tr)$; (iii) a guarding condition $C^g_{t,tr}$ on variables being true for the transition t if t is the initial transition of the shortest path of $Path(t, tr)$ considering the current valuation of the variables. For every pair of a state s of the SUT EFSM and a trap tr the following is generated: (i) constraint $C_{s,tr}$ being a sufficient feasibility condition for the shortest paths of $Path(t, tr)$ where s is the source state of t; and its length $L_{s,tr}$; (ii) weakest possible constraint $C^*_{s,tr}$ being a sufficient feasibility condition for any path in $Path(t, tr)$ where s is the source state of t; and the length $L^*_{s,tr}$ of the longest such path. The exact rules for calculating the constraints are presented in section 2.3.

2.1 Example

We demonstrate the result of offline computation and on-line test data generation on a simple model of a double counter depicted in Figure 1 to get an intuition before we explain the method more precisely. The model has one state variable x and input variable i, both of integer type with a range $[0, 10]$ and initialised to 0. Every transition is attributed by a label, guard and optional update. The table shows constraints generated by the off-line computation for the trap $(T2, true)$. The constraints C in the third column are satisfied only for some values of x and i that make the shortest paths with length L on the EFSM control structure reachable. For example the condition $C_{T-,(T2,true)}$ (abbreviated to $C_{T-,T2}$) means that the shortest path with length 2 to the trap starting with transition $T-$ is feasible only when the value of x is 5 and input must be chosen to be greater than 4. The weakest conditions C^* on the fifth column give the largest set of values of the variables that can be used for reaching the trap. For any input value satisfying the constraint, there is a path to the trap not longer than L^*. The result of the constraint $C^*_{T1,T2}$ seems unintuitive at first. It is clear that a path starting with $T1$ can eventually lead to the trap independent of the value of x in state $S0$, but it is not reflected in the constraint. The reason is that the calculation reaches a fixpoint for $S1$ on step 4, as can be seen from the values of $C^*_{S0,T2}$ and $L^*_{S0,T2}$ due to presence of transition $T0$. $C^*_{T1,T2}$ expresses condition on the state variables for paths no longer than 4, but it is sufficient for our purposes and there is no need to generate more general constraint. Guarding constraints C^g are generated only for transitions and a condition $C^g_{t,tr}$ is satisfied in the current valuation of the data variables when the shortest path to trap tr starts with transition t. The conditions are used to guide the tester towards the trap. It can be seen most clearly from the conditions $C^g_{T+,T2}$, $C^g_{T-,T2}$, and $C^g_{T2,T2}$ for the transitions $T+$, $T-$, and $T2$ leaving from state $S1$.

A tester must select concrete inputs on-line using the generated constraints. Suppose that the tester is in the state $S0$ and state variable x has value 5 and the

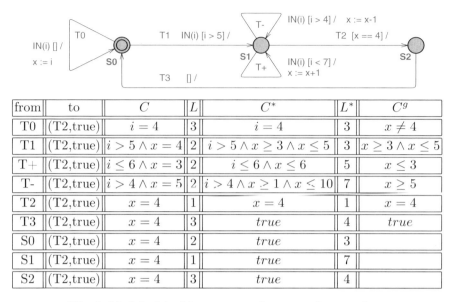

Fig. 1. Model of double counter and generated constraints

goal is to cover the trap $(T2, true)$. Firstly the check is performed that the trap is reachable using the constraints $C_{S0,T2}$ and $C^*_{S0,T2}$. The guarding constraints of the transitions $T0$ and $T1$ are used for choosing the next transition. Both $C^g_{T0,T2}$ and $C^g_{T1,T2}$ are satisfiable and do not constrain the choice, because the path with length 3 is possible both ways. We have a non-deterministic model and nothing in the model forces $T1$ to be taken, but let us assume that the random choice works for our favour this time. Choosing transition $T1$ gives a concrete instance $i > 5 \land 5 \geq 2 \land 5 \leq 6$ of constraint $C^*_{T1,T2}$ to be solved and e.g. an input $i = 6$ is generated. Guarding constraints $C^g_{T+,T2}$, $C^g_{T-,T2}$, and $C^g_{T2,T2}$ determine that $T-$ is the transition of choice from state $S1$ with $x = 5$. Just solving $C_{T-,T2}$ for determining the input i can give a value 5 which can trigger $T+$ also. Solving $C^*_{T-,T2} \land \neg guard_{T+} \land \neg guard_{T2}$ gives value 7 for the input and resulting $T-$ to be taken and x to be equal to 4. Next step does not depend on input, but the guard of $T2$ is satisfied and taken eventually.

2.2 On-Line Computation

The goal of on-line computation during a test run is to find the shortest possible path covering the maximal number of traps while keeping the on-line computation as efficient as possible. The planning, based on pre-computed constraint set, is done repetitively, i.e. before executing each EFSM transition. Planning is performed in three steps (Algorithm 1) : (i) the succession of traps is planned; (ii) the path from the current state to the next trap is planned; (iii) the input

Algorithm 1. On-line planning
```
s=initial state
while exist uncovered traps do // at state s
  //(i) select next trap tr (greedy)
  select trap tr with
    min(L_{s,tr},L*_{s,tr}) and corresponding C_{s,tr} or C*_{s,tr} satisfiable
  //(ii) select next transition t
  select t with source state s and C^g_{t,tr} satisfiable
  //(iii) generate and communicate inputs
  select input variables valuation by solving C_{t,tr} or C*_{t,tr}
  communicate the inputs to the SUT and observe the output
  if the output does not conform to the model
    stop(test_failed)
  move to the next state s
end while
stop(test_passed)
```

variable valuation is generated for the SUT to ensure the progress of test along the preferred path.

The next trap to reach from the current state is selected in the step (i) using the lengths $L_{s,tr}, L^*_{s,tr}$ to the traps found off-line. The lengths serve as interval estimates of the distances to traps and are used for planning the order the traps have to be taken. The actual test length depends on the valuation of the variables and cannot be determined off-line. There are several strategies for selecting the order of traps starting from the greedy approach to guide the test towards the closest uncovered trap; and ending with the global planning approach that involves solving NP-complete asymmetric travelling salesman problem (ATSP). This can be computationally quite expensive on-line when the number of traps is large. Still, this is not an issue because the intended order of covering traps can be computed off-line. Fast heuristic approximating ATSP algorithms can be applied also later in on-line phase to refine the plan when the SUT deviates from the planned path due to non-determinism. Alternatively, the greedy approach does all the planning on-line trying to reach the closest trap from the current state taking into account data constraints. The planning horizon can be parametrically tuned from greedy to global planning by setting how many traps ahead the planning covers.

To guide SUT towards the trap chosen in the step (i) the next transition is selected in the step (ii) using the guarding constraints $C^g_{t,tr}$ of outgoing transitions t from the current state s. The guarding constraints of the outgoing transitions are mutually exclusive except when two transitions prefixing two different paths to the same trap tr have equal lengths and non-contradictory data constraints. For checking the constraints $C^g_{t,tr}$ we apply a simple heuristic that chooses constraints in the order of increasing values of $L_{t,tr}$.

To take the transition chosen in step (ii) a suitable set of input variable values must be generated in step (iii) by solving constraint $C_{t,tr}$ or $C^*_{t,tr}$. The choice of the constraint is determined in step (i) depending if $L_{s,tr}$ or $L^*_{s,tr}$ determined the choice of the trap tr. The constraint solving can be guided by random choice, border value, or corner value data coverage strategy. We assume that the constraints involving propositional logic and linear inequalities can be solved efficiently by standard methods.

Generated inputs may enable also some other transitions guards and lead the testing process to non-desired direction due to non-deterministic nature of the model. The non-deterministic behaviour may avoided if the conjunction of the chosen constraint and negations of the guards of neighbouring transitions is satisfiable and used for generating the inputs.

2.3 Offline Computation

The generation of the reachability constraints that guide the on-line testing process is carried out off-line. The reachability constraints for transition-trap and state-trap pairs are constructed by backwards breath-first traversal starting from the traps. The shortest path constraints C are constructed when the transition or state with constraint not equal to $false$ is encountered first in that traversal. For finding the weakest condition C^* the computation continues and the constraints are weakened at each step until the fixpoint is reached or the traversal depth bound (planning horizon) is reached. The fixpoint is guaranteed to exist as long we restrict the model to be of finite domain, but finding it may be computationally infeasible and the computation is cancelled at some traversal depth. In that case the constraints express the conditions for the paths with length up to the planning horizon.

Algorithm 2 presents the procedure for finding the constraints and path lengths. The algorithm employs the monotonic nature of the constraint derivation. It carries over only the changes C^Δ discovered at each traversal step and adds the result to the previous value $C^{*'}$ of the constraint C^* as a new disjunct (lines 8, 12). The state condition change $C^\Delta_{s,tr}$ is calculated (line 6) by eliminating all the input variables I from the disjunction of constraint changes of the outgoing transitions of the current state s. The transition condition change $C^\Delta_{t,tr}$ is a conjunction of two constraints (line 11). The first conjunct $guard_t$ is the guard of the transition t. The second conjunct is *the weakest precondition* of the current transition's update $update_t$ and of the condition change $C^\Delta_{s,tr}$ of that transition's target state s. The *weakest precondition* calculation is a straightforward substitution in case the update is a collection assignments. The calculation of the guarding constraints C^g (line 14) is the most complicated step. The update of the constraint $C^g_{t,tr}$ can be interpreted as the valuation of the state variables that satisfy the transition's constraint change $C^\Delta_{t,tr}$ but do not satisfy the constraint $C^{*'}_{source(t),tr}$ of the source state of the transition t and will be used to extend the interpretation set of the $C^{*'}_{source(t),tr}$ in the next iteration. Constraints C_s, C_t for the shortest paths are determined when satisfiable constraint

Algorithm 2. Off-line constraint generation

```
find constraints(Trap tr)
1.  initialise C_{i,tr} to false
2.  initialise Li_{i,tr} to 0
```
3. $C_{tr,tr} \leftarrow C^*_{tr,tr} \leftarrow C^\Delta_{tr,tr} \leftarrow guard_{tr} \wedge condition_{tr}$
4. while fixpoint or max depth level is reached
5.   for each state s in the *depth* level do
6. $C^\Delta_{s,tr} \leftarrow$ simplify$(\exists I : \bigvee_{ti} C^\Delta_{ti,tr})$ where $source_{ti} = s$
7.   if sat$(\neg(C^\Delta_{s,tr} \Rightarrow C^{*'}_{s,tr}))$ then   // if $C^*_{s,tr}$ changed
8. $C^*_{s,tr} \leftarrow$ simplify$(C^{*'}_{s,tr} \vee C^\Delta_{s,tr})$; $L^*_{s,tr} \leftarrow depth$
9.   if $C'_{s,tr} = false$ then $C_{s,tr} \leftarrow C^*_{s,tr}$; $L_{s,tr} \leftarrow L^*_{s,tr}$
10.   for each transition t having s as target state do
11. $C^\Delta_{t,tr} \leftarrow guard_t \wedge wp(update_t, C^\Delta_{s,tr})$
12. $C^*_{t,tr} \leftarrow$ simplify$(C^{*'}_{t,tr} \vee C^\Delta_{t,tr})$; $L^*_{t,tr} \leftarrow depth + 1$
13.   if $C'_{t,tr} = false$ then $C_{t,tr} \leftarrow C^*_{t,tr}$; $L_{t,tr} \leftarrow L^*_{t,tr}$
14. $C^g_{t,tr} \leftarrow$ simplify$(C^{g'}_{t,tr} \vee ((\exists I : C^\Delta_{t,tr}) \wedge \neg C^{*'}_{source(t),tr}))$

change C^Δ_s, C^Δ_t is found (line 9, 13). The fixpoint is reached when no weakening happens on the traversal step and it is checked by satisfiability procedure (line 7). Some simplification procedures are applied to all intermediate results to reduce the size of the formula.

Tuning the planning horizon or depth level of the search allows a trade-off to be found between close to optimal (in terms of test length) and the scalability of tester behaviour with computationally feasible expenses.

3 Experimental Results and Conclusions

To show the feasibility of the RPT synthesis method we performed experiments on a case-study where the SUT is the Feeder Box Control Unit (FBCU) of a street lighting subsystem. The model represents the power-up scenario of the FBCU. The strongly connected state model of the FBCU includes 31 states and 78 transitions. The model is non-deterministic. Pairs of non-deterministic transitions depart from seven states of the model and a triple of non-deterministic transitions departs from one state of the model. The minimum length of the sequences of transitions from the initial state to the farthest transition is 20 transitions. The minimum test sequence length for all transitions is 207 steps. Using the maximum planning horizon 20 the reactive planning tester managed to cover all the transitions of the SUT model with test sequence of length in average 1.5 times longer than the minimum. The difference from the optimum is mainly due to the non-determinism of the model. For comparison, the anti-ant and random choice tester generated test sequences that were in average 57 and 146 times longer, respectively. Tuning the planning horizon of the RPT allows a trade-off to be found between close to optimal (in terms of test length) and scalability of tester behaviour with computationally feasible expenses. Deep loop counters in another example have been tried successfully up to 1000 steps.

The proposed method is intended for the non-deterministic models but it works well on deterministic models also and converges to deterministic suboptimal paths. Generation of test inputs for all the test goals investigated in [3] resulted the optimal paths.

The current results have been obtained by a prototype implementation using Z3 SMT-solver library functions [8] for quantifier elimination, simplification and checking satisfiability of the constraints in off-line phase and constraint solving for input variable values generation in the on-line phase. The restrictions caused by Z3 presumes using linear arithmetic in the guards and update functions.

References

1. Nachmanson, L., Veanes, M., Schulte, W., Tillmann, N., Grieskamp, W.: Optimal strategies for testing nondeterministic systems. In: ISSTA 2004. Software Engineering Notes, vol. 29, pp. 55–64. ACM, New York (2004)
2. Godefroid, P., de Halleux, P., Nori, A.V., Rajamani, S.K., Schulte, W., Tillmann, N., Levin, M.Y.: Automating software testing using program analysis. IEEE Software 25, 30–37 (2008)
3. Derderian, K., Hierons, R.M., Harman, M., Guo, Q.: Estimating the feasibility of transition paths in extended finite state machines. Automated Software Engg. 17(1), 33–56 (2010)
4. Williams, B.C., Nayak, P.P.: A reactive planner for a model-based executive. In: Proc. of 15th International Joint Conference on Artificial Intelligence, IJCAI, pp. 1178–1185 (1997)
5. Vain, J., Raiend, K., Kull, A., Ernits, J.: Synthesis of test purpose directed reactive planning tester for nondeterministic systems. In: 22nd IEEE/ACM International Conference on Automated Software Engineering, pp. 363–372. ACM Press, New York (2007)
6. Kull, A., Raiend, K., Vain, J., Kääramees, M.: Case study-based performance evaluation of reactive planning tester. In: Model-based Testing in Practice: 2nd Workshop on Model-based Testing in Practice (MoTiP 2009), Enschede, The Netherlands. CTIT Workshop Proceedings Series WP09-08, pp. 87–96 (2009)
7. Hamon, G., de Moura, L., Rushby, J.: Automated test generation with SAL. CSL Technical Note (1995)
8. De Moura, L., Bjørner, N.: Z3: An efficient SMT solver. In: Ramakrishnan, C.R., Rehof, J. (eds.) TACAS 2008. LNCS, vol. 4963, pp. 337–340. Springer, Heidelberg (2008)

A Generic Approach to Run Mutation Analysis

Siamak Haschemi[1] and Stephan Weißleder[2]

[1] Humboldt Universität zu Berlin, D-12489 Berlin, Germany
haschemi@informatik.hu-berlin.de
[2] Fraunhofer Institut FIRST, D-12489 Berlin, Germany
stephan.weissleder@first.fraunhofer.de

Abstract. Estimating the quality of test suites is an important and difficult task. Mutation analysis is one approach to measure test quality by injecting faults in a correct version of the system under test and measuring the percentage of faulty systems that are detected by the tests. There are several automatic mutation analysis tools. Each of them, however, is restricted to a comparatively small range of execution environments. In this paper, we introduce a generic approach to run mutation analysis and present a corresponding prototype implementation.

1 Introduction

Testing is one of the most important means of quality management for systems under test (SUT). One of the most important properties of a test suite is its fault detection capability, i.e., the number of detected faults divided by the number of all faults of the SUT. Since the number and kind of faults are not known until they are found and solving the problem of finding all faults is usually impossible in finite time, the fault detection capability can only be estimated. One means of estimating this capability is *mutation analysis*. In mutation analysis, faults are injected into a correct version of the SUT. The more of these faulty version (*mutants*) can be detected by the test suite, the higher is the test suite's estimated fault detection capability.

There are several issues in mutation analysis. For instance, the repeated execution of test suites for each mutant requires many resources. Furthermore, semantically equivalent mutants are hard to detect [1]. In this paper, we focus on problems of automatically running mutation analysis: the mutation tool's dependence on the SUT's execution environment, the missing transparency of mutation analysis, and the impossibility to (re-)run mutation analysis only for selected mutants. Our contributions are a metamodel for describing mutants, a concept to use this metamodel for integrating existing mutation analysis tools, and a prototype implementation of the integration approach that is also able to analyze a wider range of SUTs than the integrated mutation analysis tools.

The paper is structured as follows. We introduce the concepts of mutation analysis in Section 2. In Section 3, we present the motivation for our paper. We describe our approach in Section 4 and the corresponding prototype implementation MuUnit [2] in Section 5. We present the related work in Section 6. In Section 7, we conclude, discuss our approach, and present future work.

2 Mutation Analysis

Mutation analysis (or mutation testing) is a wide-spread approach to measure the fault detection capability of a test suite. It can be applied at different levels of abstraction, e.g., at models [3] or at source code [4].

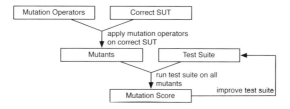

Fig. 1. The basic process of mutation analysis

We apply mutation analysis to source code with the aim to find uncovered parts of the source code. The idea of mutation analysis is depicted in Figure 1: First, faults are injected into a correct SUT implementation using *mutation operators*. The faulty implementations are called *mutants*. Then, the test suite is executed on each mutant with the goal to detect (*kill*) mutants. The number of all killed mutants divided by the number of all mutants is the *mutation score*. In a closed loop, the test suite can be improved until the mutation score reaches the desired value.

Mutation analysis was proposed in 1971 by Richard Lipton and first publications about mutation analysis were from Hamlet [5] and DeMillo et al. [6]. The *coupling effect hypothesis* [7] shows that using small mutations covers a big portion of larger mutations. Andrews et al. [4] show that mutation analysis is a good means to predict the actual fault detection capability for real faults.

Mutation operators define how to change details of an implementation or a model. Formal mutation operators allow for automation, which offers a significant decrease of the costs for mutation analysis. Several mutation operators have already been declared for software [8] and for specifications [3]. Several languages have been used for mutation analysis, e.g., Fortran77 [9] or Java [10].

3 Motivation

The motivation for our investigations are the experiences in the *SOSEWIN* (Self-Organizing Seismic Early Warning Information Network) project [11]. It comprises an alarm protocol for distributed consensus-based earthquake detection.

Since a fault in this protocol can result in high costs in terms of lives and money, ensuring a minimal number of remaining faults in this SUT is of utmost importance. We decided to use mutation analysis to measure the fault detection capability of our test suite. Our SUT is implemented in Java using the component-oriented approach of the OSGi [12]. The test suite is created for integration testing, in which system components can be (de-)activated at test runtime. Running mutation analysis for the SOSEWIN alarm protocol test suite with available tools for Java was challenging for the following three reasons: the restricted execution environment, the lack of transparency, and high costs for running mutation analysis always on all mutants.

Execution Environment. All mutation analysis tools are restricted to a certain execution environment. In our case, the test suite and the SUT components need to be executed inside a OSGi runtime. Existing mutation tools, e.g., Javalanche [1] or MuClipse [13], cannot be executed for OSGi-based applications and modifying them correspondingly is very expensive.

Lack of Transparency. Mutation analysis tools typically use the SUT and a set of mutation operators to generate mutants. After running the test suite on all mutants, they return the number of killed mutants to the user but seldom a description of undetected mutants. This description would allow for a detailed investigation of the reasons for missing this mutant.

Mutant Selection. For running mutation analysis, the whole test suite has to be executed for all mutants. Moreover, if not all detectable mutants are detected in the first run, mutation analysis has to be repeated: After adapting the test suite, all mutants have to be tested again. An explicit description and selection of mutants would allow for investigating only undetected mutants and, thus, for a significant decrease of mutation analysis costs.

4 Approach

In this section, we present our approach to tackle the described problems of existing mutation analysis tools. The ideas are to separate mutant creation and test execution and to integrate existing mutation tools. For that, our framework uses abstract information about mutants that are provided by the integrated mutation tools to create the mutants in a separate execution environment.

To clarify the idea of our approach, we present our adapted process of mutation analysis in Figure 2. The arrows describe the single steps in our approach: First,

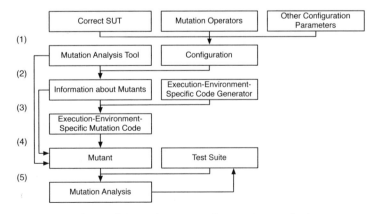

Fig. 2. Adapted process of mutation analysis

we collect the correct SUT, the mutation operators, and other configuration parameters for the integrated mutation tool like, e.g., a database script, and use it as *configuration* for the integrated mutation analysis tool (1). This tool uses the configuration to create information about possible mutants, e.g., their numbers, types, and code positions (2). Afterwards, the information about the mutants is used to generate execution-environment-specific code (3), e.g., for JUnit or OSGi. This generated code calls the integrated mutation analysis tool to create a mutant (4). Subsequently, the test suite is executed on this mutant (5). Step 4 and 5 are repeated for all mutants. It is also possible to execute step 4 and 5 for selected mutants. This permits the mutation analysis to be rerun with an extended test suite only for yet unkilled mutants.

To apply this adapted process, we designed a mutation analysis integration framework that caters for the three issues mentioned in Section 3 by reusing existing mutation analysis tools instead of creating new ones. This allows to reuse features like, e.g., the implemented mutation operators.

The core features of this framework are:

- the separation of collecting information about mutants, creating mutants, and executing the test suite on all mutants,
- the reuse of existing mutation analysis tools, and
- the support of several test execution environments.

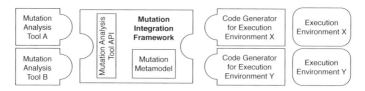

Fig. 3. Mutation integration framework

The essential parts of the framework are described in Figure 3. To enable the core features, our mutation analysis framework has to bridge between mutation analysis tools (A, B) and execution environments (X, Y) for SUTs.

In the following, we present the three key elements of the mutation analysis integration framework: the mutation analysis tool API in Section 4.1, the mutation metamodel in Section 4.2, and the used code generators in Section 4.3.

4.1 Mutation Analysis Tool API

One feature of our framework is to integrate existing mutation analysis tools. The main tasks of these tools are to choose a set of mutation operators, to apply these mutation operators to the SUT, and to execute the test suite on each of the resulting mutants. The simplicity of this behavior structure allows for defining an interface that consists just of these three tasks. We designed such an interface and modified two mutation analysis tools, Jumble [10] and Javalanche [1], to implement this interface. Both tools are designed for Java and apply mutation operators on Java bytecode. The interface, however, is free from any Java-specific implementations and can be used for other programming languages. The interface comprises the following operations:

Life Cycle Operations:
- *start()*, *stop()*: explicit initialization and shut down sequences, e.g., for database initialization in Javalanche.

Configuration Operations:
- *setSourcePath(String)*, *setTargetPath(String)*: location of the SUT described as a file system path; *source path* references the unmodified SUT; *target path* describes the location of the generated mutants.
- *setIncludes(String)*: mutation operators may be restricted to parts of the SUT, e.g., the part under test; *setIncludes(String)* defines inclusion patterns for classes and operations (see Figure 4 for the grammar).

Mutation Operations:
- *getMutationCount()*: returns the number of possible mutants.
- *getMutation(Integer)*: returns the description of a mutation as an instance of our mutation metamodel (see Section 4.2).
- *applyMutation(Integer)*: creates mutant for given index at *target path*.

```
       Filter       ::=  FilterEntry (',' FilterEntry)*
       FilterEntry  ::=  Class '{' Method (';' Method)* '}'
       Method       ::=  MethodName '(' (MethodParam (',' MethodParam)*)? ')'
       MethodParam  ::=  PrimitiveType | Class
       PrimitiveType ::= int | long | float | char | boolean
       Class        ::=  Namespace '.' ClassName
       Namespace    ::=  Identifier ('.' Identifier)*
       ClassName    ::=  Identifier
       MethodName   ::=  Identifier
       Identifier   ::=  [a-zA-Z] [A-Za-z0-9]*
       example           "com.foo.Bar{methodA(int);methodB(char,float)},
                          com.foo.Test{methodC(com.foo.Foo)}"
```

Fig. 4. Grammar for inclusion filters to specify mutations of a SUT

The interface makes two assumptions on mutation analysis tools:
- Mutation analysis tools are able to calculate the possible mutations in a deterministic manner: Given a fixed configuration, two calls of *getMutationCount()* return the same number. Furthermore, *getMutation(Integer)* always returns the same mutation for a fixed index *idx* and *applyMutation(Integer)* always applies the same mutation for a fixed index *idx*.
- The configuration of the mutation analysis tool is done outside of our framework. For instance, the mutation operators have to be specified with the tool's configuration mechanism. The only exceptions are configuration operations like *setSourcePath(String)* or *setIncludes(String)*.

4.2 Mutation Metamodel

Mutation analysis tools implementing the *getMutation(Integer)* operation of the above interface return descriptions of mutants. This description is an instance of the metamodel shown in Figure 4.2. The metamodel consists of the root element *MutationMM*, which refers to a list of *Mutation* elements representing the possible mutations of a SUT. The *Mutation* class is abstract. Derived classes have to add necessary information like, e.g., the method name in *MethodMutation*. This metamodel has been designed using the mutation analysis tools Jumble and Javalanche. It can be easily extended if necessary.

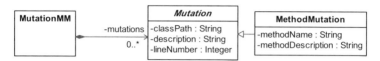

Fig. 5. Metamodel for mutations

4.3 Code Generators

The third and most important part of our framework is the support of several mutation analysis execution environments. As stated in Section 3, existing mutation analysis tools are restricted to a certain execution environment.

Our code generators create an execution-specific code skeleton with mutation patterns. The mutation patterns interact with the integrated mutation analysis tool to create mutants. The skeleton enables mutation analysis to be run in an arbitrary environment. It consists of execution-environment-specific code that also integrates the mutation patterns. The generated code calls the mutation analysis tool to create a mutant for mutation analysis, executes the test suite on that mutant, and checks if the mutant is killed by the test suite. The advantage of this approach is that these steps can be aligned with execution-environment-specific calls, i.e., specific initialization or specific storage mechanisms. For example, the code generators can produce code for the Java runtime environment, code for OSGi, or human readable documents containing information about the possible mutations.

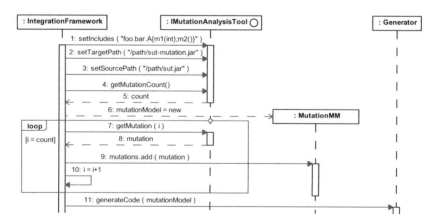

Fig. 6. Behavior of the mutation integration framework

4.4 Behavior of the Mutation Integration Framework

Figure 6 shows the behavior of our integration framework: It defines all tool-independent configurations (step 1 to 3), collects information about possible mutants (step 4 to 10), and forwards them to a code generator (step 11). For this, the framework solely relies on the defined interface, the inclusion grammar, and the mutation metamodel.

5 Implementation

In this section, we present *MuUnit* [2], a prototype implementation of the mutation integration framework. We created this prototype to show the general applicability of our approach and to prepare mutation analysis for the SOSEWIN project (see Section 3). As depicted in Figure 7, MuUnit is written in Java and relies on various third-party Java frameworks: The *Eclipse Modeling Framework* (EMF) is used to implement and process the metamodels and models. The *Eclipse Modeling Workflow Environment* (MWE) is used to implement the code generators. MuUnit plug-ins provide access to mutation analysis tools and code generators. They are implemented using the OSGi component framework. Until now, Javalanche and Jumble have been integrated. They can be used to generate mutation code for JUnit and OSGi. A wizard for the Eclipse Platform improves usability of the prototype. It is implemented in *SWT/JFace*.

Fig. 7. Overview of the software architecture of MuUnit

The most important aspects of MuUnit are:

- the implementation of the mutation analysis tool API and the metamodel,
- the plug-in mechanism for mutation analysis tools and code generators,
- example plug-ins for mutation analysis tools and code generators, and
- use with or without an Eclipse wizard as a graphical user interface.

In the following, we describe the details of the implementation.

Mutation Analysis Tool API and Metamodel. The mutation analysis tool API is implemented as a Java interface. The Eclipse Modeling Framework (EMF) has been used for creating and processing the mutation metamodel based on the Ecore [14] format.

Plug-In Mechanism. In MuUnit, the plug-in mechanism of OSGi [12] is used to integrate mutation tools and code generators. OSGi is a modularization layer for Java. It encapsulates a set of Java packages and classes in *bundles*. The OSGi runtime is able to install, start, and stop these bundles. Bundles communicate using a *service* mechanism. They can register instances of Java interfaces in the OSGi service registry. Other bundles can ask for service instances.

Mutation Analysis Tool Plug-Ins. The plug-in mechanism of MuUnit has been used to integrate Jumble [10] and Javalanche [1]. For this, the mutation analysis tool API has to be implemented and internal mutant representation has to be transformed into mutation metamodel instances. We found that the effort to integrate these tools depends on the implemented optimizations. While Jumble implements no special optimizations, Javalanche implements two optimizations that made it difficult to integrate: First, Javalanche supports modifications of the SUT that contain several mutants, each of which can be switched on and off at runtime [15] using an additional flag. While this approach reduces the overhead for mutant creation, it forces the execution environment to manage these conditional statements. The second optimization is the on-the-fly manipulation of the SUT at runtime to introduce faults. This approach also reduces the overhead of creating mutants, but is incompatible with our SOSEWIN environment using OSGi where modification of bundles is impossible most of the time.

Code Generator Plug-Ins. The Eclipse Modeling Workflow Environment [16] (MWE) is used for code generation. MWE provides a framework to define code generators based on the template language XPAND. We create code generation plug-ins for the component-based SOSEWIN environment and for standard Java execution environment. For both code generators, we decided to produce code based on JUnit [17], a widely used unit testing framework for Java. Thus, JUnit serves as an execution framework for our mutation analysis. For the SOSEWIN environment, we added environment-specific code and bundled a separate plug-in to enable mutation analysis for the component-based environment.

Performing Mutation Analysis. MuUnit is designed to be executable in different environments. For example, it is possible to execute MuUnit in a headless mode without any graphical user interface. This can be necessary if mutation analysis is done automatically and continuously on a build server. MuUnit is also flexible enough to run inside different environments, i.e., the Eclipse IDE. In order to demonstrate this flexibility, but also with the intention of providing a user friendly access to mutation analysis with MuUnit, we created an Eclipse plug-in which integrates with the user interface of the Eclipse IDE.

6 Related Work

Mutation analysis is a means to measure the quality of test suites. There are many books that provide surveys of testing [18,19]. There are also several publications about mutation analysis [3,4,20]. Many mutation operators have already been declared for software [8] and for specifications [3]. There are several case studies [4,20] describing that mutation analysis is a good predictor for the test suite's fault detection capability of real faults. Mutation analysis has been applied to many programming languages, e.g., Fortran77 [9] or Java [10]. The mutation analysis site (*http://www.mutationtest.net/*) provides references to many mutation analysis tools such as Mothra, MuJava, MuClipse, Jumble, JesTer, NesTer, PesTer, and Javalanche. To our knowledge, all existing mutation analysis tools are restricted to a certain execution environment. In contrast, we provide a framework that separates the creation of mutants from the mutation analysis execution environment.

7 Conclusion, Discussion, and Future Work

In this paper, we presented a generic mutation analysis framework and the corresponding prototype implementation MuUnit. The major advantages are the reuse of existing mutation analysis tools in new execution environments and the explicit selection of mutants for (repeated) mutation analysis runs.

Our first results are promising. There is, however, room for discussion. First, we reduced the integrated mutation analysis tools to their basic functions (creating mutants and running test suites). As a result, features beyond the correspondingly defined interface are not integrated: For instance, Javalanche is also able to measure the code coverage of the test suite. We think that measuring code coverage is out of focus for a mutation analysis tool. To deal with such issues, however, we plan to offer a tool-dependent interface to include such additional features. Second, the integration of additional tools might rise the necessity to extend the described metamodel for mutants. Since MuUnit is generated based on this metamodel, we expect only little effort for extending it. Finally, the focus of our framework is on decoupling mutant creation and test execution. The language of the SUT is not exchangeable, i.e., mutation tools for Java (Jumble, JesTer, ...) cannot be applied to SUTs that are implemented in C or Perl.

In the future, we plan to apply MuUnit to the test suites of the SOSEWIN project to improve their fault detection capability. Furthermore, we plan to implement extensions of MuUnit like highlighting the mutated code in an IDE, generating environment-specific templates for running mutation analysis in several environments, and generating a human-readable form of mutants.

Acknowledgment. We like to thank the anonymous reviewers for comments on preliminary versions of this paper. This work was supported by grants from the DFG (German Research Foundation, research training group METRIK) and the BMBF (Bundesministerium für Bildung und Forschung) via innovation alliance SPES2020.

References

1. Schuler, D., Zeller, A.: (Un-)Covering Equivalent Mutants. In: 3rd International Conference on Software Testing, Verification, and Validation (ICST) (April 2010)
2. Haschemi, S.: MuUnit (2010), http://code.google.com/p/muunit/

3. Black, P.E., Okun, V., Yesha, Y.: Mutation operators for specifications. In: ASE 2000: Proceedings of the 15th IEEE International Conference on Automated Software Engineering, Washington, DC, USA, p. 81. IEEE Computer Society, Los Alamitos (2000)
4. Andrews, J.H., Briand, L.C., Labiche, Y.: Is mutation an appropriate tool for testing experiments? In: ICSE 2005: Proceedings of the 27th International Conference on Software Engineering, pp. 402–411. ACM, New York (2005)
5. Hamlet, R.G.: Testing Programs with the Aid of a Compiler. IEEE Transactions on Software Engineering 3(4), 279–290 (1977)
6. DeMillo, R.A., Lipton, R.J., Sayward, F.G.: Hints on Test Data Selection: Help for the Practicing Programmer. Computer Journal 11(4), 34–41 (1978)
7. Offutt, A.J.: Investigations of the Software Testing Coupling Effect. ACM Transactions on Software Engineering and Methodology 1(1), 5–20 (1992)
8. Offutt, A.J., Lee, S.D.: An Empirical Evaluation of Weak Mutation. IEEE Transactions on Software Engineering 20(5), 337–344 (1994)
9. Offutt, VI, A.J., King, K.N.: A Fortran 77 Interpreter for Mutation Analysis. In: SIGPLAN 1987: Papers of the Symposium on Interpreters and Interpretive Techniques, pp. 177–188. ACM, New York (1987)
10. Irvine, S.A., Pavlinic, T., Trigg, L., Cleary, J.G., Inglis, S.J., Utting, M.: Jumble Java Byte Code to Measure the Effectiveness of Unit Tests. In: TAICPART-MUTATION: Testing: Academic and Industrial Conference Practice and Research Techniques - MUTATION (2007)
11. Zschau, J., Gasparini, P., Papadopoulos, G., Filangieri, A.R., Fleming, K.: The SAFER Consortium: SAFER - Seismic eArly warning For EuRope. In: EGU General Assembly, Vienna, Austria (April 2007) (poster)
12. OSGi Alliance: OSGi Service Platform Core Specification, V4.1 (April 2007)
13. Smith, B.H., Williams, L.: An Empirical Evaluation of the MuJava Mutation Operators. In: TAICPART-MUTATION: Testing: Academic and Industrial Conference Practice and Research Techniques - MUTATION (2007)
14. Steinberg, D., Budinsky, F., Paternostro, M., Merks, E.: EMF: Eclipse Modeling Framework, 2nd edn. (Eclipse), 2nd (rev. edn.). Addison-Wesley Longman, Amsterdam (January 2009)
15. Schuler, D., Dallmeier, V., Zeller, A.: Efficient mutation testing by checking invariant violations. In: ISSTA 2009: Proceedings of the eighteenth international symposium on Software testing and analysis, pp. 69–80. ACM, New York (2009)
16. Eclipse Foundation: Modeling Workflow Engine,
http://wiki.eclipse.org/Modeling_Workflow_Engine_MWE
17. Massol, V., Husted, T.: JUnit in Action. Manning Publications Co., Greenwich (2003)
18. Ammann, P., Offutt, J.: Introduction to Software Testing. Cambridge University Press, New York (2008)
19. Binder, R.V.: Testing Object-Oriented Systems: Models, Patterns, and Tools. Addison-Wesley Longman Publishing Co., Inc., Amsterdam (1999)
20. Andrews, J.H., Briand, L.C., Labiche, Y., Namin, A.S.: Using Mutation Analysis for Assessing and Comparing Testing Coverage Criteria. IEEE Transactions on Software Engineering 32, 608–624 (2006)

The Practical Assessment of Test Sets with Inductive Inference Techniques

Neil Walkinshaw

Department of Computer Science, The University of Sheffield, Sheffield, UK

Abstract. Inductive inference is the process of hypothesizing a model from a set of examples. It can be considered to be the inverse of program testing, which is the process of generating a finite set of tests that are intended to fully exercise a software system. This relationship has been acknowledged for almost 30 years, and has led to the emergence of several induction-based techniques that aim either to generate suitable test sets or assess the adequacy of existing test sets. Unfortunately these techniques are usually deemed to be too impractical, because they are based on *exact* inference, requiring a vast set of examples or tests. In practice a test set can still be adequate if the inferred model contains minor errors. This paper shows how the Probably Approximately Correct (PAC) framework, a well-established approach in the field of inductive inference, can be applied to inductive testing techniques. This facilitates a more pragmatic assessment of these techniques by allowing for a degree of error. This evaluation framework gives rise to a challenge: To identify the best combination of testing and inference techniques that produce practical and (approximately) adequate test sets.

1 Introduction

Software testing and inductive inference are two sides of the same coin. In software testing the challenge is to identify a finite set of tests that will fully exercise some software system. In inductive inference the challenge is to work out what the (hidden) system is from a finite sample of observations of its behaviour.

Work that relates the two areas is well-established, and has appeared sporadically over the past 30 years, and especially over the last decade [1–11]. Techniques have exploited the intuitive symmetry between model-inference and test-generation. A model that is inferred from a test set makes explicit the extent to which the test set explores the behaviour of the system. If the model is equivalent to the underlying system, the test set can be considered to be *adequate* [1, 2]. If it is not equivalent, the test set needs to be augmented. Some techniques exist only to assess the adequacy of a test set, and leave it up to the test-generator to generate further tests. Others are more proactive, and use the inference to drive the test-set generation in an iterative fashion until no conflicting test cases are found (this idea is referred to as *inductive-testing* in this paper).

Although the idea sounds appealing in theory, practical attempts to implement it tend to share the same problem: inference techniques are only considered to be successful if the inferred model is *exactly* equivalent to the software system. There is no explicit allowance for a degree of error. In reality, for any reasonably detailed model of a non-trivial system, an inductive inference technique will require an impractically large number of tests to arrive at an exact result. This renders inductive testing techniques too expensive to be of practical value.

A more pragmatic approach that is now routinely used in the inductive inference community is to explicitly allow for a degree of error. In most areas of inductive inference, merely allowing for a small degree of error tends to result in a significant reduction in the number of inputs required to infer a model that is nonetheless reasonably accurate. Valiant [12] used this idea to propose the *Probably Approximately Correct (PAC)* framework, which provided the community with a formal basis to quantify this degree of error, without requiring them to produce exact results.

When applied in the context of test generation, the PAC framework provides several appealing features. Instead of a test set either being adequate or not, it is possible to account for a margin of error. If a model that is inferred from a test set is approximately correct with respect to the underlying software system, the test set can be deemed to be *approximately adequate*. Furthermore, it provides a useful basis for empirically comparing the relative capabilities of different combinations of testing and inference techniques.

This paper makes two contributions. (1) It shows how the PAC framework can be applied in a general inductive testing setting. (2) It sets out a challenge: to identify the combination of test and inductive inference technique that produce the smallest approximately adequate test sets.

2 Background

2.1 Motivation: Generating and Assessing Test Sets

The testing challenge is to, within a finite set of test cases, exercise the full range of behaviour that can be exhibited by the software system (identifying any inputs that cause it to fail in the process). If this is the case a test set is deemed to be *adequate* [1]. Generating an adequate test set is challenging, especially when there is no available model of how the program is supposed to behave. The predominant approach to approximating whether a test set is adequate is to measure the extent to which it covers the structure of the source code (e.g. branch coverage), although this is often an unsatisfactory approximation [1].

2.2 Inference-Based Adequacy Criteria

Inductive testing techniques attempt to circumvent the problems of structural coverage techniques. The essential idea of inductive testing is as follows: test executions are used to infer a model or program that encapsulates what the test set has tested, and if it is shown to be equivalent to the underlying program, then the test set can be deemed to be adequate. Implementations of this approach can be broadly separated into two camps. The earlier approaches were based on the idea of "program synthesis", where inference techniques synthesise an executable program from test cases, which is in turn compared to the original program. The more recent approaches have attempted to infer behavioural models of the software systems, but can serve the same purpose of establishing the adequacy of the test set. The theoretical relationship between testing and inference is explored in depth by Zhu et al. [3, 4]. A brief summary of existing techniques that infer models from tests is presented below.

Inferring Programs. Given that a test set is supposed to fully exercise a program, Weyuker [1] proposed that it should therefore contain a sufficient amount of information to enable an inference engine to infer the program from the test sets alone. Given such an inference engine, the test set can be deemed to be *inference-adequate* if the inferred program is equivalent to the specification and the program under test. She suggested that this equivalence could be estimated by generating random tests and comparing their outcomes in the inferred program against the expected outcomes from the actual program, or a specification if available. Any difference in outcomes would imply that the inferred program is not equivalent to the actual program, indicating that the test set used to infer the program is not adequate. Weyuker demonstrated the approach with respect to a simple case study. Test sets were generated for programs written in PL/I, the test sets were fed to an inference system [13] that inferred programs in a subset of LISP.

Subsequent work by Bergadano and Gunetti [2] adopted a similar approach. Whereas Weyuker's aim had primarily been to assess test-set adequacy, their primary aim was to construct the test set itself. They made the explicit assumption that there exists no prior specification. Instead, given a particular program, they enable the developer to specify the set of possible alternative (mutated) versions of the program. They generate tests randomly, and consider a test set to be adequate if it can distinguish between the given program and all of the supplied alternative versions. If, for a given test set, the inferred program corresponds to one of the explicitly specified alternative programs, the test set is expanded with an input that differentiates between the subject program and the inferred program, and the whole procedure iterates. Otherwise the test set is considered to be adequate. The approach was demonstrated with respect to a PROLOG system.

Inferring Models. Model inference approaches can have a dual purpose; either the main purpose is to reverse-engineer the model, and the tests are a mere by-product, or vice-versa. Although some of the techniques to be discussed have not explicitly been devised with test-adequacy in mind, the basic principle still applies: the more accurate an inferred model is, the more likely it is that the test set is adequate. Model-based approaches have the added benefit that certain types of models are associated with well-understood strategies for the construction of test sets, and the properties that are required of test sets to enable their exact inference.

Finite-state machines are associated with well-established testing strategies [14], and are well-studied in the domain of inductive inference [15]. Several approaches have been developed [8–10], which are based on the inference algorithm by Angluin [16]. Angluin's algorithm will start off from a (potentially empty) test set, and will systematically generate "membership queries" (test cases in our setting). Once it has produced a model, it relies on the ability to identify a "counter example" (a further test case in our setting) that will distinguish the hypothesis from the actual system if the two are not equivalent. Due to the fact that the test-generation strategy employed by Angluin's algorithm can be prohibitively expensive, Walkinshaw et al. have combined heuristic inductive algorithms [17] with random testing strategies to enable the inference of state machines with smaller test sets.

Not all model-inference techniques are founded on state-machine models. Harder et al. [5] and Xie and Notkin [6] show how the Daikon invariant inference technique can be used to infer pre-/post-condition abstractions from test executions, which can in turn be used to refine the underlying test sets. Although clearly relevant, these models are only partial in the sense that they are not meant to exactly characterise program behaviour as is the case with state machines or the program-inference techniques described previously. For this paper we will only consider inference of models or programs that can be compared to the system under test in terms of their equivalence.

2.3 Problem: Assessing Model Accuracy (and Test Set Adequacy)

All of the inductive approaches discussed above, both program and model-based, suffer from the same problem: there is no accepted way of quantifying how accurate the inferred model is, because the challenge of comparing a model to a hidden system is undecidable. When the models are used as a basis for test-set generation (i.e. for inductive testing), a model is simply deemed to be *exact* if further tests can find no conflicts, and inexact otherwise. The problem with this approach is that, in practice, a detailed model of a realistic system is unlikely to be exact, because model inference techniques are known to require an impractically large set of test cases for this to be the case [18–20]. Consequently, the corresponding test sets can not be deemed to be adequate with any confidence.

3 Applying the Probably Approximately Correct (PAC) Framework

The problems discussed in the previous section are not unique to the inductive testing setting, and are well-established in the broader field of inductive inference. The widespread acknowledgement of these problems has triggered a shift towards more realistic aims - i.e. the ability to learn models that are *reasonably* correct, and to do so within reasonable bounds (i.e. polynomial time and space). With this in mind, Valiant [12] introduced the Probably Approximately Correct (PAC) Framework. This enables the relaxation of the constraints within which a learner can be deemed to be successful. In short it makes it possible to apply and evaluate inductive techniques (that may have previously been deemed to be prohibitively expensive) in a practical and applied environment.

3.1 The Probably Approximately Correct (PAC) Framework

This section only provides a brief, high-level introduction to the PAC framework. For more a more formal overview the reader is referred to Valiant's original paper [12], for a more comprehensive high-level overview the reader is referred to Mitchell's book [21]. The PAC framework is presented in relatively abstract terms, but these are illustrated with respect to the established challenge of inferring state machines.

The PAC setting assumes that there is some *instance space* X. As an example, if a technique is supposed to infer the language produced by a state machine with an alphabet Σ, X could be the set of all strings in Σ^*. A *concept* $c \subset X$ corresponds to the target to be inferred (in our case it is the language, which is a subset of strings in Σ^*). Given some element x (in our case a string), $c(x) = 0$ or 1, depending on whether it belongs to the target concept. It is assumed that there is some selection procedure $EX(c, D)$ that randomly selects elements in X following some distribution D (we do not need to know this distribution, but we do assume that it does not change).

PAC learning enables the success conditions for a learner to be specified in two dimensions. First, the learner may fail to successfully infer a model every so often, and the probability that it will fail is specified by the confidence parameter δ. Second, the models it generates are not required to be 100% accurate; we specify an error parameter ε that puts an upper limit on the probability that a model may mis-classify a given input. Thus δ states the extent to which the learner will *probably* succeed, and ε states the extent to which models can be *approximate*.

The basic learning scenario is that some learner is given a set of examples as selected by $EX(c, D)$. After a while it will produce a hypothesis. The correctness of the hypothesis is subsequently evaluated with respect to a further selection from $EX(c, D)$. The hypothesis is deemed to be approximately correct if the proportion of subsequent selections that are wrongly classified is smaller than ε. The problem is deemed to be *PAC-learnable* by the learner if the probability of it approximately inferring the model is $(1 - \delta)$.

3.2 Establishing Test Adequacy within the PAC Framework

Adapting the existing inductive testing techniques to the PAC framework is straightforward[1], and the high-level process is shown in figure 1. The test-set generator generates a test set A, which is used to infer a model. This is the test set that will be assessed in terms of its adequacy. The choice of test-set generator is up to the user; it may be random, it may be a model-based tester that is using some existing model (that is independent from the model inferred by the inductive process). The generator generates a further test set B, which must be generated in an identical manner to A, but must not contain the same tests (in practice it is possible to use the generator to generate one large test

---

[1] In her work on DFA-inference Angluin [16] does discuss how her technique can be adapted to the PAC framework, but to the best of the author's knowledge this has not been implemented in current Angluin-based inductive testing approaches.

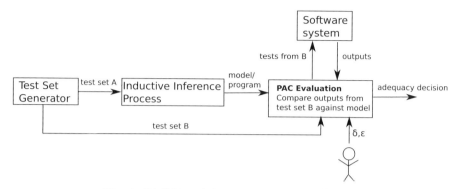

Fig. 1. PAC Test-Adequacy Assessment Process

set, and to draw the two samples from this large set). The inferred model and test set B are passed to the PAC evaluator, along with the parameters δ and ε. The PAC evaluator component executes the complete test set B on the software system under test, using the inferred model as a test oracle, and recording the proportion of tests that fail. If the proportion of failed tests falls below ε, the evaluator either returns a true value indicating that test set A is adequate, otherwise it returns a false value.

The PAC framework makes an important assumption about the circumstances under which it is used, and any test-set adequacy conclusions that are drawn within this framework have to be interpreted with care. For a given test-set generator, it must be capable of eventually deriving a test set that leads to the inference of an exact model. If the generated test sets are not capable of encapsulating the complete behaviour of the system, the final model will only be evaluated against a subset of the actual system behaviour, and could be falsely deemed to be adequate as a consequence.

The manner in which test set similarity is quantified is flexible. One approach that has been used by the authors in previous work is to use straightforward binary classification measures to compare test outputs [22]. Test case B is executed on the inferred program / model, and results in a binary string, where a 0 indicates a failed test and a 1 indicates a passed test. A similar binary string is produced by running test set B on the actual program. The error margin between the two can then be computed as an F-Measure, or the Balanced Classification Rate (several possible alternative measures are detailed by Sokolova et al. [23]).

The PAC approach is useful on two levels; it can be used to evaluate individual test sets, but also provides a useful basis for evaluating general combinations of test-generation and inductive inference techniques. So far, the focus has been placed on individual test sets - a straightforward process, which can be modulated by the degree of error ε that the user is prepared to allow. However, the prospect of being able to systematically evaluate different configurations of testing and inference techniques is at least as interesting. PAC facilitates this because all of the elements in the process as shown in figure 1 are decoupled; it is straightforward to evaluate the performance of different inference techniques with respect to a particular test-set generation technique or vice versa, because they can simply be replaced without affecting other parts of the system.

4 Conclusions

Research that combines inductive inference with software testing has been around for 30 years, and has become increasingly popular over the past decade. Unfortunately, most techniques are difficult to apply because a test set is never deemed to be adequate unless it is impractically large. This is because most techniques assume that, to be adequate, a test set must result in the inference of a model that is perfect and exact.

This paper argues that this is an unrealistic requirement, and that techniques can produce adequate test sets even if the inferred model is not necessarily exact. The presented approach is inspired by more practical approaches to problems that have traditionally been held to be unsolvable in the machine learning community. The PAC framework enables a user to quantify a margin of error, within which the model can still be deemed to be *approximately correct*. A test set that can infer such a model can therefore be deemed to be *approximately adequate*.

Besides portraying the performance existing techniques from a more practical perspective, the framework has additional benefits. It provides a framework within which different combinations of testing and induction techniques can be empirically compared against each other. The challenge for future research is to identify the ideal combination of inference and testing techniques, that will produce approximately adequate test sets of a reasonable size, for a broad range of programs.

References

1. Weyuker, E.: Assessing test data adequacy through program inference. ACM Transactions on Programming Languages and Systems 5(4), 641–655 (1983)
2. Bergadano, F., Gunetti, D.: Testing by means of inductive program learning. ACM Transactions on Software Engineering and Methodology 5(2), 119–145 (1996)
3. Zhu, H., Hall, P., May, J.: Inductive inference and software testing. Software Testing, Verification, and Reliability 2(2), 69–81 (1992)
4. Zhu, H.: A formal interpretation of software testing as inductive inference. Software Testing, Verification and Reliability 6(1), 3–31 (1996)
5. Harder, M., Mellen, J., Ernst, M.: Improving test suites via operational abstraction. In: Proceedings of the International Conference on Software Engineering (ICSE 2003), pp. 60–71 (2003)
6. Xie, T., Notkin, D.: Mutually enhancing test generation and specification inference. In: Petrenko, A., Ulrich, A. (eds.) FATES 2003. LNCS, vol. 2931, pp. 60–69. Springer, Heidelberg (2003)
7. Berg, T., Grinchtein, O., Jonsson, B., Leucker, M., Raffelt, H., Steffen, B.: On the correspondence between conformance testing and regular inference. In: Cerioli, M. (ed.) FASE 2005. LNCS, vol. 3442, pp. 175–189. Springer, Heidelberg (2005)

8. Raffelt, H., Steffen, B.: Learnlib: A library for automata learning and experimentation. In: Baresi, L., Heckel, R. (eds.) FASE 2006. LNCS, vol. 3922, pp. 377–380. Springer, Heidelberg (2006)
9. Bollig, B., Katoen, J., Kern, C., Leucker, M.: Smyle: A tool for synthesizing distributed models from scenarios by learning. In: van Breugel, F., Chechik, M. (eds.) CONCUR 2008. LNCS, vol. 5201, pp. 162–166. Springer, Heidelberg (2008)
10. Shahbaz, M., Groz, R.: Inferring mealy machines. In: Cavalcanti, A., Dams, D.R. (eds.) FM 2009. LNCS, vol. 5850, pp. 207–222. Springer, Heidelberg (2009)
11. Walkinshaw, N., Derrick, J., Guo, Q.: Iterative refinement of reverse-engineered models by model-based testing. In: Cavalcanti, A., Dams, D.R. (eds.) FM 2009. LNCS, vol. 5850, pp. 305–320. Springer, Heidelberg (2009)
12. Valiant, L.: A theory of the learnable. Communications of the ACM 27(11), 1134–1142 (1984)
13. Summers, P.: A methodology for LISP program construction from examples. Journal of the ACM 24(1) (January 1977)
14. Lee, D., Yannakakis, M.: Principles and Methods of Testing Finite State Machines - A Survey. Proceedings of the IEEE 84, 1090–1126 (1996)
15. Gold, M.: Language Identification in the Limit. Information and Control 10, 447–474 (1967)
16. Angluin, D.: Learning Regular Sets from Queries and Counterexamples. Information and Computation 75, 87–106 (1987)
17. Lang, K., Pearlmutter, B., Price, R.: Results of the Abbadingo One DFA Learning Competition and a New Evidence-Driven State Merging Algorithm. In: Honavar, V.G., Slutzki, G. (eds.) ICGI 1998. LNCS (LNAI), vol. 1433, pp. 1–12. Springer, Heidelberg (1998)
18. Gold, M.: Complexity of automaton identification from given data. Information and Control 37, 302–320 (1978)
19. Angluin, D.: On the complexity of minimum inference of regular sets. Information and Control 39, 337–350 (1978)
20. Walkinshaw, N., Bogdanov, K., Holcombe, M., Salahuddin, S.: Improving Dynamic Software Analysis by Applying Grammar Inference Principles. Journal of Software Maintenance and Evolution: Research and Practice (2008)
21. Mitchell, T.: Machine Learning. McGraw-Hill, New York (1997)
22. Walkinshaw, N., Bogdanov, K., Johnson, K.: Evaluation and Comparison of Inferred Regular Grammars. In: Clark, A., Coste, F., Miclet, L. (eds.) ICGI 2008. LNCS (LNAI), vol. 5278, pp. 252–265. Springer, Heidelberg (2008)
23. Sokolova, M., Lapalme, G.: A systematic analysis of performance measures for classification tasks. Information Processing and Management 45(4), 427–437 (2009)

Mining API Popularity

Yana Momchilova Mileva, Valentin Dallmeier, and Andreas Zeller

Saarland University, Saarbrücken, Germany
{mileva,dallmeier,zeller}@cs.uni-saarland.de

Abstract. When designing a piece of software, one frequently must choose between multiple external libraries that provide similar services. Which library is the best one to use? We mined hundreds of open source projects and their external dependencies in order to observe the popularity of their APIs and to give recommendations of the kind: *"Projects are moving away from this API element. Consider a change."* Such **wisdom of the crowds** can provide valuable information to both the API users and the API producers.

1 Introduction

Nowadays, hardly any software project exists that does not use external libraries and their APIs. However, despite this strong connection between projects and external libraries, no proper manner of evaluating the quality and success of an API exists. Means like emails, newsgroups and bug-tracking systems are indeed present, but they do not serve such a purpose. The absence of a bug report, for instance, might mean that the API is not being used at all, or that it is being very successful and free of bugs. *In our research we consider the popularity of an API to be indicative of its success. We also consider the lack of popularity or the decrease in popularity to be indicative of lack of success.*

In order to leverage the wisdom of the crowds of API users, we need to mine a large body of projects. For this purpose we collected information from hundreds of open-source projects and analyzed the overall global API elements usage trends. To explore the choices made, we mined information from the source code history of 200 Apache[1] and Sourceforge[2] projects. To this end, we developed a tool prototype that provides popularity information regarding the usage of API elements (classes and interfaces) and gives recommendations regarding the future usage trend of API elements. For example, as it can be seen from Figure 1, the *java.io.StringBufferInputStream* class is not being very popular and its usage is declining. Investigation of the reasons behind this drop in popularity showed that the class is in fact defective. Such information regarding API elements can serve both the API users as well as the API producers.

The remainder of this paper is organized as follows. Section 2 discusses the benefits of API popularity data. Section 3 presents our approach to finding

---
[1] http://www.apache.org/
[2] http://sourceforge.net/

API usage trends. Section 4 discusses the usage recommendations we offer to the API users. The correctness of those recommendations is evaluated in Section 4.1. Some of the possible threats to the validity to our results are discussed in Section 5; related work is discussed in Section 6. We conclude the paper with a summary and ideas for further improvement of the presented approach (Section 7).

2 API Popularity

Even though external libraries are an important part of projects' source code, no direct feedback means exist that can determine and display the popularity of an API. When analyzing API popularity we focus on the "weak spots" on the API, i.e. those elements that are unpopular or declining is popularity. Having such information available can be beneficial in two ways:

Library users. The software developers who use external libraries in their projects can profit from knowing which are the "weak spots" in an API. If a lack of or a decrease in the usage of an API element exists this is an indication that the majority of the users prefer not to use it. Such information will help the software developers make better choices regarding the usage of API elements by avoiding the indicated bad experience of their peers.

Library producers. In order to deliver a better product, the library developers need to know how their API is being used by the end user. Once they identify the "weak spots" of their API, they can direct their attention to investigating why the popularity is such. Similarly to product survey results, such data can help the API producers provide a better product as a whole based on the preferences of their users.

After discussing the importance of API popularity data, in the next section we present our approach to collecting and analyzing API usage trends.

3 Collecting Usage Data

For our analysis we used projects from both Apache and Sourceforge — two of the most popular open-source repositories. We downloaded and analyzed the source code of 200 projects (50 from Sourceforge and 150 from Apache) for the period beginning of January 2008 — end of January 2009.

To analyze the popularity of a library API at the given time period, we counted the number of projects in which each API element was used in that period. In order to do that we analyzed the number of projects per month that used a specified **import statement**. From January 2008 to January 2009, in the 200 projects, we detected the usage of 23 401 **unique** import statements.

Our prototype tool analyses the collected data and plots the usage trend for a specified API element (see Figure 1). The data is accumulated over the entire number of projects that use the specified import statement.

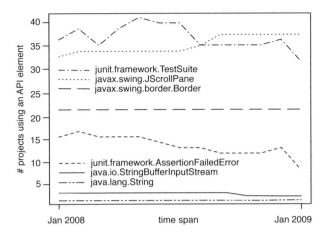

Fig. 1. Examples of the four usage trend types: increasing trend — *javax.swing.JScrollPane*, decreasing trend — *junit.framework.AssertionFailedError*, stable trend — *javax.swing.border.Border* and undecided trend — *junit.framework.TestSuite*.

Such accumulated usage trends can give valuable information to the libraries producers as of how popular their API and its elements are (also in comparison to other similar libraries) and to thus assist them in taking future maintenance and management decisions.

As mentioned earlier, such usage or popularity data is also useful for the users of an API. Our prototype tool is able to offer usage recommendations, based on the past usage trends of an API element. More specifically, if a decrease in or low popularity of the specified API element is observed, our prototype tool is going to warn against the usage of this element. We evaluate the correctness of such recommendations in Section 4.1.

Let us now discuss some concrete examples of decreasing API elements usage trends. One can expect that with the evolution and growth of projects the usage of the specific import statements will increase. This is indeed true for those libraries and their APIs that are widely used by the software developers (see Figure 1, *javax.swing.JScrollPane*). However, there are cases where the usage is decreasing. As mentioned before, we are mainly interested in those cases where a decrease in the usage is present or the actual usage is very low. We assume that such usage (or low popularity) of a specific import statement indicates that this API element is considered to be outdated, obsolete or is simply defective.

In Figure 1, one can see examples of classes with decreasing or low usage. We investigated the possible reasons behind some of those trends:

java.lang.String: Even though the *String* class is not a deprecated class on its own, there is an explicit rule in the Java Coding Convention stating that this class should never be imported. Thus a developer importing it violates the Java Coding Conventions and introduces a **code smell** in the source code.

java.io.StringBufferInputStream: In this case, the class *StringBufferInputStream* is declared deprecated as it does not correctly convert characters into bytes. Even though the documentation of the API explicitly states that the *StringReader* class should be used instead, there are still projects that use the deprecated *StringBufferInputStream* class. Based on the reasons why this class was deprecated (wrong conversion of characters) one can assume that those projects that are still using it are susceptible to **code defects**.

junit.framework.AssertionFailedError: In the case of this class we found a commit log message reporting an issue with *AssertionFailedError* when using it in combination with the *jmock* library. This is an example of a library **compatibility problem**.

These examples show real source code problems, introduced due to the inappropriate usage of API elements. This allows us to make the following statement:

> *Before using a specific API element, one should consider its usage popularity.*

4 Predicting Usage Trends

Our popularity analysis is straightforward in its nature — we compute the number of times per month a specific API element is used throughout the 200 open-source projects we mine. The usage recommendations, however, that our prototype tool gives based on this popularity analysis are not so straightforward.

Due to the diverse nature of software projects development, the API elements usage trends are also quite diverse in their shapes. As it is not possible to frame the trends into any other general way, we differentiate between four main **types of trends**: *increasing, decreasing, stable* and *undecided* (see Figure 1) — based on the slope of the trend line. All kinds of trends carry valuable information, but the ones that are most interesting for us are the *decreasing* ones. A decrease in the usage of an API element can be due to factors like: defects in the API, deprecated classes or methods (see Section 3), or the availability of a different and better API. However, no matter what the reasons behind a usage drop are, the API users should be warned about this element. When our prototype tool detects a decreasing trend or an unpopular API element (element used by less than 1% of the projects) the tool issues a warning of the kind: *"Projects are moving away from this API element. Consider a change."*

4.1 Evaluating the Recommendations

In this paper we take a look at the past usage trends of API elements as accumulated over all the 200 analyzed projects. Based on the notion that *the type of the past accumulated usage trend will not change in the future*, we give usage recommendations regarding a specific API element. In this section we evaluate the statement that:

> *The past usage trend of an API element is predictive of the future usage trend of the same element.*

Due to the diverse nature of the shapes of the trends curves, it is hard to find a predicting method that will work for all types of curves. However, as we are interested only in the general direction of a trend, i.e. if the trend is *increasing, decreasing* or *stable*, linear regression will give us descriptive enough results for our evaluation.

In order to evaluate the correctness of our recommendations we took the usage trends of the import statements for the period beginning of January 2008 — end of January 2009 (13 months) and split it into two parts. We wanted to see if the trend that we observe in the first period will continue to have the same shape during the second period. In order to check that we used linear regression on the first period January 2008 — October 2008 (8 months) and on the entire period (all 13 months) and compared the results for each import statement for the first period and for the entire period.

Table 1. Precision of the import statements usage trends recommendations

	Trends	Actual		
		Increasing	Stable	Decreasing
Predicted	Increasing	**67%**	33%	0%
	Stable	1%	**98%**	1%
	Decreasing	0%	18 %	**82%**

As it is evident from Table 1, we have very high *precision* values when it comes to predicting that an increasing trend will continue increasing, a stable trend will remain stable and a decreasing trend will keep on decreasing. Note that, due to the nature of software projects development, it is very rare to observe an accumulated usage trend that has no fluctuations in its shape. The *recall* values are also quite high - ranging from 0.82 to 0.95 (complete recall values table is not presented here, due to space limitations). Finally, our evaluation showed that in total in 84% of the cases our prediction of the future trend and thus our recommendations are valid.

Those results are a clear evidence that our recommendations regarding the future behavior of usage trends are accurate. In conclusion of the evaluation of our hypothesis, we can state that:

> *The past usage trend of an API element is indeed predictive of the future usage trend of the same element.*

5 Threats to Validity

As any empirical study, this study has limitations that must be considered when interpreting its results.

The approach may cancel itself. When one gives recommendations based on past trends, there is always the question: what will happen if everybody indeed starts following the recommendations — won't those recommendations cancel the future refreshment of their own source? This issue is solved by the introduction of the notion of **early adopters** and **late followers** [2]. This notion states that there will always be users, who take the role of early adopters of a technology (in our case API element), despite the risks and the recommendations.

People do not delete unused imports. We found evidence in the commit log files clearly stating that people are removing unused import statements. However, even if there are some unused imports that are still present in the code, they will not majorly influence the decreasing or unpopular trends of a library, and those are the trends we base our recommendations on.

The approach is applicable only to Java projects. It might seem at first glance that our approach is designed strictly for Java projects. However the analysis of the import statements can be easily transferred to analysis of imports in any other language — the way we scan through a Java source file, can be used to scan through any other programming language source file.

6 Related Work

Analyzing popularity and success factors of software projects is a relatively new research field. PopCon [1] is a prototype tool that collects popularity information regarding the Eclipse API. Based on the usage frequency of the API elements, the authors direct the library users to using the popular elements. For this research, the authors used data from a fixed point in time and investigated the usage of the Eclipse API. In comparison, we used data that spans a period of one year and goes through the code history of 200 projects. Thus our approach presents richer and much more general results for estimating API popularity.

Schuler and Zimmermann [4] collect information about the popularity of library methods and thus help the library developers plan and prioritize the development effort. They also present the notion of usage expertise, which manifests itself whenever developers call an API method.

The AKTARI tool [2] collects information regarding the popularity of different library *versions* of the same library and provides means for evaluating the quality of those versions. The data used for this analysis is limited to open-source projects that use the Maven[3] platform.

A lot of related work has been also done to support developers in adjusting their code to a new version of an API. SpotWeb [5] is a tool that crawls open source repositories to mine frequent usage patterns for libraries. These patterns are then presented to the developers who want to start using a library. In contrast to this work, our approach tries to suggest whether a developer should at all use the specific library API and its elements.

---

[3] http://maven.apache.org/

Perkins [3] presents an approach to refactoring deprecated API methods. The author directly offers the API users a substitute code for the deprecated methods, by replacing those methods with their bodies and appropriate replacement code.

The MAPO [6] tool helps developers understand API usages better and write API client code more effectively. Given a query that describes an API element, this tool mines source code search engines results and presents a short list of frequent API usages.

To the best of our knowledge, our approach is the first that tries to recommend or dissuade from using a specific API element based on its global usage history as inferred from a large body of projects.

7 Conclusions and Future Work

In this paper we investigate the question of API popularity. Our conclusions are based on data collected from 200 open-source projects and thus leverage the wisdom of a crowd of experts.

We have developed a tool prototype that analyzes the collected information and plots API elements usage trends. This information can be of great value for the API producers, when identifying the weak spots of their product. Based on the past usage trends, we are also able to give usage recommendations to the API users. The large and diverse set of projects that we analyze, as well as our good evaluation results, ensure that the recommendations offered by our tool prototype are valid. As we have seen in Section 3, neglecting the vote of the majority can lead to introducing defects and code smells in the project's code.

In conclusion we can state that:

> *API elements usage trends are a method for displaying the preferences of the API users in the past and for predicting their future.*

We believe that collecting usage information accumulated over the development history of hundreds of software projects has the potential to issue valuable cross-project recommendations. As we want to further explore the potential of mining the wisdom of such a crowd of experts, we have already identified a number of ways the here presented work can be extended and improved:

Give more targeted recommendations. We want to be able to not only give recommendations regarding the popularity of a specific API element, but also to be able to give the reasons behind such recommendation. One possible approach would be to mine commit log messages. Once we find a log message describing the problem with the usage of this element, we can present it to the API user. In the case of the *AssertionFailedError* class used in combination with the *jmock* library — we will not only recommend against using this class and give the reasons behind this recommendation, but we will also be able to recommend this only to projects that use both libraries (thus targeting better the end user).

Analyze More Data. We have traversed the entire Apache repository but so far we have used historical data for only a small fraction of the repository. In this respect we plan to redo our experiments on the entire repository.

Evaluation of the usefulness of our recommendations. We are planning to perform a more extensive evaluation of the value that our recommendations bring. Here we have presented a few examples, but it would be interesting to put our approach to the test by examining in how many of the cases real developers (API users and producers) find our recommendations useful.

For further information about the project, visit

http://www.st.cs.uni-saarland.de/softevo/

Acknowledgments. Yana Mileva is funded by the Max-Planck-Institut Informatik and by Microsoft Research Cambridge Lab. Valentin Dallmeier is a member of and supported by the Saarland Graduate School of Computer Science. The authors thank the anonymous reviewers as well as David Schuler, Kim Herzig and Andrzej Wasylkowski for their valuable comments on previous versions of this paper.

References

1. Holmes, R., Walker, R.J.: Informing eclipse api production and consumption. In: eclipse 2007: Proceedings of the 2007 OOPSLA workshop on eclipse technology eXchange, pp. 70–74. ACM, New York (2007)
2. Mileva, Y.M., Dallmeier, V., Burger, M., Zeller, A.: Mining trends of library usage. In: IWPSE-Evol 2009: Proceedings of the joint international and annual ERCIM workshops on Principles of software evolution (IWPSE) and software evolution (Evol) workshops, pp. 57–62. ACM, New York (2009)
3. Perkins, J.H.: Automatically generating refactorings to support api evolution. SIGSOFT Softw. Eng. Notes 31(1), 111–114 (2006)
4. Schuler, D., Zimmermann, T.: Mining usage expertise from version archives. In: MSR 2008: Proceedings of the 2008 international working conference on Mining software repositories (May 2008)
5. Thummalapenta, S., Xie, T.: Spotweb: detecting framework hotspots via mining open source repositories on the web. In: MSR 2008: Proceedings of the 2008 international working conference on Mining software repositories, pp. 109–112. ACM, New York (2008)
6. Zhong, H., Xie, T., Zhang, L., Pei, J., Mei, H.: MAPO: Mining and recommending API usage patterns. In: Drossopoulou, S. (ed.) ECOOP 2009. LNCS, vol. 5653, pp. 318–343. Springer, Heidelberg (2009)

Automatic Discovery of Unspecified Behaviors in Automotive Control Software

Muzammil Shahbaz and Robert Eschbach

Fraunhofer IESE, Germany
{muzammil.shahbaz,robert.eschbach}@iese.fraunhofer.de

Abstract. Modern vehicular systems include Electronic Control Units (ECUs) equipped with software that implements vehicle functions. The composition and validation of ECUs is a complex task since they include propriety software in which functional details are often unspecified. These details also vary from one supplier to another which has a greater impact on the behavior of the entire composed system. This paper presents the application of model inference approach for automatic discovery of unspecified behaviors in an electronic door control unit supplied by our industrial partner. The final results can be used to address the problem of selecting quality components, validation and maintenance of component variants and their integration in embedded control systems.

1 Introduction

The designers in embedded system industry are facing challenges for producing high quality and reliable products. Especially, the automotive industry has to deal with performance issues when complying with new market trends. As a consequence, a modern vehicle has become a complex system that involves several electronic and software components from multiple vendors. The economics of product engineering demands cost-effective solutions and suggests designers to obtain components from specialized vendors rather than develop in-house. On top of these requirements, the designers make frequent use of component variants to satisfy larger group of customers and thereby increase market share and product volume [7].

One of the main problems in component based engineering is the improper understanding of specifications. Studies show that a major source of system failure comes from erroneous or incomplete specifications [10]. The incompleteness is often compensated with domain expertise, hence having implicit requirements. Generally, component vendors follow a de-facto context for component development and vary in implementation details. As a result, components of similar functionalities from different vendors come with numerous configurations and variants which are also not documented properly. This situation raises issues with respect to selecting quality components, validation and maintenance of component variants and their integration into a system.

To address these issues, we propose to use the approach of model inference in order to explore the component behaviors systematically. The behaviors could be useful in analyzing "fitness for use" of the components in the global system in a formal way. The approach does not require knowledge on the internal structure/design of a component but the interfaces with which the designer would interact to integrate in the system. This paper presents our experiences with the approach for embedded control systems in automobiles. The approach has been applied on the electronic door control unit (DCU) of a Mercedes-Benz automobile and discovered unspecified behaviors of its power window and mirror control units.

The rest of the paper is structured as follows. Section 2 describes the model inference technique used in our experiments with the control unit. Section 3 describes the system for which our experiments setup. Section 4 gives a full account of our experiments. Section 5 concludes the paper.

2 Model Inference Approach

The idea of model inference is to derive a formal model of underlying behaviors of a component automatically. There are several statistical and algorithmic methods that infer models in different contexts. For example, model inference for network protocols has been studied previously in the reverse engineering context [1]. Inferring grammars, regular [4] and context-free [5], from arbitrary input data has also been studied extensively.

In our work, we use algorithms in grammar inference assuming that the underlying component behavior can be represented as a regular language. In this context, we use the learning algorithm [12] that learns a Mealy machine model from a black box component. Assuming that the input alphabet of the component is known, the algorithm calculates tests from the alphabet and applies those tests to the component. Based upon the observations in the result of these tests, the algorithm calculates more tests and thus collects more observations from the component. It iterates in this fashion until some conditions are satisfied on the overall observation pack, and finally calculates a Mealy machine model that is consistent with the observations. The discussion on the algorithmic complexity and properties of the inferred model is referred to the original paper [12]. Here, we demonstrate the algorithm with the help of a simple example.

Let the input alphabet of the unknown component be $\{a, b\}$. Then, the inputs in the set are applied on the initial state of the component. Suppose the component responses with 0 and 0 respectively. Then, these observations are recorded in some data structure. Here, we use a tree for recording the observations as shown in Figure 1(a). Then, more tests are calculated from each leaf node of the tree. In this example, we apply aa, ab, ba and bb to the component and extend the tree with new observations as shown in Figure 1(b). After each extension, we check whether the extended node is equivalent to some previous node in the tree. Two nodes $n1$ and $n2$ are equivalent if i) $n1$ and $n2$ have same number of outward edges and ii) for each outward edge of $n1$ with label x/y, there is an outward edge of $n2$ with label x/y. For example, node 2 is equivalent to node 1 in Figure 1(b). In this case, we stop extending further the subtree of root node 2,

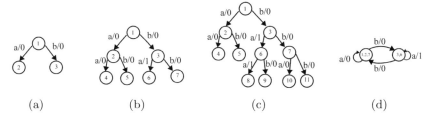

Fig. 1. Demonstration of the learning algorithm

assuming that all future behaviors from node 2 would be same as of node 1. However, node 3 is not equivalent to any of its preceding nodes. Therefore, we continue extending the leaf nodes 6 and 7, as shown in Figure 1(c). Here, node 6 and node 7 are equivalent to node 3 and node 1 respectively. Thus, we stop extending further the subtrees of root node 6 and 7. Now, we merge the equivalent nodes in the tree, i.e., 1, 2, 7, and 3,6, which shapes a Mealy machine as shown in Figure 1(d). The inferred machine is consistent with respect to all recorded observations in the tree. It is also *minimum*, i.e., no two states are equivalent. It is also *input-enabled*, i.e., for each state and each input, there is an outward transition.

3 Automotive Control Units

An advanced vehicle includes a number of Electronic Control Units (ECUs) equipped with software that controls one or more system or subsystems. For example, a power window ECU manages functions related to the window.

Figure 2 depicts the conceptual view of an ECU with its i/o boundaries. Current practice builds on top of a reusable "software platform", which consists of a hardware abstraction layer with device drivers and possibly a software (component) framework that is typically vendor specific. This software platform is accessible through an Application Programmers Interface (API). Different vendors, presenting the same API, can have different realization of different parts in the software platform [7].

In our experimental setup, we focused on the ECUs of power window and mirror that are embedded in a superior Door Control Unit (DCU). The ECUs can be accessed individually with the help of provided APIs. The I/O communication is held

Fig. 2. Conceptual view of an ECU

via CAN-bus or LIN-bus. The I/O boundaries are complete since all inputs can be received and all outputs can be forwarded through their specialized interfaces.

4 Inference of the DCU Behaviors

4.1 Inputs Chart

One of the main challenges of inferring DCU behaviors was to identify all possible signals that could stimulate the observable behaviors of the embedded components. The selection of signals for observing the corresponding behavior of the DCU on a specific input, and eventually, the mapping of input and output signals was also crucial. We identified most of the signals from the requirements [3] by selecting all signals that were described in the context of the i/o interfaces and determining their relevance. While many inputs broadcast via CAN-bus for example, not all were relevant. To further reduce complexity, all inputs were checked for the possibility of abstraction. In our case, sets of inputs having logical connection were aggregated and named, usually sequences of inputs that always occur in the same order. Table 1 shows a part of resulting inputs.

Table 1. Part of the Input Chart

Symbolic name	Signal values	Description
$START$	0,...,20	Key operations and Engine Ignition
$MRUN$	1,0	Motor Start
OP	1,0	Open window (Control Panel)
CP	1,0	Close window (Control Panel)
OTP	1,0	Open window completely (Control Panel)
CTC	1,0	Close window completely (Control Panel)
CV	0,...,254 (MPH)	Car Velocity
SM	1,0	Switch to right or left mirror
MU	1,0	Move mirror up
MD	1,0	Move mirror down
ML	1,0	Move mirror left
MR	1,0	Move mirror right
FE	1,0	Fold/Expand mirror
AT	-40,...,85 (Celsius)	Air Temperature

4.2 Automation

RALT [11] was used as the inference tool that implements the learning algorithm for Mealy machines [12]. Initialized with an inputs set, the tool provides tests for the real system and finally infers behavioral models based upon the test results.

ProveTech:TA [6] tool was used as a test runner that automates the test execution process for the DCU. It uses WinWrap Basic for writing test scripts in which signal values were set for each ECU.

Thus, the generated tests from RALT were transferred to ProveTech:TA test scripts. Similarly, the results of the tests from ProveTech:TA were then transferred into abstract symbols for RALT to interpret. The real time interfacing

Fig. 3. Position of DCU in the door   **Fig. 4.** Testing Setup

between ProveTech:TA and DCU was provided by dSPACE [2] that eventually applied tests to the target ECUs and received output signals accordingly. Figure 3 shows the position of DCU in a car door. Figure 4 shows the physical testing setup in which the car door and the dSPACE unit are visible. Once the test setup was prepared, the inference process was completely automatic.

4.3 Initialization

The preconditions of the experiments were set according to the following initialization setup. The door was locked and all ECUs were switched off. The window was closed completely and the mirror was folded. These conditions were also viewed as system reset before applying each test during inference.

In order to control timing issues, we kept a delay of 3 seconds between any two inputs in a test sequence. This delay was selected after a careful study of the physical latencies in the system. For example, it takes almost three seconds for the power window ECU to open/close window completely starting from the initial point. Similarly, the recording of the observations for each input was also taken care of with appropriate timing delays.

The condition of *input-enabled* in the inference process was also adjusted, since it is always possible to check signal values in ProveTech:TA at any given time. In reality, when an input signal does not trigger an observable system response, then the corresponding output signal contains a zero value (or a negative value in some cases). This particular situation was dealt by denoting a special symbol, named "KO", suffixed with the abstract output.

Continuous stimuli (time, temperature) were partitioned and the transition from one partition to another was treated as an input. Only few values were selected for such stimuli to avoid exhaustive testing and state explosion in the inference results.

4.4 Inference Results and Analysis

The models for power window and mirror ECUs were learned individually by restricting the input set only to these units each time. It took half an hour for

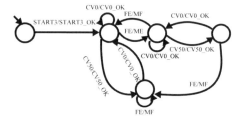

(a) Showing that window closing does not function if preceded by opening. The delay between inputs was 3 sec.

(b) Showing that mirror expansion and folding mechanism depends upon the car velocity.

Legends:

-*x_OK*: operation *x* done	-*x_KO*: operation *x* failed
-*START*3: *START* with value 3	
-*CV*0: *CV* with value 0	-*CV*50: *CV* with value 50
-*ME*: Mirror Expanded	-*MF*: Mirror Folded

Fig. 5. Snippets of the inferred models of power window and mirror ECUs

the power window ECU and inferred a five state model using 802 tests. The mirror ECU was learned in about two hours with nine states using 1952 tests. Figure 5 shows a part of the inferred models produced by RALT.

The inferred models were compared with the available specification of the DCU. The specification was originally documented in a natural language which was converted into a formal representation through Sequence Based Specification (SBS) [9] process. SBS is a stepwise construction of a traceably-correct black box specifications that is based on a sequence enumeration procedure and basic requirements analysis skills. The end result can be easily converted into state machines or other formal representations. In our case, we developed Mealy machine representation of the available specification of DCU using SBS process.

The formal comparison of inferred models and specifications reported many differences in the functional behaviors of power window and mirror ECUs. Some of these differences occurred due to inconsistencies, unclear statements and vague formulations in the original specification document. In most of these cases, the differences were resolved by consulting the general knowledge about the possible implementation (e.g, voltage, sensor readings) and conceptual issues (e.g., mechanical maneuvers). Rest of the behavioral differences were analyzed with respect to the equivalence of responses for the same input sequences.

It is found that inferred models discovered behaviors which were either missing altogether from the original specification or specified partially. For example, the input sequence *OTP* opens the window completely but the sequence *OTP-OTP* starts opening the window but stops in the middle of the frame. The former behavior was learned as expected, however, the latter was not mentioned in the available specification. In another sequence, *OTP-CP* should open the window completely and then close it according to the specification. However, the inferred model prescribes that it starts opening the window for the first input but stops

Table 2. Description of the inferred behaviors of power window and mirror ECUs that were unspecified or partially specified in the original specification

Description of the Inferred Behaviors	Status
Any input preceded by OTP with in the span of 5 seconds stops the opening of the window at the middle of the frame.	Unspecified
Any input preceded by OTP with in the span of 5 seconds does not produce any observable behavior. For example, the sequence OTP-CP opens the window for the first input but does not close the window for the second input.	Unspecified
Mirror can only be expanded (by $FE = 1$) when the mirror is in folded position previously and $CV < 50$ (approx).	Partially Specified
Mirror heating turns on automatically when $MRUN = 1$, $AT <$ 10 (approx) and battery voltage is 12V.	Partially Specified
$START = 10$ folds the mirror and turns off the ECUs. $START = 3$ turns on the ECUs and expands the mirror. However, if the mirror was already in folded position before given $START = 10$, then the following $START = 3$ does not expand the mirror.	Unspecified
$START = 12$ folds the mirror and turns off the ECUs. ($START = 10$ and $START = 12$ have same impact on power window and mirror ECUs.)	Unspecified

in the middle of the frame, remains mute for the second input and does not close the window. All inferred behaviors that were discovered unspecified or partially specified were rechecked for their reproducibility. Table 2 summarizes some of these important behaviors. The first column describes the inferred behaviors and the second column labels its status (unspecified or partially specified) according to the original specification.

5 Conclusion

We studied the application of a model inference approach to the electronic door control unit (DCU) of a Mercedes-Benz automobile. The experiments were conducted with the objective of discovering behaviors of DCU that were unspecified or partially specified in the original specification document provided by our industrial partner. The inferred models depicted several unknown behaviors related to power window and mirror ECUs which are important with respect to validating their dependencies and overall system response of an automobile. For example, it is also found that the behavior of the mirror ECU is dependent upon the telemetric recordings of car velocity.

The composition and validation of third-party components is a complex task since they include propriety software in which functional details are often unspecified. Moreover, a component behavior may have a hidden impact on the functionality of other components in the system. Thus, it is difficult to judge the quality of components without having a complete knowledge over their behavioral spectrum. We hope that the results presented in this paper will pave a way towards building rigorous techniques for embedded systems to deal with issues related to selecting quality components, validation and maintenance of component variants and their integration into a system.

These experiments can also be viewed important for the application of model inference approach on real world systems. It is known that inference algorithms does not always lead towards inferring correct and precise models. The cost of hypothetical perfect model is exponential in the theoretical context [8]. At the same time, model inference in embedded system domain deduce relatively good approximations in a "reasonable" time which are appropriate enough for designers in practice. The main reason is that the applications in this domain mainly concern with control parts, e.g., ECUs, which do not subject to scale up in state space like in other domains such as web services.

References

1. Cui, W.: Discoverer: Automatic protocol reverse engineering from network traces. In: Proceedings of the 16th USENIX Security Symposium (2007)
2. dSPACE, http://www.dspaceinc.com
3. Houdek, F., Paech, B.: Das türsteuergerät. eine beispielspezifikation. Technical Report 002.02/D, Fraunhofer IESE (2002)
4. Kearns, M.J., Vazirani, U.V.: An introduction to computational learning theory. MIT Press, Cambridge (1994)
5. Lehman, E., Shelat, A.: Approximation algorithms for grammar-based compression. In: Proceedings of the 13th annual ACM-SIAM symposium on Discrete algorithms, pp. 205–212 (2002)
6. MBtech: Provetech:ta, http://www.mbtech-group.com
7. Möller, A., Fröberg, J., Nolin, M.: Industrial requirements on component technologies for embedded systems. In: Crnković, I., Stafford, J.A., Schmidt, H.W., Wallnau, K. (eds.) CBSE 2004. LNCS, vol. 3054, pp. 146–161. Springer, Heidelberg (2004)
8. Peled, D., Vardi, M.Y., Yannakakis, M.: Black box checking. Journal of Automata, Languages and Combinatorics 7(2), 225–246 (2002)
9. Prowell, S.J., Poore, J.H.: Foundations of sequence-based software specification. IEEE Trans. Softw. Eng. 29(5), 417–429 (2003)
10. Schach, S.R.: Classical and Object-Oriented Software Engineering. McGraw-Hill Professional, New York (1995)
11. Shahbaz, M.: Reverse Engineering Enhanced State Models of Black Box Components to support Integration Testing. PhD thesis, Grenoble Institute of Technology (2008)
12. Shahbaz, M., Groz, R.: Inferring mealy machines. In: Cavalcanti, A., Dams, D.R. (eds.) FM 2009. LNCS, vol. 5850, pp. 207–222. Springer, Heidelberg (2009)

An Empirical Evaluation to Study Benefits of Visual versus Textual Test Coverage Information

Vahid Garousi and Negar Koochakzadeh

Department of Electrical and Computer Engineering, University of Calgary, Canada
{vgarousi,nkoochak}@ucalgary.ca

Abstract. The code coverage tools (e.g., CodeCover for Java) and the textual coverage information (e.g., only metric values) they produce are very useful for testers. However with increasing size and complexity of code bases of both systems under test and also their automated test suites (e.g., based on JUnit), there is a need for visualization techniques to enable testers to analyze code coverage in higher levels of abstraction. To address the above need, we recently proposed a test coverage visualization tool. To assess the usability, effectiveness and usefulness of this tool in unit testing and test maintenance tasks, we have conducted a controlled experiment, the results of which show that the tool can benefit testers more compared to textual coverage information.

1 Introduction

Various test coverage criteria (e.g., statement or decision coverage) have been defined to help testers in determining how much testing effort is required for a System Under Test (SUT). Testers also refer to coverage information to perform software and test maintenance tasks such as fault localization [1].

To support automated code coverage measurement and analysis, test coverage values are conventionally shown in percentages and are visualized by progress-bar-like green/red boxes in the existing coverage tools (e.g., the CodeCover plug-in [2] for the Eclipse IDE). In the state-of-the-practice, covered source-code statements of the SUT by a test suite are also usually colored by various tools using green, yellow, and red colors.

Although the existing test coverage and test visualization tools and the information they produce are very useful for testers, however with increasing size and complexity of code bases of SUTs and also their automated test suites (e.g., based on JUnit), there is a need for visualization techniques to enable testers to analyze code coverage in higher levels of abstraction and in holistic manners, e.g., one might ask a question such as: which packages of the SUT are covered by a specific set of test cases?

To achieve the above need, we recently proposed a graph-based test coverage visualization tool [3] that displays all test and SUT artifacts in a graph-based representation. In this graph, unit test artifacts covering SUT source code artifacts are interconnected by edges. To the best of our knowledge, this idea has never been proposed before.

The tool is actual an Eclipse IDE plug-in called TeCReVis (Test Coverage and Test Redundancy Visualization), which is now part of the CodeCover tool [2]. To evaluate our test visualization framework and tool, we have performed a controlled experiment to assess whether it would help testers in improving fault localization efficiency. The experimental results (reported in this short paper) support the effectiveness of our visualization methodology both qualitatively and quantitatively.

The remainder of this article is structured as follows. A quick overview of the visualization tool is discussed in Section 2. Experimental evaluation of the tool is discussed in Section 3.

2 Test Coverage Visualization

The concept behind the recently proposed TeCReVis test visualization tool [3] is a graph, in which SUT source code artifacts covered by unit test artifacts (e.g., in the JUnit framework) are inter-connected by edges. This graph is referred to as a Test Coverage Graph (TCG).

Figure 1 shows a sample TCG generated by our TeCReVis tools for an open-source java SUT called Allelogram [4]. This TCG contains three test methods (nodes on the left side) and seven SUT methods (nodes on the right side). Various granularities can be selected for both groups of items. Method, package and class (similar to grouping mechanisms in Java) are available for both groups. We have primarily developed our visualization technique for JUnit and the Eclipse framework. However, the idea and the tool can be easily ported (extended) to other test frameworks and platforms.

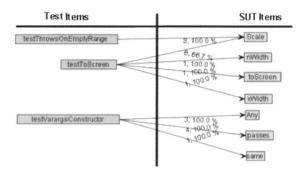

Fig. 1. A sample TCG Graph generated by the TeCReVis tool

For instance, when code branch level is selected in the TeCReVis tool, each of the source code branches (i.e., SUT items) is shown by a node in TCG. When the statement level is selected in this tool, each of the Java code statements in the SUT is shown by a node in TCG. In the example TCG shown in Figure 1, test method and source code method levels are chosen for both of the test and SUT items. Test method `testToScreen` calls the methods `Scale` and `nWidth` from the SUT (i.e., Allelogram), 8 and 1 time(s), respectively. The coverage ratios are 66.7% and 100%, respectively (statement coverage is selected in this case).

3 Empirical Evaluation

The approach we have used in our experiment is the Goal, Question, Metric (GQM) methodology. Using the GQM's goal template, the goal of the experiment is to analyze the benefits of *test coverage visualization*, for the purpose of *evaluating its effectiveness on fault localization* from the point of view of *project managers and software testers* in the context of *software maintenance*. Based on the above goal, we raise the following research question: Does TeCReVis help human testers on average to localize faults more efficiently compared to the use of conventional code-coverage tools (which show textual and progress-bar like coverage information)?

As participants, we invited 204 graduate students and a few testers from the local industry. From the pool of respondents, eight graduate students (studying at the University of Calgary) in the field of software engineering were selected to take part in this experiment. To evaluate the effect of using TeCReVis on the efficiency of fault localization, the eight participants of this experiment were divided into two groups with TeCReVis being available only for the experimental group, while the control group used the CodeCover coverage tool.

In grouping the participants, we utilized rigorous methods as defined by empirical software engineering experts [5], e.g., random assignment and careful blocking. We did our best to make sure that the accumulative testing knowledge and experience of both groups were almost equal (details in [6]).

Based on our experiment goal and our research question, we formulated our hypothesis as follows. *Hypothesis (H_1)*: TeCReVis helps human testers on average to localize faults more efficiently. *Null Hypothesis (H_0)*: TeCReVis does not assist human testers with fault localization. We used statistical hypothesis testing (i.e., one-sided t-test) to assess our hypothesis.

To measure fault localization efficiency, we designed a metric as follows. Suppose that we have injected n faults into a SUT. A human debugger usually spends some amount of time to locate those faults in the system by analyzing test results and source code. More time spent would result in less efficiency. Also the number of located faults at the end of the process of fault localization should be considered in measuring the efficiency. Based on the above discussions, equation (1) shows the metric we defined to measure fault localization efficiency for each human debugger in our experiment. In equation (1), d is a human debugger and t_i is the amount of time that he/she has spent to locate the i-th fault. In our experiment, all the faults we injected were almost equally challenging to be located and thus this weight factor was not considered in measuring the efficiency of fault localization.

$$FLE(d) = \sum_{i=1}^{n} \frac{1}{t_i} \quad (1)$$

As the object of this experiment, we chose an open-source ATM machine simulation software [7]. We decided to choose this system because it is easily understandable for most software engineering graduate students (as per our interviews, all of them had seen this system as an example in their earlier courses). To provide a size scale of this system, it has 2,541 Java LOC. To perform the fault localization process, we slightly revised this system by injecting in it three faults.

To perform this experiment, as there was no unit test suite provided with the ATM implementation provided in [7], we created a test suite (containing 23 JUnit test methods) for version 1 of this system. This test suite was constructed to achieve full path coverage on the SUT's UML state-chart diagram. For replicability purposes, all of the developed JUnit test suite and the system's UML design models are available online from [8].

Participants were asked to find and locate three injected faults in the ATM system. Participants were asked to report the time of locating each fault, which were analyzed later by the authors to measure fault localization efficiency. The time to locate each fault by each participant was carefully recorded.

Time duration data of localizing each fault by each participant is shown in Table 1. In this table, G1 is the first group which was asked to use TeCReVis during the experiment (experimental group), while G2 is the other group (control group). A '*' in Table 1 denotes that the participant was not able to find the fault.

By monitoring the participants and also according to the data in Table 1, we observed that the first fault location time contained "learning curve" (program comprehension) as well, i.e., to learn about the SUT and also fault localization by using the available tools. Thus, the time of locating the first fault is higher compared to the others. For example, for P_1, $Fault_1$ was located in 20 minutes, while $Fault_2$ and $Fault_3$ were located in 2 and 1 minutes respectively. The values of fault localization efficiency for each of the participants in each group are also calculated by applying the metric in equation (1). These values are also shown in Table 1.

Table 1. Results of the Experiment (* means that the fault was not found by the participant.)

Group	Participant	Time of locating Fault 1	Time of locating Fault 2	Time of locating Fault 3	Efficiency (FLE)
		All time values are in minutes.			
Experimental Group (used TeCReVis)	P1	20	2	1	1.55
	P2	24	*	*	0.04
	P3	18	1	2	1.55
	P4	23	2	*	0.54
Control Group (used CodeCover)	P5	*	*	*	0
	P6	27	*	*	0.03
	P7	22	7	1	1.18
	P8	*	*	*	0

To analyze the result and conclude about our hypothesis, the t-test was applied. Two types of experiment errors (α and β) were as follows: α=0.12, and β=0.47. Reminder: $α = P(H_0 \text{ is rejected} \mid H_0 \text{ is true})$ and $β = P(H_0 \text{ is accepted} \mid H_0 \text{ is false})$.

The values of α show that, by considering 95% as our confidence level (α=0.05), the null hypothesis (H_0) cannot be rejected. Confidence level of rejecting this null hypothesis is 88% (1- α).

We believe that, although we had tutorial part in our experiment first, learning curve in limited time of performing fault localization task in the experiment has affected our results. While as Table 1 shows, participants in the experimental group have used the benefits of TeCReVis to localize second and third faults more effectively, compared to the control group using the CodeCover tool.

In other words, learning curve caused less effectiveness of using TeCReVis in localizing faults in limited time, which has led to less confidence for rejecting the null hypothesis of this experiment.

Limitation in subject selection made us to have only eight participants. As reported in [9], the sample size of a selected pool of experimental software engineering papers which applied t-test in their experiment ranged from 5 to 136 participants. Thus, our sample size (i.e., 8) lies in the low extreme of similar studies from this perspective.

In this experiment, in addition to measuring fault localization efficiency, we asked participants of experimental group about their feedback on the usefulness of TeCReVis for locating the faults. All of the participants' answers were supportive of the usefulness of TeCReVis for fault localization. For instance, a participant of the experiment group said: "*I feel that, in large systems, this graph-based visualization can be very useful*".

On the other hand, one of the participants in the control group said that it was very time consuming for him to open all files that he had guessed are covered by a failing test to find which part of the source code are colored according to coverage information.

4 Conclusions

Possible threats to the validity of our experiment are explained next. *Internal validity:* The result of this experiment might be from some other factors which we had no control on or we did not measure. For instance, the bias and knowledge of the participants about programming in Java can be such a factor. However, we used the placement test results and also our knowledge from the participants' background in the testing course to make sure that the two groups had almost similar Java skill levels accumulatively.

Construct validity: As this validity is concerned with the relation between theory and observation in the experiment, we should make sure if the outcome of the experiment reflect the effect considered in hypothesis well. In this experiment, we measured fault localization efficiency by equation (1) which is only one possible metric for this purpose.

We plan to investigate the possible usages of our visual test coverage tool in interactive test evolution and Search-based Software Testing (SBST) applications.

References

1. Masri, W.: Fault Localization based on Information-Flow Coverage. To appear in the Wiley Journal on Software Testing, Verification and Reliability (2010)
2. CodeCover Team: CodeCover, http://www.codecover.org (Last accessed: March 2010)
3. Garousi, V., Koochakzadeh, N.: TeCRevis Home Page, http://www.softqual.ucalgary.ca/sw_tools.html (Last accessed: March 2010)
4. Manaster, C.: Allelogram, http://code.google.com/p/allelogram/ (retrieved on 08/20/2008)
5. Wohlin, C., Runeson, P., Host, M., Ohlsson, M.C., Regnell, B., Wesslen, A.: Experimentation in Software Engineering: An Introduction. Kluwer Academic Publishers, Dordrecht (2000)
6. Koochakzadeh, N.: A Measurement, Detection, and Visualization Framework for Software Test Redundancy. MSc Thesis, Department of Electrical and Computer Engineering, University of Calgary (April 2009)
7. Bjork, R.C.: http://www.math-cs.gordon.edu/courses/cs211/ATMExample/ (Last accessed: February 2010)
8. Garousi, V., Koochakzadeh, N.: Supplementary Project Data-JUnit Test Suite, pp. 1–13, http://www.softqual.ucalgary.ca/projects/2010/VG_NK_TAIC_PART (Last accessed: February 2010)
9. Kampenes, V.B., Dybå, T., Hannay, J.E., Sjøberg, D.I.K.: Systematic review: A systematic review of effect size in software engineering experiments. Information and Software Technology 49(11-12), 1073–1086 (2007)

A Multi-criteria Decision Making Framework for Real Time Model-Based Testing

Mohammad Saeed Abou Trab, Bachar Alrouh, Steve Counsell, Rob M. Hierons, and George Ghinea

Department of Information Systems and Computing, Brunel University, Uxbridge, UK
Mohammad.aboutrab@brunel.ac.uk

Abstract. Testing Real-Time Embedded Systems (RTES) is a non-trivial task - time adds a new dimension to the complexity of the testing process. In previous research, we introduced a 'priority-based' approach which tested the logical and timing behaviour of an RTES modelled formally as Uppaal timed automata. In this paper, we develop a novel Analytical Hierarchy Process (AHP) decision-making framework for our priority-based testing approach that provides testers with a systematic approach through which they can prioritize the available testing sets that best fulfils their testing requirements.

Keywords: AHP, decision making, real-time model-based testing.

1 Introduction

Testing a Real-Time Embedded System (RTES) to ensure that its implementation is relatively error-free before deployment is essential; errors in such systems can range from a slight system deviation to severe damage to the environment [1, 2, 3]. In previous research [4], we proposed a new 'priority-based' test case generation approach for RTES modeled as Uppaal timed automata [3]. Our focus was to test RTESs and we chose clock regions as a selection criterion for generating test cases that covered the timed state space of the specification model. Dividing the generated test traces into three separate sets (i.e., boundary, out-boundary and in-boundary), our Priority-Based approach considered the testing environment by enabling the tester to choose between the proposed test sets (or any combination thereof). According to that choice, our approach established a trade-off between increasing confidence in SUT correctness and limited testing resources such as time, effort and cost. Choosing the "best-suited" test set to be deployed for a certain application in a particular organization is a complex decision-making task facing the tester. The urgent necessity of making a best decision according to the testing requirement highlights the need of adopting a systematic decision-making model such as AHP [5].

2 The Analytical Hierarchy Process

The Analytical Hierarchy Process (AHP) [5] is one approach for multi-criteria decision making. The widespread acceptance of AHP is due to its simplicity and ease of use.

AHP assists in analyzing the decision problem logically and in establishing judgments based on decision makers' opinions which can be validated, questioned and reviewed by others. In addition, AHP utilizes a hierarchy structure, which aims to reduce the complexity of a certain problem by decomposing it into sub-problems. Saaty and Vargas [6] describe the steps to implement the AHP method as follows:

1. *Hierarchy*: the problem is decomposed into a hierarchy of goal, criteria, sub-criteria and alternatives. At the root of the hierarchy is the goal or objective of the problem being studied and analyzed. The leaf nodes are the alternatives to be compared. In between these two levels are various criteria and sub-criteria.
2. *Pair-wise Comparisons Matrices*: Elements in lower levels are pair-wise compared with respect to the element immediately above them. Data can be collected from experts/decision-makers or through empirical experiments corresponding to the hierarchic structure.
3. *Eigenvector*: The principal Eigenvalue and the corresponding normalized right Eigenvector of the comparison matrix is calculated to give a relative importance for the various criteria being compared.
4. *Consistency Ratio*: The consistency of the matrix of order n is evaluated using the ratio CR = CI/RI; CI: comparison matrix consistency index, RI: random matrix consistency index. Saaty [6] suggests the value of CR should be < 10%.
5. *Ratings*: The rating of each alternative is multiplied by the weights of the sub-criteria and aggregated to get local ratings with respect to each criterion. The local ratings are then multiplied by the weights of the criteria and aggregated to obtain global ratings.
6. *Integrating Group Judgments*: When the judging process involves multiple experts or data are collected from multiple experiments, then a single consolidated judgment is calculated using a geometric mean to integrate the multiple measures.

3 Decision Making Model

As we aim to develop an AHP hierarchy or Framework for selecting test sets that are most appropriate for certain applications, we recognized that four facets need to be defined: (a) goal; (b) alternatives; (c) criteria; and (d) sub criteria. We then define the decision alternatives. For this purpose, we deliberately prioritize seven test options as a result of predefined three testing sets of our priority-based approach [4] and any possible combination between them: Boundary (B), Out-Boundary (OB), In-Boundary (IB), B+OB, B+IB, OB+IB, B+OB+IB. Fig.1 represents the AHP framework including the decision criteria and sub criteria. In the following, we discuss the decision making criteria and give a brief explanation about each of them stating whether it can be measured (represented by a value) or should be judged (represented by a rank).

Test Adequacy (measurable). The adequacy criteria are considered to be main criteria to rank the quality of the proposed test sets. The test adequacy criteria we followed in our decision model cover the fault and structural converges.

Fault Coverage: A fault model is one of the parameters essential in determining the power of produced test cases in detecting faults in an implementation and hence play an important role in the decision-making process.

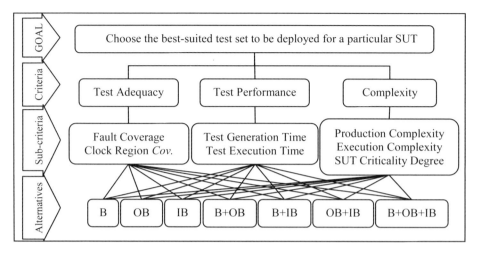

Fig. 1. AHP framework

- The fault model we use is introduced in [7]. The fault coverage sub-criterion can be calculated and compared as ratio for each of the test sets according to (1).

$$Fault\ Coverage\ Ratio = \frac{number\ of\ faults\ dected\ by\ a\ chosen\ set}{total\ number\ of\ faults\ in\ the\ fault\ model} \quad (1)$$

- *Structural Coverage:* As we chose the clock region coverage as a coverage criterion is to direct the selection process of the test points. Calculating the degree of region coverage that each of the proposed test sets can achieve according to (2) plays an important role in the decision-making process.

$$Clock\ Region\ Coverage\ Ratio = \frac{number\ of\ clock\ regions\ covered\ by\ a\ chosen\ set}{total\ number\ of\ clock\ regions\ of\ the\ spec\ model} \quad (2)$$

Test Performance (measurable). It is essential to compare two testing sets to find which performs best. As a result, we cannot ignore them in the decision-making framework. First, **Test generation time**: The time required for each test set to be generated is measured and used for our model. Second, **Test execution time:** Test execution time determines how fast a SUT performs under a particular test set. Since the tester will always prefer a test set that needs the least time to execute, calculating each set execution time for a particular SUT it is important for the tester to make the decision.

Complexity. Each testing set differs according to its inherent difficulty; this can range from the length of the test trace and test suite it generates to the degree of difficulty of executing it on the SUT.

- *Generation Complexity* (measurable): This sub-criterion value can be represented by the number of timed transitions taken within one test trace and the number of test traces in the generated test suite.
- *Execution Complexity* (judgment): Each test set may get different execution complexity rate according to the execution algorithm and therefore the execution steps they follow.

- *SUT Criticality degree* (judgment). The failure of the RTES systems can range from a slight system deviation to severe damage to the environment and people lives. The reason for putting the SUT criticality degree under the complexity criterion is that the more critical SUT requires a larger testing set in order to increase the confidence in SUT correctness.

4 Conclusions

This paper has described a novel Analytical Hierarchy Process (AHP) decision-making framework that provides testers with a systematic and manageable approach through which they can prioritize the available testing sets that best fulfils their testing requirements. We are currently testing the proposed decision making model by various case studies to prove its validity and improve it.

References

1. Mitsching, R., Weise, C., Kolbe, A., Bohnenkamp, H., Berzen, N.: Towards an Industrial Strength Process for Timed Testing. In: International Conference on Software Testing, Verification and Validation Workshops, Denver, Colorado, pp. 29–38 (2009)
2. En-Nouaary, A.: A scalable method for testing real-time systems. Software Quality Control 16, 3–22 (2008)
3. Hessel, A., Larsen, K.G., Mikucionis, M., Nielsen, B., Pettersson, P., Skou, A.: Testing Real-Time Systems Using UPPAAL. In: Hierons, R.M., Bowen, J.P., Harman, M. (eds.) FORTEST. LNCS, vol. 4949, pp. 77–117. Springer, Heidelberg (2008)
4. AbouTrab, M.S., Counsell, S.: Fault Coverage Measurement of a Timed Test Case Generation Approach. In: IEEE International Conference on the Engineering of Computer-Based Systems, Oxford, UK, pp. 141–149 (2010)
5. Saaty, T.L.: Decision making with the analytic hierarchy process. International Journal of Services Sciences 1, 83–98 (2008)
6. Saaty, T.L., Vargas, L.G.: Models, methods, concepts and applications of the analytic hierarchy process. Springer, Heidelberg (2000)
7. En-Nouaary, A., Khendek, F., Dssouli, R.: Fault coverage in testing real-time systems. In: Sixth International Conference on Real-Time Computing Systems and Applications, RTCSA 1999, Hong Kong, China, pp. 150–157 (1999)

Improved Testing through Refactoring: Experience from the ProTest Project

Huiqing Li and Simon Thompson

School of Computing, University of Kent, UK
{H.Li,S.J.Thompson}@kent.ac.uk

Abstract. We report on how the Wrangler refactoring tool has been used to improve and transform test code for Erlang systems. This has been achieved through the removal of code clones, the identification of properties for property-based testing and the definition of testing-aware refactorings and test-framework-specific refactorings. While some of the observations are Erlang-specific, others apply to test code in general.

We argue that refactoring is particularly valuable within testing. The Wrangler tool for Erlang provides support for clone detection and removal, and this has been used effectively both for clarifying test code and in extracting higher-level properties from test suites. We also report on refactorings within particular test frameworks, and on the constraints on refactorings that test frameworks impose.

1 Background

ProTest [1], EU FP7 grant 215868, concerns property-based testing. The interactions of refactoring and testing are the responsibility of the Kent team.

Erlang [2] is a strict, impure, dynamically typed functional programming language with support for higher-order functions, pattern matching, concurrency, communication, distribution, fault-tolerance, and dynamic code loading. There are a number of test frameworks for Erlang, including EUnit [3] and Common Test [4] as well as the property-based, random testing tool, Quviq QuickCheck [5]. Each of these tools imposes a number of constraints on the way that test code is written including naming, macro definitions and callback functions.

Wrangler [6] is an interactive tool for refactoring Erlang programs. Wrangler is integrated with Emacs and also with Eclipse through ErlIDE. Wrangler supports a collection of refactorings, including renaming, function extraction and generalisation, folding and inlining definitions and moving definitions between modules. All refactorings work across multiple-module projects. Wrangler also has a set of "code smell" inspection functionalities as well as facilities to detect and eliminate code clones and to improve the module structure of projects.

Wrangler 'similar' code detection is based on the notion of *anti-unification* [7] to detect code clones in Erlang programs; it also has a mechanism for automatic clone elimination under the user's control. The *anti-unifier* of two terms denotes their *least-general common abstraction*, and we say that two expression/expression sequences, A and B, are *similar* if there exists a 'non-trivial' least-general common abstraction, C, and two substitutions which take C to A and B respectively. By 'non-trivial' we mean that the size of the least-general common abstraction should satisfy some threshold relative to the clone instances. To eliminate a clone, we define a function whose body is the anti-unifier: each instance is given by transforming the substitution into the actual parameter list. More details of the implementation are in [8].

2 Improving Test Code by Clone Elimination

We have been able to use *clone detection and elimination* to make test files simultaneously more concise and more comprehensible. A case study with Ericsson SW Research is reported in detail in [9]: we review the conclusions here.

The case study examined the test code for part of an Erlang implementation of the SIP (Session Initiation Protocol). Working with engineers Adam Lindberg and Andreas Schumacher from Ericsson and Erlang Solutions Ltd. we reduced the code from 2658 lines of code to 2042 in a series of twelve clone eliminations. At the conclusion further clone eliminations and other refactorings were possible. The basic pattern of refactoring was to repeatedly perform these steps.

– Run the clone detection report.
– Choose a clone for removal.
– Introduce the common generalisation as a new function definition.
– Rename the function and the parameters.
– Eliminate the instances by 'folding' them against the function definition.

At first sight this appears to be an entirely mechanical process, but the case study showed that it was quite the reverse: we look at the reasons now.

Which of the reported clones? The first clone detection reports 31 clones, from one of 86 lines, repeated once, to one of 6 lines, appearing 15 times. Which should be chosen? Our experience was that it was best to choose a smaller clone (repeated many times) rather than a larger one. The reason for this *bottom up* approach was that it was substantially easier to understand and therefore to name the former rather than the latter.
Include all the reported code? The clone report has certain threshold parameters: e.g. the default search is for clones of at least five statements. We found cases where a clone contains *sub-clones* which had not been reported because of thresholding, but where we chose to eliminate the sub-clone (first).
What are their names? We were working with engineers who were familiar with the SIP environment, even if they had not written the tests themselves. Only with their insights were we able to give appropriate names to the new functions and their formal parameters.
When and how to generalise? How general should code be? We saw situations where we chose not to further generalise code even when that was

possible, since we would prefer to keep separate versions of similar code with different names. On the other hand, we encountered situations where we had generalised prematurely, and so we had to inline our generalisations in order to make a more general clone elimination. In both cases it was a matter of "programmers' taste" as to when to (stop) generalising.

'Widows' and 'orphans'. We saw cases where the detected clone contained a clear piece of functionality, but by accident, as it were, an extra line appeared at the start or end, because this functionality was usually preceded or succeeded by a particular action. Despite this, we chose to eliminate the meaningful clone, rather than including the maximum number of lines, since naming the former would be possible while naming the latter would not.

Taken together, these reasons show that this cannot be a "push button" automatic operation, but rather it can only be accomplished in collaboration with domain experts. On the other hand, we found that without the automated facilities of Wrangler for finding candidates to eliminate, and generalisations to eliminate them, it would have been impossible to perform an exercise like this.

3 Extracting Properties from Tests

QuickCheck testing involves the statement of properties, which are typically universally quantified, and checking whether they hold of randomly generated values. One of the aims of the ProTest project is to extract properties from tests, and the latest release of Wrangler provides one mechanism for this, thus:

- Identify a clone which consists of a complete test case, with the function `body` giving the common generalisation.
- Replace clone instances by function calls: `body(args1)`, `body(args2)` etc.
- Define a QuickCheck generator `args()` for `[args1, args2, ...]` and a universal property stating "`body(X)` holds for any value in `args()`".
- Generalise the generator to `arg_types()`, which generates arbitrary tuples of the argument types.
- Generalise the property to "`body(X)` holds for any value in `arg_types()`".

Future work will identify its applicability and limitations, as well as extensions.

4 Making Refactorings Testing Framework-Aware

The refactorings in Wrangler have been designed to respect the conventions of the testing frameworks for Erlang. This affects not only the transformations themselves but also the pre-conditions for their applications. This is reported in detail in [10]: we summarise the pertinent points here.

Naming Conventions. When a naming convention is enforced by a testing framework, the refactorer must ensure that this naming convention is observed. For example, the suffix `_test_()` has a particular significance in EUnit. Changing names in this way must therefore be checked.

Callback Functions. QuickCheck testing with state machines requires the tester to implement certain callback functions. A callback function has a specified function interface, and refactorings need to respect this.

Meta-programming. Each of the testing frameworks uses meta-programming. For example, symbolic function calls of the form {call, Mod, Fun, Args} are used by QuickCheck abstract state machines. Frameworks for other languages may well use reflection for similar purposes.

Macros. QuickCheck testing code uses macros very heavily: this can cause problems for semantic analysis, which is at the foundation of pre-condition checking for refactorings. Pre-processors (e.g. CPP) are used in other frameworks.

Evidently most of the points raised here are equally applicable to testing frameworks for other programming languages.

5 Refactoring within Test Frameworks

Recent releases of Wrangler support a number of refactorings for test code *within* the QuickCheck framework. These were developed together with the QuickCheck team to support particular use cases of the tool, and include:

- Refactorings to introduce local definitions (?LET) and to merge local definitions and quantifiers (?FORALL).
- In state-machine based testing it is usual to begin with the state machine data being a simple value, but during test development for it to become a record. We support this transformation.

The latter *data type* refactoring is possible because of the stylised way that the state data is handled in QuickCheck. It would be much more difficult to perform in general because of the dynamic type system of Erlang.

This work in progress is to be supplemented in due course with refactorings within EUnit and Common Test.

6 Conclusions

We have shown the various ways that refactoring tools can improve testing for Erlang programs, and reflected on aspects of each of these. While some points relate specifically to Erlang, the main arguments of the paper apply equally well to testing in other languages and frameworks.

References

1. ProTest project, http://www.protest-project.eu/
2. Cesarini, F., Thompson, S.: Erlang Programming. O'Reilly Media, Inc., Sebastopol (2009)
3. Carlsson, R., Rémond, M.: EUnit,
   http://svn.process-one.net/contribs/trunk/eunit/doc/overview-summary.html

4. Common Test, http://www.erlang.org/doc/apps/common_test/index.html
5. Arts, T., et al.: Testing Telecoms Software with Quviq QuickCheck. In: Proceedings of the Fifth ACM SIGPLAN Erlang Workshop. ACM Press, New York (2006)
6. Li, H., Thompson, S., Orosz, G., Töth, M.: Refactoring with Wrangler, updated. In: ACM SIGPLAN Erlang Workshop 2008, Victoria, British Columbia, Canada (2008)
7. Plotkin, G.D.: A note on inductive generalisation. Machine Intelligence 5 (1970)
8. Li, H., Thompson, S.: Similar Code Detection and Elimination for Erlang Programs. In: Carro, M., Peña, R. (eds.) PADL 2010. LNCS, vol. 5937, pp. 104–118. Springer, Heidelberg (2010)
9. Li, H., et al.: Improving your test code with Wrangler. Technical Report 4-09, School of Computing, University of Kent (2009)
10. Li, H., Thompson, S.: Testing-framework-aware Refactoring. In: Third ACM Workshop on Refactoring Tools, ACM Digital Library (2009) (to appear)

Towards Run-Time Monitoring of Web Services Conformance to Business-Level Agreements

Konstantinos Bratanis[1], Dimitris Dranidis[2], and Anthony J.H. Simons[3]

[1] South East European Research Centre (SEERC),
Research Centre of the University of Sheffield and CITY College,
Mitropoleos 17, 54624, Thessaloniki, Greece
kobratanis@seerc.org,
http://www.seerc.org/

[2] Computer Science Department, CITY College,
International Faculty of the University of Sheffield,
Tsimiski 13, 54624, Thessaloniki, Greece
dranidis@city.academic.gr,
http://www.city.academic.gr/

[3] Department of Computer Science, University of Sheffield,
Regent Court, 211 Portobello Street, Sheffield S1 4DP, UK
a.simons@dcs.shef.ac.uk,
http://www.sheffield.ac.uk/

Abstract. Web service behaviour is currently specified in a mixture of ways, often using methods that are only partially complete. These range from static functional specifications, based on interfaces in WSDL and preconditions in RIF, to business process simulations using executable process-based models such as BPEL, to detailed quality of service (QoS) agreements laid down in a service level agreement (SLA). This paper recognises that something similar to a SLA is required at the higher business level to govern the contract between service producers, brokers and consumers. We call this a business level agreement (BLA) and within this framework, seek to unify disparate aspects of functional specification, QoS and run-time verification. We propose that the method for validating a web service with respect to its advertised BLA should be based on run-time service monitoring. This is a position paper towards defining these goals.

Keywords: run-time verification, business-level agreements, QoS, Web services, Stream X-Machines.

1 Business-Level Agreement

Web services enable the outsourcing of business processes to different service providers. Each provider may offer a similar service with different behaviour, i.e. different functional or non-functional characteristics. Before the service provision the service provider and the service consumer will have to agree on the concrete behaviour of the service.

The functional characteristics concern the implementation of the individual operations in a Web service and the allowed sequence of messages. For example how a payment is being handled and what are the preconditions for performing a payment. The non-functional characteristics concern quality attributes from a technical perspective such as accessibility, responsiveness and throughput, as well as quality attributes from a business perspective such as orders fulfilled in a day and payments handled per hour. For the quality of the technical aspect of the service provisioning a service-level agreement (SLA) is often established. For the business aspect, however, we believe that another type of agreement is required that captures both the functional and the non-functional business characteristics of the service provisioning.

Inspired from what already exists in the real business world, we call this new type of agreement a business-level agreement (BLA). Another inspiration for the term is [14], according to whom, the term BLA describes an agreement between two business partners who will be participating in business processes using Web services. To clarify the need and the contents of BLA, we discuss an example in the next paragraph.

As an example, in a pharmaceutical industry pharmacies order the medical supplies from a pharmaceutical company. The pharmaceutical company uses a third-party logistics (3PL) provider to handle the inventory and the shipment of medical supplies. A pharmacy places an order using the OrderManagmentService provided by the pharmaceutical company. After the necessary validations and in order for the ordered items to be shipped to the pharmacy, the pharmaceutical company uses the WarehouseService provided by the 3PL.

Both the pharmaceutical company and 3PL have signed BLA that states the following: (i) In the case that for a particular item, contained in the pharmacy's order, there is not enough reserve in the 3PL's warehouse, 3PL should not withhold the pharmacy's order, but partially execute the order by shipping the rest of the items, while at the same time 3PL should notify the pharmaceutical company for producing the item that is out of stock. Thus, the item that was not available remains as an outstanding order that will be fulfilled when the item will be available from the pharmaceutical company. (ii) 3PL should fulfil at least 5 orders for each pharmacy on a daily basis, and (iii) 3PL should complete the fulfilment of an order within 3 hours. It is evident that the first clause concerns the functional aspect in terms how 3PL should handle the fulfilment of an order, whereas the other two clauses concern the non-functional aspect in terms of time constraints that have to be respected to impose a specific quality level for the outsourced service.

2 Run-Time Monitoring of Conformance to BLAs

A BLA is a contract between a service provider and a service consumer that describes the agreed functional and non-functional characteristics of a Web service. In order to assure conformance of a service to BLA, it is necessary to perform monitoring during the execution of a Web service for a number of reasons: (i) Dynamic changes/upgrades in implementation may unwittingly break previous contracts after testing is formally over; (ii) Conditions at run-time may introduce non-determinism (particularly when sharing resources) that requires monitoring and compensation at run-time; (iii) The existence of a conformance monitoring capability is a kind of guarantee for the consumer that redress is possible if the BLA is not honoured.

To support run-time monitoring, a representation of the BLA is required which allows to express both functional and non-functional characteristics in a machine-readable way. This representation should be abstract enough to hide the actual implementation of a service, while exposing the steps, rules and dependencies that comprise the workflow of a business process, together with the qualitative characteristic of this workflow. Additionally, it should be complementary and separated from existing descriptions for Web services.

For addressing the verification of functional characteristics we use the method presented in [15], which employs the Stream X-Machines (SXM) formalism [16] for modelling the Web services. The animation of the SXM model is supported by the JSXM tool [17] and serves as an oracle for the run-time monitoring of the service. For implementing a prototype of the run-time infrastructure for verifying the conformance of Web service to BLA, we use the JBoss application server for the deployment of Web services. We utilize SOAP message handlers provided in JAX-WS API [18] for intercepting SOAP messages. Handlers are classes that act as pre-processors and post-processors for SOAP messages. A handler forwards SOAP request/response messages to an external monitoring component. The monitoring component is a Web service itself, which transforms the forwarded messages to SXM inputs/outputs, and then it uses them to perform animation of the SXM with the JSXM tool.

The run-time conformance monitoring of Web service to BLA has been inspired by the fragmented work that exists for the run-time monitoring of Web services. For instance, [1,2,3,4] address the run-time monitoring of functional characteristics of composed Web services, as well as for individual services [5,6,7,8]. Additionally, there are existing methodologies for verifying the non-functional characteristics of atomic Web services [9,10], and approaches concerning composed services [11,12]. Each of the aforementioned works manage to solve a small fragment of the problem, and it is therefore suggested to combine the existing approaches, in order to tackle more complex monitoring of Web services [13].

3 Future Work

As future work we plan to devise an abstract and machine-readable representation for BLAs, which will be able to express business agreements that would have to exist between providers, brokers and consumers. Furthermore, while the SXM approach can address the verification of the functional aspect of a BLA, the great amount of monitoring methods available inspires us to consider an open architecture, which will facilitate the utilization of different monitoring methods under a common framework.

References

1. Baresi, L., Ghezzi, C., Guinea, S.: Smart monitors for composed services. In: Proceedings of the 2nd international conference on Service oriented computing, pp. 193–202. ACM, New York (2004)

2. Lazovik, A., Aiello, M., Papazoglou, M.: Associating assertions with business processes and monitoring their execution. In: Proceedings of the 2nd international conference on Service oriented computing, pp. 94–104. ACM, New York (2004)
3. Mahbub, K., Spanoudakis, G.: A framework for requirents monitoring of service based systems. In: Proceedings of the 2nd international conference on Service oriented computing, pp. 84–93. ACM, New York (2004)
4. Kallel, S., Charfi, A., Dinkelaker, T., Mezini, M., Jmaiel, M.: Specifying and Monitoring Temporal Properties in Web services Compositions. In: Proceedings of the 7th IEEE European Conference on Web Services (ECOWS) (2009)
5. Li, Z., Jin, Y., Han, J.: A Runtime Monitoring and Validation Framework for Web Service Interactions. In: Proceedings of the Australian Software Engineering Conference, pp. 70–79. IEEE Computer Society, Los Alamitos (2006)
6. Gan, Y., Chechik, M., Nejati, S., Bennett, J., O'Farrell, B., Waterhouse, J.: Runtime monitoring of web service conversations. In: Proceedings of the 2007 conference of the center for advanced studies on Collaborative research, pp. 42–57. ACM, Richmond Hill (2007)
7. YuYu Yin, Y.L.: Verifying Consistency of Web Services Behavior. Presented at the 2008 IEEE Asia-Pacific Services Computing Conference, December 9 (2008)
8. Simmonds, J., Gan, Y., Chechik, M., Nejati, S., O'Farrell, B., Litani, E., Waterhouse, J.: Runtime Monitoring of Web Service Conversations. IEEE Transactions on Services Computing 99, 223–244 (2009)
9. Ameller, D., Franch, X.: Service Level Agreement Monitor (SALMon). In: Proceedings of the Seventh International Conference on Composition-Based Software Systems (ICCBSS 2008), pp. 224–227. IEEE Computer Society, Los Alamitos (2008)
10. Kotsokalis, C., Yahyapour, R., Rojas Gonzalez, M.: Modeling Service Level Agreements with Binary Decision Diagrams. Service-Oriented Computing, 190–204 (2009)
11. Barbon, F., Traverso, P., Pistore, M., Trainotti, M.: Run-Time Monitoring of Instances and Classes of Web Service Compositions. In: Proceedings of the IEEE International Conference on Web Services, pp. 63–71. IEEE Computer Society, Los Alamitos (2006)
12. Xiao, H., Chan, B., Zou, Y., Benayon, J.W., O'Farrell, B., Litani, E., Hawkins, J.: A Framework for Verifying SLA Compliance in Composed Services. In: 2008 IEEE International Conference on Web Services, Beijing, China, pp. 457–464 (2008)
13. Baresi, L., Guinea, S., Pistore, M., Trainotti, M.: Dynamo + Astro: An Integrated Approach for BPEL Monitoring. In: IEEE International Conference on Web Services, pp. 230–237. IEEE Computer Society, Los Alamitos (2009)
14. Kreger, H.: Fulfilling the Web services promise. Communications of the ACM 46, 29 (2003)
15. Dranidis, D., Ramollari, E., Kourtesis, D.: Run-time Verification of Behavioural Conformance for Conversational Web Services. In: Proceedings of the 7th IEEE European Conference on Web Services (ECOWS) (2009)
16. Eilenberg, S.: Automata, Languages, and Machines. Academic Press, Inc., London (1974)
17. Dranidis, D.: JSXM: A Suite of Tools for Model-Based Automated Test Generation: User Manual. Technical Report WP-CS01-09, CITY College (2009)
18. JSR 224: JavaTM API for XML-Based Web Services (JAX-WS) 2.0. Java Community Process (2009), http://jcp.org/en/jsr/detail?id=224

A New Approach for Software Testability*

Lydie du Bousquet

Laboratoire d'Informatique de Grenoble (LIG-UJF),
BP 72, 38402 Saint Martin d'Hères cedex, France

Abstract. In this paper, we propose another point of view with respect to testability. Instead of assessing testability through metrics, the idea is to identify very good practices in testing and to check that they are really implemented in the model or in the final code.

Keywords: Software testability.

1 Introduction

Software testing is the process of executing a program with the intent of finding errors [10]. It has emerged as one of the major techniques to evaluate the implementation reliability. Unfortunately, testing is usually an expensive process. It can represent more than 40% of the total cost of the software development [12]. For this reason, being able to characterize and to produce systems easy to test (i.e. testable systems) has become a preoccupation more and more important.

Testability denotes the ability of a system to be tested. Originally, testability was defined for hardware components. For software systems, several definitions have been proposed. In [1], testability is defined as the effort needed for testing. For Binder, testability is the relative ease and expense of revealing software faults [4]. Other definitions allow a quantitative evaluation of the testing effort [11] or represents the probability to observe an error at the next execution if there is a fault in the program [3].

Lots of metrics have been proposed for software testability evaluation. These metrics can be evaluated at different stages in the development phase (i.e. model or code). They evaluate the complexity or the scope of testing, or both [4]. The *scope* evaluates how many test cases have to be produced. The *complexity* indicates the difficulty of producing a test. But those metrics are most of the time difficult to compute and to interpret (see Sect. 2) [13].

In this article, we propose another point of view with respect to testability. The idea is to identify very good practices in testing and to check that they are really implemented in the model or in the final code. This approach can be compared to design patterns [6]. Section 2 summarizes some testability metrics and approach. Section 3 introduces the approach.

---
* This work was supported by the ANR project no. ANR-07-TLOG-019 (SIESTA).

2 Metrics for Testability

Software testability is the subject of several different works in the literature. J. Voas proposed the PIE analysis that aims at computing the sensitivity of individual locations in a program [15]. The sensitivity of a program location refers to the minimum likelihood that a fault at that location will produce incorrect output, under a specified input distribution. It relies on the fact that for discovering a fault in a program, three conditions should be met: (1) the statement that contains the fault should be executed, (2) the state of the variable should be infected, and (3) it should be propagated to an output. Testability of a software statement is expressed by the product of the probability of the statement execution, the probability of internal state infection, and the probability of error propagation. The sensitivity analysis was adapted by J. Voas and K. Miller to focus of the specification level [14], in order to evaluate the information loss through the program.

The Domain-Range Ratio (DRR) of a specification is the ratio between the cardinality of the domain to the cardinality of the range. J. McGregor and S. Srinivas proposed an extension of DRR for object-oriented programs called *Visibility Component* (VC) [9]. It takes into account inheritance and encapsulation.

Two measures have been proposed by R. Freedman, based on the concepts of observability and controllability, which are classical in hardware testability [5]. The *domain testability* evaluates how much input and output domains should be enlarged to achieve the maximum observability and controllability.

S. Jungmayr proposes a testability measurement in the context of static dependencies within object-oriented systems [8]. The idea is to evaluate at the design level, how many dependencies should be removed to achieve integration testing. A similar approach was explored by B. Baudry *et al.* with the notion of testability anti-patterns [2]. Here, the purpose is to detect situations that will require specific tests at the system level.

Most of the proposed measures require sophisticated calculations or might be not calculable [13]. For instance, to compute PIE, one has to determine three probabilities for each statement (execution, infection and propagation). This can be long and/or difficult especially for long or complex programs. DRR and VC are not calculable for programs using a list, an array, an object or a pointer as input or output because these structures have infinite definition domains.

3 Proposition

Software testability metrics are difficult to use for several reasons. The main one is that the testing process is influenced by several kinds of factors among which the process, the tools, and the testing strategies [4]. Most of the proposed metrics are implicitly related to a testing strategy. For instance, PIE assumes a random data selection strategy.

Software companies need a more practical approach to build easy-to-test systems and to evaluate their testability. In this paper, we introduce a pragmatic software testability approach, which first identify design practices that ease the work of testing and formalize them as rules. Rules can be interpreted as a part of non-functional requirements. Then, an analysis is carried out to evaluate how much or how well the rules are applied. The analysis process should be automated in the development environment(s), in order to be easy to use.

The advantages of this approach are the following. This approach is very flexible: the rules can be chosen with respect to the development context or other criteria. The testability analysis is easy to interpret: a bad testability means that the rules are not (well) applied. Testability weaknesses are directly identified and can be corrected. Moreover, the evaluation of the rule application can be considered as an adequacy criteria [16].

The issues of the approach are our ability to identify the good design practices, and to formalize them. To show how it is possible, let us study an example in the context of object-oriented system. In his article [4], R. Binder underlines that object-oriented code code can be made more testable by adding some features in the class. For instance,

- A set or reset method could be added to ease the test because it allows to set the internal state (i.e. all the attributes) to a predefined internal state, regardless of its current state.
- A reporter method that returns the state of the object could also be added. It improves observability.
- If this can not be achieved, one should considered to implement set and get method for each attributes.
- Assertions decrease the test suite maintenance effort in case of modifications, because the test case oracle are embedded (and thus centralized) in the code. It also increases the documentation of the code and thus eases the maintenance of the code. Assertions can be expressed as pre and post condition for each method and also as invariant at the class level.

A formalisation of these properties could be provided. Let S be an object-oriented system. It consists of a set of classes, C. For every class $c \in C$, let $M(c)$ and $A(c)$ be the set of methods and attributes of c.

(1) $\forall c \in C, \exists m \in M(c), \text{isReseter}(m, c)$
    isReseter: METHOD $\times$ CLASS $\to$ BOOLEAN
(2) $\forall c \in C, \exists m \in M(c), \text{isReporter}(m, c)$
    isReporter: METHOD $\times$ CLASS $\to$ BOOLEAN
(3) $\forall c \in C, \forall a \in A(c), \exists m \in M(c), \text{isGetter}(m, a, c)$
    $\forall c \in C, \forall a \in A(c), \exists m \in M(c), \text{isSetter}(m, a, c)$
    isGetter: METHOD $\times$ ATTRIBUTE $\times$ CLASS $\to$ BOOLEAN
    isSetter: METHOD $\times$ ATTRIBUTE $\times$ CLASS $\to$ BOOLEAN
(4) $\forall c \in C, \forall m \in M(c), \text{hasExplicitPrecondition}(m, c)$
    $\forall c \in C, \forall m \in M(c), \text{hasExplicitPostcondition}(m, c)$
    $\forall c \in C, \text{hasExplicitInvariant}(c)$
    hasExplicitPrecondition: METHOD $\times$ CLASS $\to$ BOOLEAN
    hasExplicitPostcondition: METHOD $\times$ CLASS $\to$ BOOLEAN
    hasExplicitInvariant: METHOD $\to$ BOOLEAN

Our current work on this approach is to

- show that those patterns increase testability through mutation analysis [7]. It is expected that test suites using the methods added by testability patterns kill more mutants.
- demonstrate that those patterns can be automatically be detected thanks to an automatic procedure.
- evaluate its interest and its possible usage in an industrial context.

References

1. Bache, R., Mullerburg, M.: Measures of testability as a basis for quality assurance. Software Engineering Journal 5(2), 86–92 (1990)
2. Baudry, B., Le Traon, Y., Sunyé, G., Jézéquel, J.-M.: Measuring and improving design patterns testability. In: 9th IEEE Int. Software Metrics Symposium (METRICS 2003), Sydney, Australia, p. 50–59 (September 2003)
3. Bertolino, A., Strigini, L.: On the use of testability measures for dependability assessment. IEEE Trans. Software Eng. 22(2), 97–108 (1996)
4. Binder, R.V.: Design for testability in object-oriented systems. Communications of the ACM 37(9), 87–101 (1994)
5. Freedman, R.S.: Testability of software components. IEEE Trans. Software Eng. 17(6), 553–564 (1991)
6. Gamma, E., Helm, R., Johnson, R., Vlissides, J.: Design Patterns: Elements of Reusable Object-Oriented Software. Addison Wesley, Reading (1995)
7. Jia, Y., Harman, M.: An Analysis and Survey of the Development of Mutation Testing. Technical Report TR-09-06, CREST Centre, King's College London, London, UK (September 2009)
8. Jungmayr, S.: Identifying test-critical dependencies. In: Int. Conference on Software Maintenance (ICSM), Montreal, Quebec, Canada, pp. 404–413. IEEE, Los Alamitos (2002)
9. McGregor, J.D., Srinivas, S.: A measure of testing effort. In: Second USENIX Conference on Object-Oriented Technologies (COOTS) (1996)
10. Myers, G.: The Art of Software Testing. Wiley-Interscience, Hoboken (1979)
11. Institute of Electrical and Electronics Engineers. IEEE Standard Computer Dictionary: A Compilation of IEEE Standard Computer Glossaries. Technical report. IEEE, New York, USA (1990)
12. Salem, A.M., Rekab, K., Whittaker, J.A.: Prediction of software failures through logistic regression. Information & Software Technology 46(12), 781–789 (2004)
13. Shaheen, M.-R., du Bousquet, L.: Survey of source code metrics for evaluating testability of object oriented systems. Research Report RR-LIG-003, LIG, Grenoble, France (2010)
14. Voas, J.M., Miller, K.W.: Software testability: The new verification. IEEE Software 12(3), 17–28 (1995)
15. Voas, J.M.: PIE: A dynamic Failure-Based Technique. IEEE Trans. Software Eng. 18(8), 41–48 (1992)
16. Zhu, H., Hall, P.A.V., May, J.H.R.: Software unit test coverage and adequacy. ACM Comput. Surv. 29(4), 366–427 (1997)

DOM Transactions for Testing JavaScript

Phillip Heidegger, Annette Bieniusa, and Peter Thiemann

Albert-Ludwigs-Universität Freiburg, Germany
{heidegger,bieniusa,thiemann}@informatik.uni-freiburg.de

Abstract. Unit testing in the presence of side effects requires the construction of a suitable test fixture before each test run. We consider the problem of providing test fixtures for unit testing of client-side JavaScript code that manipulates its underlying web page. We propose using techniques from software transactional memory to restore the test fixture after each test run.

1 Introduction

Unit testing often requires the construction of a test fixture before running a test. As a test run may change a fixture arbitrarily, unit testing frameworks like JUnit (http://junit.org/) contain hooks for setting up and tearing down a fixture and perform each test run on a fresh instance of the class under test, tacitly assuming that the test run does not affect state outside the current instance.

Now consider unit testing for client-side JavaScript code using AJAX. AJAX code runs in the context of an HTML document. It sends asynchronous requests to a server and each response triggers a callback that dynamically modifies the HTML document. Thus, the fixture consists of the browser's internal DOM (document object model [5]) representation of the HTML document, a sophisticated network of objects with strong invariants. The code under test routinely modifies the DOM representation as well as other parts of the browser's state.

Setting up such a fixture involves running the browser to parse a slew of HTML, construct its DOM representation, render it, and run initialization scripts (e.g., onload handlers). JavaScript test frameworks either restart the browser to reset the fixture or they only offer testing on mock objects (e.g., Blue-Ridge http://github.com/relevance/blue-ridge). Neither approach is desirable, because mock objects do not offer the full functionality of the real thing and a full browser restart is too time consuming. Just consider the slowdown imposed on random testing where there are hundreds of test runs each of which takes only a tiny fraction of the time needed for a browser restart.

We propose to apply techniques from software transactional memory to the problem of restoring a test fixture. The general idea is to set up the fixture first, and then perform each test run in the body of a transaction, collect the results of the test, and rollback the transaction to restore the fixture.

To evaluate the idea, we have built an implementation based on the technique of transactional boosting [4]. To this end, our test suite intercepts calls to browser methods as well as assignments that may modify state that is shared between

```
1  <html><head>...</head>              1  function insertRow(log) {
2  <body>                               2    var tr = document.getElementById('myTable')
3   <table id="myTable">                3        .insertRow(1);
4    <tr>                               4    var td1 = tr.insertCell(0), td2 = tr.insertCell(1);
5     <th>Date/Time</th>                5    var d = new Date();
6     <th>From, Subject</th>            6    td1.appendChild(document.createTextNode(d));
7    </tr>                              7    td2.appendChild(document.createTextNode(log));
8   </table>                            8  }
9   <div id="status"></div>             9  function adjustStatus(str) {
10 </body>                             10    var div = document.getElementById('status');
11 </html>                             11    while (div.childNodes.length > 0)
                                       12      div.removeChild(div.childNodes[0]);
                                       13    div.appendChild(document.createTextNode(str));
                                       14  }
```

Fig. 1. HTML code of the fixture and insert row into table and adjust status

runs. For each modification, a compensating action that reverses the effect of the modification is pushed on an *undo stack*. When a test run is finished, the compensating actions are executed in a LIFO manner such that their total effect is to rollback the global state (including the DOM) to its original state.

2 Motivating Example

In the context of an AJAX project, consider the task of keeping up-to-date a table of incoming emails and a status line that contains the number of unread emails in the inbox (Fig. 1 left). To this end, the project contains some JavaScript code that periodically contacts a server for the information and then asynchronously updates the HTML document in a callback. The functions insertRow and adjustStatus (Fig. 1 right) are invoked from the callback. The former extends the table with a new line whereas the latter changes the status text.

Suppose we want to find bugs in the function insertRow using random testing with the fixture described by Fig. 1 (left). For each test run, the testing framework first has to generate a random string, then run the function against the fixture, and afterwards use DOM functions to check if the expected change has been performed on the document structure.

To use the same fixture for each test run, our test framework rewrites the code of insertRow and adjustStatus by inserting code that registers actions for all side effects. The resulting code for a test run needs to be wrapped in a transaction. Before executing the test suite, starting the browser and loading the program under test creates the fixture (the initial HTML page). During the test run, the compensating actions are transparently pushed on an undo stack. After the test run, the result is verified. Then, the transaction is rolled back by triggering the processing of the undo log to restore the initial state for the next test run.

3 Implementing a Transactional Layer in JavaScript

To perform test runs in a transaction, it is necessary to rewrite the code under test such that each operation with global side effects registers a compensating action. Such side effects are assignments to global variables and properties of globally reachable objects as well as calls to native DOM methods that modify the DOM. Unfortunately, JavaScript's `with` statement prevents a static analysis of the scope of a variable in general. Similarly, in many cases it is not possible to statically decide which method is called. Thus, the rewriting implements the following strategy:

- For each assignment, push a closure on the undo stack that assigns the old value to the variable or object property.
- For a method call, the decision whether a user method or a native DOM method is invoked is taken dynamically in a library method, which checks the method's closure against the known DOM methods. For each DOM method, the library provides a factory to create a compensating operation. An example is given in Fig. 2. For a user method, no compensation is needed because each side effect inside the user method creates an entry in the undo stack.

```
1  function(node) {
2      function undo() {if (parent) {parent.insertBefore(node,next);}}
3      var parent = this;
4      var next = node.nextSibling;
5      return undo;
6  }
```

Fig. 2. Example of the factory undo operation for removing a child of a DOM node

Under a closed world assumption where no additional code is loaded at run time or generated using `eval`, this transformation is safe in the sense that it does not change the semantics of the code under test and that it faithfully registers compensating actions for all relevant side effects.

We integrated the transformation in our tool JSConTest[3][1], a random test generator for JavaScript based on contract annotations. To increase performance of the test suite, the annotation ~noEffects informs the transformation that the function is free from side effects.

4 Related Work

Dhawan and co-authors [1] propose to augment the language and runtime of JavaScript with transactions for monitoring security policies. In contrast, we transform the code under test. Hence, the tool can be used in all browsers which implement the current ECMA Script standard.

Checkpointing [2] is a related technique that creates recovery points for long running software to avoid restarting such applications from scratch. In browsers

---
[1] http://proglang.informatik.uni-freiburg.de/jscontest/

which offer the possibility to construct a checkpoint and revert to it, the rollback of a fixture could be performed without administration of transactions. It has also been used to construct debuggers that support backward evaluation [6].

There are also proposals for testing programs involving databases using transactions. Again, the rationale is to avoid the cost of recreating an expensive fixture between test runs.

5 Conclusion and Outlook

We have shown how transactions enable the construction of an effective JavaScript testing framework that works in the original browser environment and avoids the repeated reconstruction of test fixtures / HTML pages from scratch. This approach simplifies the setup of a AJAX testing environment enormously and allows for testing under real-world conditions. We have constructed a proof-of-concept implementation as an extension of our tool JSConTest[3]. Our tool offers both a transactional and a set-up/tear-down test setup. We plan to investigate their respective overhead in more detail.

The implementation can be further improved in several ways. Due to their irreversible nature, I/O operations like sending HTTP requests have to be treated differently. For example, if a testing environment includes a server, this server has to be reset for each run. Similarly, methods on the window object should be redirected to a mock object to avoid human interactivity during the tests.

Compensating actions should be inverses of the original actions. This property should be (mechanically) proved.

Program analysis can improve the performance of the rewritten code. In ongoing work, we explore the partial inference of scope information so that local and global variables can be distinguished outside of `with` statements.

References

1. Dhawan, M., Shan, C., Ganapathy, V.: The case for JavaScript transactions. In: PLAS 2010: Proceedings of the ACM SIGPLAN Fifth Workshop on Programming Languages and Analysis for Security, Toronto, Canada. ACM Press, New York (June 2010)
2. Elnozahy, E.N.M., Alvisi, L., Wang, Y.-M., Johnson, D.B.: A survey of rollback-recovery protocols in message-passing systems. ACM Comput. Surv. 34(3), 375–408 (2002)
3. Heidegger, P., Thiemann, P.: Contract-driven testing of JavaScript code. In: TOOLS, Malaga, Spain. Springer, Heidelberg (June 2010) (to appear)
4. Herlihy, M., Koskinen, E.: Transactional boosting: a methodology for highly-concurrent transactional objects. In: PPoPP 2008: Proceedings of the 13th ACM SIGPLAN Symposium on Principles and practice of parallel programming, pp. 207–216. ACM, New York (2008)
5. Le Hégaret, P., Whitmer, R., Wood, L.: W3C document object model (August 2003), http://www.w3.org/DOM/
6. Tolmach, A., Appel, A.W.: A debugger for Standard ML. Journal of Functional Programming 5(2), 155–200 (1995)

The GZoltar Project: A Graphical Debugger Interface

André Riboira and Rui Abreu

Faculty of Engineering, University of Porto
Rua Dr. Roberto Frias, s/n 4200-465 Porto, Portugal
andre.riboira@fe.up.pt, rui@computer.org
http://www.gzoltar.com/

Abstract. Software debugging is one of the most time-consuming and expensive tasks in software development. There are several tools that contribute to this process to become faster and more efficient, but are not integrated with each other, nor provide an intuitive interface. These tools can be integrated to create an IDE plug-in, which gathers the most important debugging information into one place. GZoltar is a new project to create that missing plug-in. The main goal of GZoltar project is to reduce debugging process time and costs.

Keywords: Debug, Spectrum-Based Fault Localization, Code Dependency Graphs, Project Hierarchy Trees.

1 Introduction

In software development, debugging (localization and correction of software faults) is one of the most expensive tasks [1,3]. Although existing automatic debugging tools are quite powerful, some developers tend to use basic manual debug functionalities that their Integrated Development Environment (IDE)'s offer. There are plenty of tools to help developers to find the faults of their software. Unfortunately, those tools tend to not be integrated with each other, and the developer does not have a place to get all the information he wants at the same time. Moreover, debugging tools traditionally provide an unattractive output and sometimes also rather confusing, especially with regard to large software projects. Code coverage tools, such as Zoltar [1], allows developers to know which lines of code were executed in a given test. Usually, those tools use source code lines highlight in different colors to show if a line was executed or not. Code dependencies graphs [2] allows the creation of a graph of the entire project, in which the nodes of the graph represent the different modules of the project and the links represent the dependencies between these modules. This information allows an overview of the project and makes it possible to analyze fault propagations between modules. With tree-mappings is possible to have a clear understanding of the different components of the project, and the way they are related hierarchically. This is useful because we can easily navigate through the different levels of detail on our software projects, and have a clearer picture of sub-modules of a given module. Furthermore, there are tools available that automatically calculate the failure probability of each software module. Lately there has been a clear interest in developing tools for automatic debugging. These tools are mainly based on Model-based software debugging (MBSD) or Spectrum-based fault localization (SFL) [3]. These tools are all very useful, but may work much better if they collaborate with each other. Integrating some of these functionalities would give to the developer a very powerful tool for all debugging processes. But although the results of these tools would be very useful, they should also be presented in a way that the developer can quickly assimilate all the information, and navigate through it intuitively. The integration of these features will have a better result if it is done in an IDE.

2 Zoltar: A Toolset for Automatic Fault Localization

On automatic debug field, SFL techniques are shown to have better performance than those of MBSD [3]. Zoltar is a tool that implements SFL [3] and can predict, with a high success rate, the localization of software faults. Zoltar hosts a range of spectrum-based fault localization techniques featuring BARINEL [3]. The toolset provides the infrastructure to automatically instrument the source code of software programs to produce runtime data, which is subsequently analyzed to return a ranked list of diagnosis candidates [1]. Despite the usefulness of this tool, its output can be difficult to analyze because it is mainly textual. As output we obtain a listing of code blocks with the failure probability of each of these blocks. In a long project this list can become quite confusing and the navigation can be particularly difficult.

3 GZoltar: A Graphical Debugger Interface

This paper proposes a new project, that uses Zoltar's output, as well as a generated code dependency graph and a project hierarchy tree as input. The main goal of this project is to build a useful graph where the developer could not only better understand the organization of his project, but also the module dependencies and failure probability of each module. This rich information could then be used to ease the debugging process, therefore reducing the overall debugging time. The startup view of this GZoltar tool would be a tree with the software hierarchy, so that the developer could have a general view of all the project. User would be able to navigate through that tree, like zooming in and out in the different levels of detail. That navigation would give the developer a sense of depth, that would help him to more clearly understand the location of each module in the whole system. Please see Figure 1 for a prototype. All this modules would be colored differently to represent their failure probability. At all times, the developer would be able choose to see the dependency graph of a given module. This would help the developer to analyze the possibility of having errors propagated by the modules due to its dependency.

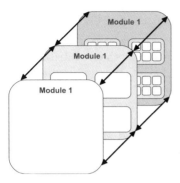 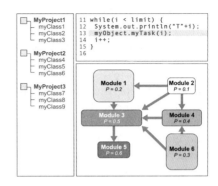

Fig. 1. Sense of depth in GZoltar Hierarchical View

Fig. 2. GZoltar Code Dependency Graph View in IDE integration

Sometimes the origin of a fault is not in the most affected module itself, but is inherited of another module that it depends on. GZoltar tool could be integrated on a popular IDE like Eclipse [4] for developer comfort, that could reduce the learning curve of the tool and increase its use. A GZoltar plug-in would bring a useful tool to all Java coders. Such a tool could allow the programmer to quickly identify a faulty module in a global overview, and expand that module to see which sub-modules are problematic. Even if the failure is not implicit to that given module, he is able to analyze the module dependencies to try to find out where is the failure origin. Please see Figure 2 for a prototype. Surely the time and costs devoted to debugging would be reduced considerably with the use of this tool. We can use available open source tools, like EclEmma [5] to get the project code coverage to be used as Zoltar input, recode Zoltar in Java, to provide a better integration in Eclipse, and use a tool like PDE Incubator Dependency Visualization [6] to provide the code dependency graph, and a tool like Tree Views for Zest [7] to provide the project treemap. An OpenGL view was also taken into consideration, to provide a powerful navigation though all the project modules. This view can provide a 3D map of the application, where all the nodes features like its size, color, transparency and position would have a special meaning, like the number of code lines of a given module, its failure probability, the number of times it was executed or its detail level. GZoltar will be released as an open source tool, so anyone can contribute to it in the future. This also gives greater versatility to any organization that wants to implement GZoltar. The purpose of this tool is to provide a powerful and integrated view of a software project, with a good navigation system and the indication of the fault probability of each module, allowing the programmer to quickly find and correct software faults. Being a free open source tool that is able to free the programmer from consuming steps of finding software faults, we believe that it will certainly help to reduce the overall cost of debugging process.

4 Conclusions

Software debugging is the most time-consuming and expensive phase of the software development cycle [1,3]. There are several tools that contribute to the debugging process to become faster and more efficient, but unfortunately these tools are not integrated with each other, nor provide an intuitive interface for their use is the mass. These tools can be integrated to create a single tool, which allows the developer to obtain all the needed information in one place, preferably inside his IDE. From the output of Zoltar as base, and adding a code dependency graph and a hierarchy tree of the project, we can build a very useful tool, allowing a pleasant way to pass to the developer not only the structure of his project but also the dependencies of each module and their failure probability. Navigation through all of this information should also have a special attention. In long projects, visualization is particularly important because it should allow the developer to, at the same time, have an overview of the whole project, but also be able to achieve high levels of detail to identify exactly where the location of the faults of his project. This tool could be created as an Eclipse plug-in [4] to increase the developer convenience. A plug-in like this could greatly improve the debugging process, reducing time and cost of it.

References

1. Janssen, T., Abreu, R., van Gemund, A.J.C.: Zoltar: A toolset for automatic fault localization. In: International Conference on Automated Software Engineering, New Zealand (2009)
2. Balmas, F.: Displaying dependence graphs: a hierarchical approach. In: Workshop on Analysis, Slicing and Transformation, Germany (2001)
3. Abreu, R.: Spectrum-based Fault Localization in Embedded Software. PhD Thesis, Delft University of Technology, Netherlands (2009)
4. Eclipse.org, http://www.eclipse.org/
5. EclEmma - Java Code Coverage for Eclipse, http://www.eclemma.org/
6. PDE Incubator Dependency Visualization, http://www.eclipse.org/pde/incubator/dependency-visualization/
7. Tree Views for Zest, http://wiki.eclipse.org/Tree_Views_for_Zest

Author Index

Abou Trab, Mohammad Saeed 194
Abreu, Rui 215
Alrouh, Bachar 194
Amin Jolly, Shahnewaz 118

Bazdell, Gary 39
Benac Earle, Clara 23
Bessayah, Fayçal 137
Bieniusa, Annette 211
Böhm, Klemens 56
Bokil, Prasad 8
Bratanis, Konstantinos 203

Cavalli, Ana 137
Chang, Chien-Hsing 39
Counsell, Steve 194

Dallmeier, Valentin 173
Dean, Thomas R. 104
Derrick, John 23
Dranidis, Dimitris 203
du Bousquet, Lydie 207

Eichinger, Frank 56
Eschbach, Robert 181
Eskandar, Matt M. 118

Fredlund, Lars-Åke 23

Garousi, Vahid 118, 129, 189
Ghinea, George 194
Grieskamp, Wolfgang 7
Große, Philipp W.L. 56
Guo, Qiang 23

Haschemi, Siamak 155
Heidegger, Phillip 211
Hierons, Rob M. 194
Hoare, Sir Tony 5
Hoffman, Daniel 39

Jääskeläinen, Antti 72

Kääramees, Marko 147
Kam, Ben W.Y. 104
Koochakzadeh, Negar 129, 189

Li, Huiqing 198

Maja, Willian 137
Martins, Eliane 137
Meyer, Bertrand 1
Mileva, Yana Momchilova 173
Muske, Tukaram 8

Nica, Mihai 88
Nica, Simona 88

Pankratius, Victor 56

Raiend, Kullo 147
Riboira, André 215

Shahbaz, Muzammil 181
Shrotri, Ulka 8
Simons, Anthony J.H. 203
Stevens, Brett 39
Suman, P. Vijay 8

Thiemann, Peter 211
Thompson, Simon 198

Vain, Jüri 147
Valenti, Andre Willik 137
Venkatesh, R. 8

Walkinshaw, Neil 165
Weißleder, Stephan 155
Wiederseiner, Christian 118
Wotawa, Franz 88

Yoo, Kevin 39

Zeller, Andreas 173

Printing: Mercedes-Druck, Berlin
Binding: Stein+Lehmann, Berlin